Praise for *3:15—The Genesis of All Prophecy*

By Rabbi

MW00441154

Who better to author a relevant ar Genesis to the modern era than Rabbi Eric Walker? No one in my opinion. This revelatory book opened my faith and mind to fit together the pieces of history from the beginning in such a way that for the first time I could fathom the Scriptures in the context of God's grand design through a series of prophetic realizations. This book goes on my top shelf of books that I most prize. It grew my love for God and confirmed my faith both intellectually and in my soul. I was left praising Abba Father, Yeshua, and Ruach Ha Kodesh in thanksgiving. As someone who has met Jesus in Heaven, I know the splendor of God's truth face to face, but now my love for my beloved Jewish brothers and sisters has reached new heights. In discussing the "father" of Judaism, Abraham, Rabbi Eric Walker quotes the poet Ogden Nash in explaining that God chose the Jews because the Jews chose God, and, as the author says, "Abraham chose God." I love that! This book may be the best bridge of Judaism to Christianity ever authored. It is certain to change hearts and minds. You HAVE to read this book—and don't skip any chapters. Savor *The Genesis of All Prophecy* like a holy wine poured through new wineskin. Thank you, Rabbi Eric. Thank you, Yahweh, for using your beloved servant to inspire us with your truth!

—RANDY KAY, bestselling author of *Dying to Meet Jesus* and *Revelations from Heaven*, pastor of Randy Kay Ministries

Messianic Rabbi Eric Walker's *3:15* will answer several very important theological questions and take you on a historical/biblical journey that will put you hot on the trail of the ultimate demise of the master deceiver, the serpent in the Garden of Eden. As you embark on this incredible journey, life will begin to make much more sense!

—MESSIANIC RABBI ZEV PORAT, founder and director of Messiah of Israel Ministries (Tel Aviv, Israel) and coauthor of the Amazon bestseller *The Rabbi, the Secret Message, and the Identity of Messiah* (Defender Publishing)

Rabbi Eric Walker has given the church an ingenious idea by focusing on Genesis 3:15—indeed, the "genesis of all prophecy." Never has the Church—even those outside the Church—become more aware of prophecy and the prophetic, especially considering the false prophecies that emerged regarding presidential elections. Rabbi Walker has written with care and avoids the spectacular or the controversial. For those who are seekers of truth and more knowledge of the Bible, this is your book. I know of no book like it. You will learn more about the Bible from a Jewish perspective that will cause you to appreciate biblical history as you have never had.

—Dr. R. T. Kendall, minister, Westminster Chapel, London (1977–2002)

In my over forty years of studying the Bible and practicing ministry, I've been incessantly told by scholars and academicians, "Think Hebrew." Skilled people were simply encouraging me to read the Bible through Jewish lenses. In this compelling book by my friend Rabbi Eric Walker, he allows us to look at the work of the evil one—and God's promise of victory over him in Genesis 3:15—through Jewish lenses. Throughout the Scripture and history, Eric shows us the devil's schemes to crush the seed of the woman and kill Jesus. But he can't. King Jesus wins! This is a great book to help us all "think Hebrew" and see God's sovereign hand guiding and fulfilling His perfect promise in Genesis 3:15.

—Dr. David Chadwick, founding pastor, Moments of Hope Church, Charlotte, North Carolina

Rabbi Eric Walker gives an effective voice to a comprehensive history of the Jews, Church anti-Semitism, Islam, and biblical passages that nurture hope. A must read. Brilliantly researched and compiled. Both the layman and erudite will benefit from this wellspring of profound nourishment.

—Dr. Jeffrey D Johnson, president, Israel Today Ministries, Arlington, Texas; Israeltodayministries.org; Facebook.com/Israel Today Ministries

3:15—The Genesis of Prophecy is one of the most profound, riveting and uniquely written books on this subject to date. Matter of fact, it's the only book of its kind that I have ever read. Rabbi Eric Walker did a splendid, careful resource and study on this ancient and eternal but historically relevant topic. In addition, this book is the only one thus far that has been penned from a Jewish believer's perspective that includes a unique perspective on Satan's insidious plans to totally eradicate the seed line of Messiah. This excellent literary work speaks from a contemporary theology while at the same time addressing the anti-Semitic rhetoric of The Squad on the floors of Congress. *3:15—The Genesis of Prophecy* is a book that is written by a truth-teller and prophetic Messianic Jewish leader, teacher, and Bible scholar. I would call Rabbi Walker a modern-day theologian and historian who understands thoroughly what God is doing here and now! This book is a bridge that takes you into the past, present, and future while also decoding the mysteries found in the fabric of the Word of God. I believe this book is a game changer! Rabbi Walker eloquently wrote it to expose the unseen threats and premise of the evil one—the devil—while equipping readers with the proper spiritual tools for rules of engagement to win this invisible battle. We cannot understand the overall plan of God through His Seed without understanding Genesis 3:15. This book helps to bridge and impart the necessary revelation knowledge and wisdom to assist in this spiritual battle and events leading up to prophetic fulfillment. A must read! I highly recommend and endorse the pages of this book. The eyes of your understanding will be enlightened after reading this book.

—Dr. Hakeem Collins, best-selling author, international
speaker, prophet, author of *Unseen Warfare*

Rabbi Eric Walker's years of deep, heart-rending study in the Scriptures and research in history culminate in this essential book for every believer to share. I have high hopes that, within ten years, this book becomes a dog-eared, oft-highlighted standard, kept within reach on every Christian's bookshelf.

—K. J. Frolander, author of *Israel Basics* and eleven other books;
founder of Ruth Israel Initiative

My friend, Rabbi Eric Walker, is a truly inspired creation. The Lord has blessed him with a deep understanding of Jewish culture and Hebraic tradition, along with a revelatory faith in Jesus the Messiah that gives him keen insight and understanding into both the Old and New Testaments. I can think of no one more qualified, or better versed, to bring forth the revelation contained in *The Genesis of All Prophecy*. In this inspired book, Rabbi Eric takes you deep into the Word and even deeper into the heart and mind of God. As you read, you will see a clear through-line of God's plans and purposes, the schemes of the enemy to thwart those plans, and how Jesus our Messiah has overcome them all. This book will open your eyes, blow your mind, and deepen your faith. You are in for quite a ride!

—ROBERT HOTCHKIN, Men on the Frontlines / Robert Hotchkin Ministries, RobertHotchkin.com

Every now and then, one has the rare opportunity to hear something that not only captures the heart but stretches the understanding as well. Rabbi Eric Walker, my dear friend and brilliant scholar, has offered us such an opportunity. In his new book, *3:15—The Genesis of All Prophecy*, we hear the prophecy God spoke in the beginning and intends to fulfill despite Satan's destructive agenda. We are taken on a journey following the biblical and historical thread of the first prophecy in Scripture from Genesis to Revelation, from a Jewish understanding, all along having our previous paradigms sifted, stretched, and shifted. It is a marvelous work. *The Genesis of All Prophecy* exposes anti-Semitism as Satan's agenda in a way most of us have never heard. The book is prophetic, insightful, convicting, and heart-rending. I rejoiced, mourned, and contemplated what I was hearing through this exceptional book. In the end, I thanked God for this opportunity to hear the word of the Lord. You will too. **This is a book that had to be written; none other like it has ever been written!**

—DR. KIM M. MAAS, Kim Maas Ministries, author of *Prophetic Community: God's Call to All to Minister in His Gifts*, and *The Way of the Kingdom: Seizing the Moment for a Great Move of God.*

Rabbi Eric E. Walker has the unique background and education to understand and explain with clear insight this most important prophecy from a unique perspective. Full of Scripture and insight, this book gives clear examples of how Yeshua/Jesus is the fulfillment of the Genesis 3:15 prophecy and how Satan has repeatedly tried to extinguish the Seed of the woman but will never succeed. This is a must-read book for those desiring a deeper understanding of what has happened and what prophetically is still to happen in the coming days.

 —Dr. Ramona Probasco, PsyD, MFT, NCC, certified
  domestic violence counselor; author, *Healing Well and Living Free*
  from an Abusive Relationship

In *3:15—The Genesis of All Prophecy*, Rabbi Walker has given us all a great gift. This scholarly, and yet easy-to-read historical and theological look at the history of the Jews and their role in Christ's final victory over Satan is compelling, and a book every Christian should read. Walker spells out in amazing detail how, over and over again throughout human history, Jewish people have been under attack by the forces of evil, and how this barrage of assaults has attempted to thwart the coming of Christ and prevent His final triumph over evil. Quite frankly, I was embarrassed to read about the times when the Christian church failed to grasp the true nature of this epic battle, and even worse, on several occasions was unwittingly on the wrong side of history in the war. If you have ever wondered why the descendants of Abraham have been so blessed in their ability to survive adversity and so often thrive in whatever they endeavor to do, then you will find this book as enlightening as I did. Walker has beautifully clarified that there is a war going on between good and evil, and thankfully, he explains how the Bible has given us the end of the story.

 —Dr. Mark W. Baker, PhD, best-selling author, *Jesus, The Greatest Therapist Who Ever Lived*

Rabbi Eric Walker's book, *3:15—The Genesis of All Prophecy*, is a beautiful new investigation of the prophetic plan of redemption first spoken by God Himself in the Garden of Eden (Genesis 3:15) from a Messianic Jewish perspective. Rabbi Walker traces God's plan and Satan's attempts to pervert it throughout the Scriptures in a fresh, new way. I believe you will find reading this book to be a revelatory experience that will energize your prayer life and expand your appreciation of God's grace and glory.

—JOAN HUNTER, healing evangelist and host of *Miracles Happen* TV show

Rabbi Eric Walker is passionate about exposing the enemy and preaching and teaching the uncompromised message of the Gospel. I consider Rabbi Walker one of the greatest Bible scholars of all time. The wisdom and truth He brings forth are unprecedented. He reveals the truth and boldness of the Scriptures with Spirit-led revelation every believer must deeply digest. This truly is a book for these prophetic times we are experiencing.

—KATHY DEGRAW, Kathy DeGraw Ministries; author, *Prophetic Spiritual Warfare*; kathydegrawministries.org

A long war began thousands of years ago in a garden on the mountain of God. Genesis 3:15 tells us that, because of the rebellion in Eden, the children of Eve and the seed of the serpent would be eternal enemies. Messianic Rabbi Eric Walker has authored a fascinating study of that verse to show how Satan and his minions have schemed against God; how they've worked from inside the church to turn Christian against Jew; and how the final fulfillment of the Genesis 3:15 prophecy will restore humanity to our rightful place in the family of God.

—DEREK GILBERT, host, SkyWatchTV

Rabbi Eric's insights are deep and profound. After reading only chapter 1, I was gripped by two things: what I did not know about Scripture, and what I wanted to know more about. I am certain you will experience the same. This book is a must read for everyone who has a true desire to envelope and be enveloped by God's Word.

—DR. MARK SHERWOOD, www.sherwood.tv

I highly recommend Rabbi Eric Walker's new book, *3:15—The Genesis of All Prophecy*. There has been a lot of thought and research put in to this writing. Those who read it will be both strengthened and stabilized in their faith.

—RABBI KIRT SCHNEIDER, Discovering the Jewish Jesus

A few years ago, I heard someone say, "Everyone needs a rabbi." I am honored to call Rabbi Eric Walker, the author of this life-giving book, "my rabbi." Our mutual thirst for truth opened the door for our friendship, and I'm honored to be a part of this amazing story of redemption. As you read this profoundly complex, yet understandable, story of God's plan for mankind, your hope will be renewed and your faith in the God of Abraham, Isaac, and Jacob will be reinforced as together we await the return of our Messiah.

—GERMAINE COPELAND, speaker and author of the best-selling *Prayers That Avail Much* book series

"It is the beginning of a love story, ultimately written in blood on a wooden cross that was erected in Judea almost two thousand years ago." Rabbi Walker's eloquence is captivating as he describes, from a Jewish believer's perspective, God's unique relationship with His chosen people, church history, and its exclusion of Messianic Jews. Rabbi Walker carefully unpacks insights from a thorough historical timeline and identifies the attempts of Satan to thwart God's plans. You will be amazed as you learn the Genesis of prophecy and how to recognize Satan's schemes, while discovering timeless mysteries revealed in Bible prophecy. And, most of all, your eyes will turn upward as you pray with urgency along with the saints, "Even so Lord, Jesus, come quickly."

—RHONDA STOPPE, No Regrets Woman; bestselling author of seven books, including *Moms Raising Sons to Be Men*

My eyes are opened and yours will be too! I am left with a holy fascination and an awe of our all-sovereign God Jehovah after reading Rabbi Eric

Walker's latest masterpiece *3:15—The Genesis of Prophecy*. Rabbi Walker follows the prophetic words of Jehovah God to us in Genesis 3:15 and how this verse plays out through the whole Bible front to back and throughout world history speaking of the full assault of Satan against "the Seed of Eve," that in the end leads up to the ultimate demise of the enemy at the hands of our all-powerful God! Rabbi Walker brings specific examples of how this prophetic picture has played out in our world through his deep knowledge of world history, and he takes you on a tour of Scripture, too, showing you as a guide how this theme manifests throughout the entirety of God's Word! As a minister of inner healing and deliverance, I believe that this book has tremendous meaning and very important implications for the deep questions and wounds of the human soul with which we all struggle. Rabbi Walker helps us to make sense of the big-picture truth that there truly is an enemy in this fallen world named Satan, who has a very real purpose to kill us and eradicate us from God's great plan to rule, reign, and relate with us His children again as He did in the beginning the Garden of Eden. Rabbi Walker explains in real examples how Satan has already been working his evil plan and how he will try to do so in the future also, empowering us to understand the times in which we live. We know our struggle is not against flesh and blood, according, to Ephesians 3:16, and our own healing and deliverance are in understanding this in context of the great spiritual battle in which we are caught, and how that battle is playing out in our world and in our everyday circumstances. I pray that you find the healing, the deliverance, and the great awe and revelation of God's holiness that I have found in these pages too!

—STEVE FAIR, LMSW, author, *Journey into the Divided Heart*,
    director of Renewal Christian Counseling Centers, and
    HeartSync Ministries coordinator of Michigan

There is a saying among Christians, "God loves you and has a wonderful plan for your life." This gives us solace, but it is only half true. Satan also has a plan for our lives. He hates us and has plans to rob, kill, and destroy. In *3:15—The Genesis of All Prophecy*, Eric Walker shows us how Satan has been trying to destroy God's plan of redemption since the very beginning. If Satan can't deceive and destroy us, he will try to interfere with and thwart God's plan. Walker calls Genesis 3:15 the most significant prophetic passage in the Bible. The bigger question, and one that plagued Walker for many years, is "Why?" As a scholar, he meticulously unpacks the reasons this is so significant. We then begin to see throughout the Bible just how sinister our adversary is, attempting at every turn (think Herod's infanticide) to crush God's redemptive plan for you and me. The good news is that God invites us to embark on a new journey toward promise, toward freedom, and toward restoration.

—DON S. OTIS, Veritas president with thirty years of experience managing successful corporate media campaigns, author publicity campaigns, and overseeing creative media writing and immediate-response releases. Otis has written four traditionally published books, and his writing has appeared in such publications as *Focus on the Family, Charisma, ParentLife, Living with Teenagers, Light & Life,* and *Christian Single.*

And I will put enmity between thee and the woman, and between thy seed and her seed; it shall bruise thy head, and thou shalt bruise his heel.

GENESIS 3:15

3:15

THE GENESIS OF ALL PROPHECY

RABBI ERIC E. WALKER

Foreword by Carl Gallups

DEFENDER

CRANE, MO

3:15—The Genesis of All Prophecy
by Rabbi Eric E. Walker
Defender Publishing
Crane, MO 65633

ISBN 13: 9781948014564

Unless otherwise noted, all Scripture quoted is from the The Holy Bible, King James Version.

To Amanda and Mila
My treasured daughter and granddaughter

Acknowledgments

To my grandfather, Robert Amper, my Poppy, who instilled in me my Jewish identity and love for Israel.

I can never underestimate the impact of the Gentile friends who twenty-five years ago encouraged me to find the Lord. Your persistence changed the course of my life and led me to Messiah.

Special thanks to my board and their families; the Lozito and the Parrish families have stood by my side with love, grace, and unwavering support for the past sixteen years.

To Tom Horn and the SkyWatchTV/Defender Publishing team, who took me in and honored me through countless interviews and ultimately brought me into the family to publish this book.

To Angie Peters, editor extraordinaire, whose gifts and talents made an immeasurable difference in taking the raw manuscript and producing this polished and professionally edited finished work.

To Ido Keynan, my Israeli guide and brother who has been so faithful to me and sustained me with love through some of the most difficult days of my life. A true brother is a special gift.

To my Messiah, above all, who orchestrated my life to lead me to faith at almost forty-five years old, and removed my stony heart and gave me His heart of flesh.

CONTENTS

Foreword

By Carl Gallups

Messianic Rabbi Eric Walker's journey to Yeshua as Messiah and Lord is one that can only be described as stunningly supernatural, divinely appointed...and almost humanly impossible. Some of the obstacles thrust in his path down through the years have been heartrending. Yet, Yeshua Ha Mashiach has brought Him through them all. And he's still standing strong as a faithful warrior for the only kingdom that truly matters...the Kingdom of Yahweh.

As a young Jewish boy growing up in Pittsburgh, Pennsylvania, Eric was steeped in Jewish orthodoxy. But his soul was restless and his mind unsettled regarding the deep truths and mysteries of God's Word.

Eric would continually come across certain passages in the Tanakh that intrigued him, yet no one of truly prominent standing in the orthodox circles seemed to possess deeper insight into these mysterious utterances. So, looking for answers, he searched out the rabbis of old through their ancient writings as well as contemporary rabbis who were teaching in some of today's influential synagogues. However, few agreed upon the biblical solutions to the puzzles, much less offered cogent rationality in seeking the ultimate truth of the matters that disturbed Eric the most.

This was especially so of the very first prophetic pronouncement found in the Word of God. To Eric, it was almost unexplainable. What made it even more intriguing is that it fell straight from the lips of Elohim Himself. That prophecy was embedded in the first few pages of the very first book in the Bible: "From the womb of a woman will come a seed…".

Eric desperately wanted to know: Who was this mysterious "seed"? What human woman could possibly bring forth that seed…the seed who would ultimately slay the Garden's vile serpent of devastating deception, then finally restore Paradise to redeemed humanity? It was within the tightly wrapped enigma of that prophetic warning that Eric's journey began. It wouldn't be a simple quest, nor would it be a puzzle easily solved. Actually, it would ultimately prove to be a decades-long journey before he got to the bottom of the matter.

What you are about to read is that amazing story—one that is still unfolding, yet one that, through the years, has brought much light and enlightenment to millions of other seekers of truth around the world.

From Eric's unique perspective of having done extensive research and taking advantage of his understanding of the Hebrew language—a language he has read from childhood—you'll now be the benefactor of what he's discovered. I'm convinced that the revelations you'll enjoy in the pages that follow will enhance your understanding of the Word of God in countless and intensely enriching ways.

But, more than that, as Rabbi Walker unravels some of the deepest mysteries of God's Word, he'll do it in a manner that will draw you even closer to the heart of God's great love for *you*. It is, perhaps, deeper than you have ever before imagined.

I've had the great honor of knowing and ministering God's Word with Rabbi Walker for years. He has become a dear friend and brother in the Lord Jesus Christ. He's a gracious, humble, and genuinely Jesus-loving scholar of God's Word. His heart for God's people is as big as any I've ever encountered. You'll see all of this for yourself as you follow along in his quest for the truth and see how it all connects to the mystery of the soon-coming restitution of all things.

This book truly "explains everything"—from ancient history all the way up to the events on the current page of today's calendar. The world, even life itself, is going to make so much more sense to you. *I promise.*

The turn of the next page will begin a journey of biblical discovery that you'll be glad you took.

—CARL GALLUPS, senior pastor since 1987; Amazon Top-60
    best-selling author of multiple books

3:15

T H E
GENESIS
O F   A L L
PROPHECY

Introduction

Nothing has gripped me more in my Jewish[1] studies than why I could not find the fulfillment of Genesis[2] 3:15 in the Tanakh[3]—the Jewish Old Testament. As I began to study in earnest as a young Jewish boy, it was this passage and prophetic promise of God[4] that I asked about in every encounter I had with my Sunday school teachers and ultimately countless numbers of rabbis.[5] The older I got, the more I pressed this issue, and the more I irritated the teachers and the rabbis. If the answer was not found in the Tanakh, when did God do what He said He would do to fulfill His first prophecy[6]?

I was always directed to read what the Talmud[7] (the source from which the code of Jewish Halakah[8] [law] is derived) had to say. It is made up of the Mishnah[9] and the Gemara.[10] The Mishnah is the original written version of the oral law, and the Gemara is the record of the rabbinic discussions. The leading authority and most-often quoted rabbi in the Talmud is Rashi.[11] (Rabbi Solomon ben Isaac [Shlomo Yitzhaki], known as Rashi [based on an acronym of his Hebrew initials], is one of the most influential Jewish commentators in history. All editions of the Talmud published since the 1520s have included Rashi's commentary in the margins.) When searching the Talmud for wisdom and insight into Genesis 3:15, Rashi simply states in Sotah[12] 9b:[13]

1

I said that the snake will walk upright, but now he shall go on his belly; I said that his food will be the same as the food eaten by a person, but now he shall eat dust. The snake said: I will kill Adam and marry Eve, but now: I will put enmity between you and the woman and between your seed and her seed. (Genesis 3:15)

That's it? That is all they had to say about the catalyst for the ongoing plot of Satan to eliminate the only one on earth who could defeat him? The most-quoted rabbi in Judaism made not one mention of a future encounter wherein the seed of the woman would crush the head of the seed of the serpent? The most venerable rabbi—in the single largest study guide for Jewish commentary, the Talmud—had nothing to say about God's first prophecy that would bring an end to all evil in the world.

Pursuing Answers

From my earliest recollection of Torah study, I was relentless in my pursuit of an answer, as there was something in this prophecy that held a key to the future of all mankind. Yet, the more I sought information, the more I was rebuffed. I was perceived as unruly, rebellious, and ultimately unteachable. I would not give up, and although the rabbis stifled my inquiry for a period of time, I took up the mantle again in my twenties after moving to Atlanta, where I joined the most respected Orthodox[14] synagogue in the city. I attended the many Bible studies offered to win favor with the rabbi so I could ultimately address this world-renowned scholar with the question that burned so deeply within me. He, too, sent me for further Talmudic study and urged me to embrace the teachings of Rashi, Maimonides,[15] and others, but still none placed the same degree of eternal significance upon this passage as I did. I pressed my agenda to discuss this as being a prophetic sign that would change the world, but, like Copernicus,[16] my theory was not taken seriously, and

I was ultimately put out of the synagogue. As I went from one teacher to the next, it was as if they had all prepared the same response: "Go to Israel and study in Yeshiva;[17] maybe they will entertain your notion."

It was now seventeen years later, and I had a senior-level position in corporate America. I could not go to live in Israel to study, yet the question about the fulfillment of Genesis 3:15 remained. I had nowhere else to turn.

Shortly after my separation from the synagogue, I began my own search. I briefly examined the Eastern religions of Buddhism[18] and Daoism,[19] and ultimately landed among a group of New Age[20] believers who were actually quite warm and engaging. They embraced the teachings of Neal Donald Walsch,[21] who claimed to have had "conversations with God," and Deepak Chopra.[22] I found their past life regressions, channeling of the dead, attributing powers to crystals, and embracing the "true god within ourselves" quite implausible and certainly in conflict with my foundational Jewish teaching. It was, however, quite spiritually eye opening as I rose to have followers of my own within just a few months. It was through this experience that I began to realize that most people will follow or subject themselves to the strongest spirit in the room without regard for its authenticity or lack thereof.

Again, I found myself alone, with nowhere to turn to find a reliable answer to my question about Genesis 3:15. I searched the Internet, but none of the Jewish commentators provided a satisfactory explanation that could be found in the Hebrew Bible.[23] Would my question ever be resolved?

Influence of Christian Friends

Several major changes had taken place in my life and career, and although I was now in my early forties, I had never had many non-Jewish friends. For the first time I was meeting new Christian[24] friends—and every time we would get together, they invited me to church.

3

I would tell them, "I am Jewish," and they would say, "I'm sorry."

"Sorry for what, me being Jewish?" I would ask. And they would just state that they didn't want to offend me.

After two years of this dialogue, they finally came to me and said, "We found a place that is really Jewish, and we would like to take you there."

Then I really was offended. What could these Gentiles know about being Jewish, or about having family members die in the Holocaust?[25]

> *I awoke one morning asking myself, "Why do I need Gentile friends to show me something that is Jewish?"*

When they gave me the name of the place, I told them to just let it go, and they did. But, something inside me wanted to know more. Without their knowledge, I began to call this synagogue, and I spoke at length many times with Susan Remer, the temporary secretary. She was kind to me and answered every question I had regarding what that place was all about: Jewish people who believed that Jesus[26] was the Messiah.

I have to admit I knew nothing about Yeshua[27]/Jesus. I did not know He was Jewish, nor was I aware that His being Jewish was a really big deal. The more the secretary explained, the more I began to wonder why I had never heard any of this before. You would think that I would have known more about Christianity, but I lived in a Jewish "bubble." Any reference I ever heard about Jesus was automatically placed in a bucket in my mind that equated Him to the God of the Gentiles.[28] Who would have told me otherwise—my grandparents? My rabbis? My Jewish friends and family? As a Jew, I knew nothing about Christianity and had no desire to know.

When I told my Christian friends that I had been talking to the secretary at the synagogue they mentioned, they were elated and said they would take me there. We made plans to go to services on Friday evening, December 27, 1996. However, I awoke the morning of Saturday, December 21, 1996, asking myself, "Why do I need Gentile friends to show me something that is Jewish?" I decided I would go to the 11 a.m. service that day and find out for myself. That was two weeks before my forty-fifth birthday.

Finding Sanctuary

When I arrived, I was met at the door by a distinctively Jewish man, and I was immediately ushered into the rabbi's office. This, in itself, wasn't a common occurrence in my synagogue life, as the rabbis I knew were scholars and weren't very accessible to just anyone walking in the door. As I entered, I had full line of sight into the sanctuary, which looked exactly as the ones I had seen all my life. The pews were filled with people wearing kippahs[29] (yarmulke) and tallit[30] (prayer shawls.) The rabbi was very talkative and asked me why I was there. I told him of my search for the answer to my question about Genesis 3:15, and he assured me that this would be the place where I would find my answer. He then ushered me into the sanctuary. The service was all too familiar, and I immediately felt comfortable. Then he began to preach. He never took his eyes off of me as he explained the lamb of God on Mount Moriah[31] who redeemed Isaac[32] and the lamb sacrificed for our freedom in Exodus12.[33] But then he began to talk about the son of a Levitical[34] priest who saw a man named Yeshua and said, "Behold the Lamb of God who takes away our sins."

A man who could take away sin? This was profound to me, as the only other reference to sin being taken away that I was familiar with was once per year, according to Leviticus 16, for the Day of Atonement.[35] The words captivated me, and the more the rabbi spoke of this Yeshua, the more intrigued I was to hear more.

And more I heard.

When presented with an invitation to have my sins forever taken away, I leapt at the opportunity, raised my hand, said a prayer of confession and atonement, and was then asked to come forward to shake the rabbi's hand. I knew in my heart I had made a life-changing decision, but was filled with even more questions—and I still wanted an answer to my most pressing one about the fulfillment of Genesis 3:15.

I quickly immersed myself in this new life as a Jewish believer in Yeshua/Jesus and was immediately placed in a discipleship program with the promise that I would find the answer to my question and so much more.

Counting the Cost

Growing up in a Jewish family in a Jewish neighborhood and being immersed in the Jewish world, there was little outside of that bubble that was discussed other than matters of importance to a Jewish family. My grandfather, Poppy, instilled a love for Israel that some might call Zionism, but being a Zionist implies that all Jews should live in Israel.

In 1959, my grandfather, Robert Amper, was named "Israel Bonds Man of the Decade." This meant he had raised more money for Israel than anyone else in the past decade. Since Israel's birth in 1948, the financial need was great, and millions of Jews were in need of food, clothing, shelter, and medical aid far beyond this new government's ability to generate from a population recovering from the decimation of the Holocaust. My grandfather saw that the need was great and devoted every free moment to advocating and raising financial support for Israel.

In 1959, David Ben Gurion, Israel's first prime minister, flew from Tel Aviv to Pittsburgh to honor my grandfather. When asked the question from the prime minister, "When do you plan to move your family to Israel?" my grandfather replied, "If all the Jews in America left to live in Israel, who would be left behind to advocate and raise money?" We were raised with this philosophy, and it was never discussed in any part of our family that we should one day move to Israel.

When I came to faith in Yeshua as my Messiah on December 21, 1996, I embraced my Jewishness with a renewed fervor and an insatiable appetite to know what life beyond Torah and the "Jewish" world was like. It was as if the catalyst that ignited the flame and made it burn brighter was that I was now connected to my Jewish roots and heritage continuously from Abraham to the present day, and it was richer and more fulfilling than anything I had experienced in my Jewish life before.

Not long after accepting Messiah, thoughts of Israel began to enter my mind. Even though I had no previous desire to even visit there, I now not only wanted to visit, but to meet and connect with other Jewish believers. Two events in my life collided, and I began to realize that not everyone shared my enthusiasm for the decision I had made to follow the teachings of Yeshua and the New Testament.

I was never close with my family, and when I shared my decision with them, it was ignored by some and passively rejected by others. Over time, I began to realize no one was talking to me anymore, and I was no longer being invited to family events. I began to hear stories about Jewish families actually holding funerals over their children who had accepted Yeshua/Jesus as their Messiah. In reality, my family just didn't care enough to go to any trouble; they just stopped talking to me.

It was during a Jewish Roots and Heritage class that I first heard that if you are a known Jewish believer in Yeshua/Jesus, regardless of your birthright, Israel will deny you the rights granted to you under the Law of Return. This law was enacted so that any Jewish person who had at least one Jewish grandparent could receive citizenship in Israel. For someone like myself who had both a Jewish mother and father and only Jewish family on both sides, there were even greater benefits offered by the State of Israel under the Law of Return. You were entitled to health benefits, housing support, educational support while learning Hebrew, and a host of other benefits reserved for those of full Jewish descent. If you were known to have made a profession of faith in Yeshua/Jesus, then you were disqualified from all benefits and treated as though you were no longer Jewish.

As my learning increased, I realized that following Yeshua was not just a matter of faith, but that I was being called into leadership and was being given a voice. I knew I was going to have to decide if I was willing to pay the price of losing my ability to be a citizen of Israel. In addition, I would be considered to have disconnected from fourteen million other Jews who would no longer consider me Jewish. My family had already gone silent, and now I knew if I became a vocal leader in advancing Yeshua/Jesus as the Jewish Messiah, I would have to pay the ultimate cost.

In November, 2006, I was ordained as a Messianic rabbi and became the founding rabbi of a congregation in Birmingham, Alabama. In 2007, I published my first book that made it abundantly clear that I still saw myself as being Jewish and lived the life of a Jew; the only difference was that I had accepted Yeshua/Jesus as my Jewish Messiah. Once Google knew, Israel knew, and the price was paid. Although I was able to place an overwhelming amount of documentation personally collected chronicling the lives of my relatives lost in the Holocaust and the birth and marriage certificates of my parents and grandparents on both sides into the hands of an attorney who worked directly with the Minister of the Interior of Israel, I was denied citizenship there because of my faith in Yeshua/Jesus. To this day, twenty-five years later, I consider it a blessing and a privilege to be able to love and support Israel and those who have rejected me because of my faith, because I am truly walking in the footsteps of my Messiah, who was also rejected for who He was.

Back to the Question...and the Finding the Answer

Over the course of my rigorous study, graduation from a Messianic yeshiva (school), being ordained as a Messianic[36] rabbi at age fifty-five, and planting and growing the world's largest Messianic synagogue, I had found my answer.

Now, twenty-five years after raising my hand and walking that aisle, I want to share with you how Genesis 3:15 is the most significant prophetic passage in the Bible and is the foundation of each of God's actions throughout the entirety of Scripture.

Following the God of Abraham, Isaac, and Jacob and believing in God's plan of salvation[37] through the shed blood of Messiah requires that a decision be made and a path of life chosen.

Following Satan[38] requires none of that: No confession. No repentance. No acceptance. No regenerated life. No decision at all. If you do

> *If you do not make the one decision, the other decision has been made for you.*

not make the one decision, the other decision has been made for you, and your lack of making a decision is your choice and your choice alone. You do not have to do anything to perish. You don't have to believe in anything, but you cannot change your final destination unless you do.

May this book bring you to a point of decision. I made mine, and it cost me much on earth, but what awaits me is so much greater. Some would say I am a fool. At least I am a fool for something, and can never look back and say I did not make a choice.

Take this journey with me and open the eyes of your heart so you may see what I have searched for my entire life.

1

In the Beginning

With only fourteen verses describing Creation,[39] referring to the fifty-chapter book of Genesis as "the story of Creation" is a misnomer. In reality, Genesis is a prophetic book of separation, covenants, promises of a conflict that will be orchestrated by one of God's most powerful—yet evil—actors, and the future redemption of all mankind through the promised seed of the woman.

A Book of Separation

God separated light from darkness. He separated the waters from above and the waters from below. He separated the waters from the land. He separated the greater light from the lesser light. He separated the dust of the earth, breathed life into it, and called it man. He separated the man's own body, and from it created woman. He separated truth from lies, and He ultimately separated man from God Himself. Darkness prevailed over light, and the fall of man and the rise of Satan's power separated death from life. And, finally, God separated man from Eden, Paradise.

First Prophecy

In Genesis 3:15, we read God's first prophecy. In speaking with the serpent (Satan), God proclaims Satan's ultimate destiny and demise:

> And I will put enmity between thee and the woman, and between thy seed and her seed; it shall bruise thy head, and thou shalt bruise his heel.

Imagine what it would be like to receive a death sentence. In the United States, all death sentences are granted an automatic appeal, and every possible tool is employed to find a way to postpone the inevitable through a stay of execution, or, ideally, with a commutation of the sentence—or, even better, by obtaining a full pardon. Every strategy is explored in the hopes that the sentence can be reversed.

We do not define God; God defines us.

In Genesis 3:15, Satan is told who will bring about his demise and how He will do it. What isn't stated is *when*. The best strategy would be for Satan to find a way to eliminate his executioner; that way, his dominion on earth would be secure forever. If he could stop the seed of the woman from coming into the world, his ultimate victory as prince of this world would be assured. Satan has already secured his first triumph by usurping man's dominion over the earth. Now he is empowered to rule and reign over mankind; ultimately, those who would choose him over God will build a demonic army equipped with a supernatural stockpile of spiritual weapons of mass destruction: pride, lies, deception, false promises, fear, envy, rage, jealousy, and an inherent hatred of all in the seed line of the woman—the Jews. If Satan can eliminate the Jews, the promised seed of the woman will never be born. Consumed with the pride that got him kicked out Heaven,[40] His battle plan and strategy are now being formulated. God makes this abundantly clear in His admonition to Cain[41] in Genesis 4:6–7:

> And the LORD said unto Cain, Why art thou wroth? and why is thy countenance fallen?
>
> If thou doest well, shalt thou not be accepted? and if thou doest not well, sin lieth at the door. And unto thee shall be his desire, and thou shalt rule over him.

Now all Satan has to do is keep a watchful eye out for how God will reveal the seed line of the woman and mount his attack. Driven by an insatiable delusion, he still believes he can ascend to the throne of Heaven and become God.

Known by many names—Lucifer, Apollyon, Abaddon, Beelzebub, Mastema, Sammael, and more—Satan is described as the most beautiful and wisest of all God's angels. His access to the throne of Heaven made him a master of God's Word. He knew that the seed of the woman was Yeshua/Jesus, that He would be born of a virgin, and that He would ultimately die. He knew and believed God's Word, but remained obsessed by pride in the belief that he could usurp God's plans and authority. His strategy would be to enlist a host of minions to thwart the birth of the seed of the woman, entirely ensuring his dominion as prince of this world.

If Satan can eliminate the Jews, the promised seed of the woman will never be born.

The death of the seed of the woman is confirmed within the Word, and its earliest mention is hidden within the genealogy included in Genesis 5. Late biblical scholar Chuck Missler made the following discovery:

Since the ten Hebrew names are proper names, they are not translated but only transliterated to approximate the way they were pronounced. The meaning of proper names can be a difficult pursuit, since direct translations are not readily available. Many study aids, such as conventional lexicons, can prove superficial when dealing with proper names. Even a conventional Hebrew lexicon can be disappointing. A study of the original roots, however, can yield some fascinating insights. (It should be recognized, however, that the views concerning the meaning and significance of the original roots are not free of controversy and are subject to variant readings. This is why we receive so many questions and comments on variations.)

Adam—The first name, Adam, comes from *adomah*, and means "man." As the first man, that seems straightforward enough.

Seth—Adam's son was named Seth, which means "appointed." When he was born, Eve said, "For God hath appointed me another seed instead of Abel, whom Cain slew."

Enosh—Seth's son was called Enosh, which means "mortal," "frail," or "miserable." It is from the root *anash*: "to be incurable"; used of a wound, grief, woe, sickness, or wickedness. (It was in the days of Enosh that men began to defile the name of the Living God.)

Kenan—Enosh's son was named Kenan, which can mean "sorrow," dirge," or "elegy." (The precise denotation is somewhat elusive; some study aids unfortunately presume an Aramaic root synonymous with "Cainan.") Balaam, looking down from the heights of Moab, employed a pun upon the name of the Kenites when he prophesied their destruction.

Mahalalel—Kenan's son was Mahalalel, from *mahalal*, which means "blessed" or "praise" and *el*, the name for God. Thus, Mahalalel means "the Blessed God." Hebrew names often included *el*, the name of God, as Dani-*el*, "God is my Judge," Nathani-*el*, "Gift of God," etc.

Jared—Mahalalel's son was named Jared, from the verb *yaradh*, meaning "shall come down." Some authorities suggest that this might have been an allusion to the "Sons of God" who "came down" to corrupt the daughters of men, resulting in the Nephilim ("Fallen Ones") of Genesis 6.

Enoch—Jared's son was named Enoch, which means "teaching" or "commencement." He was the first of four generations of preachers. In fact, the earliest recorded prophecy was by Enoch—which, amazingly enough, deals with the Second Coming of Christ.

Methuselah—The Flood of Noah did not come as a surprise. It had been preached on for four generations. But something strange happened when Enoch was sixty-five, from which time "he walked with God." Enoch was given a prophecy that as long as his son was alive, the judgment of the Flood would be withheld; but as soon as he died, it would be sent forth.

Enoch named his son to reflect this prophecy. The name Methuselah comes from two roots: *muth*, a root that means "death," and *shalach*, which means "to bring" or "to send forth." Thus, the name Methuselah signifies "his death shall bring." And, indeed, in the year that Methuselah died, the Flood came. Methuselah was 187 when he had Lamech, and then he lived 782 years more. Lamech had Noah when he was 182. The Flood came in Noah's 600th year. 187 + 182 + 600 = 969, Methuselah's age when he died. It is interesting that Methuselah's life was, in effect, a symbol of God's mercy in forestalling the coming judgment of the Flood. It is therefore fitting that his lifetime is the oldest in the Bible, symbolizing the extreme extent of God's mercy.

Lamech—Methuselah's son was named Lamech, a root still evident today in our own English word, "lament" or "lamentation." Lamech suggests "despairing." (This name is also linked to the Lamech in Cain's line, who inadvertently killed his son, Tubal-Cain, in a hunting incident.)

Noah—Lamech, of course, is the father of Noah, which is derived from *nacham*, "to bring relief" or "comfort," as Lamech himself explains.[42]

The Composite List

Hebrew	English
Adam	Man
Seth	Appointed
Enosh	Mortal
Kenan	Sorrow;
Mahalalel	The Blessed God
Jared	Shall come down
Enoch	Teaching
Methuselah	His death shall bring
Lamech	The despairing
Noah	Rest, or comfort.

Now let's put it all together: "Man is appointed mortal sorrow, but The Blessed God shall come down teaching that His death would bring those in despair, rest."

Here is a summary of God's plan of redemption, hidden within a genealogy in Genesis! You will never convince me that a group of Jewish rabbis deliberately "contrived" to hide the "Christian gospel" right here in a genealogy within their venerated Torah! The implications of this discovery are far more significant than may be evident at first glance. It demonstrates that, in the earliest chapters of the book of Genesis, God had already laid out His plan of redemption for the predicament of mankind. It is the beginning of a love story, ultimately written in blood on a wooden cross that was erected in Judea almost two thousand years ago.[43]

And it came to pass, when men began to multiply on the face of the earth, and daughters were born unto them,

That the sons of God saw the daughters of men that they were fair; and they took them wives of all which they chose.

And the LORD said, My spirit shall not always strive with man, for that he also is flesh: yet his days shall be an hundred and twenty years.

There were giants in the earth in those days; and also after that, when the sons of God came in unto the daughters of men, and they bare children to them, the same became mighty men which were of old, men of renown.

And GOD saw that the wickedness of man was great in the earth, and that every imagination of the thoughts of his heart was only evil continually.

And it repented the LORD that he had made man on the earth, and it grieved him at his heart.

And the LORD said, I will destroy man whom I have created from the face of the earth; both man, and beast, and the creeping thing, and the fowls of the air; for it repenteth me that I have made them.

But Noah found grace in the eyes of the LORD. (Genesis 6:1–8)

The wickedness of man and the dominion of darkness prevailed over all the earth so that only one righteous among the people was chosen to carry the seed of the woman into a new world. Once again, God covered the earth with the waters from above and the waters from below, and only eight remained. From those eight, God separated one family, Shem and his wife, to carry the promised seed of the woman. Satan's first attempt to destroy the seed line of Messiah failed, and God began the process of ensuring its future protection.

In Genesis 9, Noah addresses his three sons and blesses Shem:

And he said, Blessed be the Lord God of Shem; and Canaan shall be his servant.

God shall enlarge Japheth, and he shall dwell in the tents of Shem; and Canaan shall be his servant. (Genesis 9:26–27)

This is considered a Messianic prophecy in that it indicates the lineage of the Messiah—that He would be a descendant of Shem, and not Shem's brothers, Japheth or Ham. The Old Testament, especially in the book of Genesis, includes a series of prophecies about the lineage of the Messiah, and this one, Genesis 9:26—27, is viewed as the first.

Satan's Agenda

It is clear from Genesis 6 that the Nephilim were on the earth before and after the Flood, and these fallen ones rebelled against God. Throughout both the Old and New Testaments, they align themselves with the agenda of the serpent/Satan. These disembodied spirits of the fallen angels are looking for a human host to occupy or possess. Nowhere in the Bible do people possessed by demons demonstrate allegiance to God. Their sole commitment is to Satan, whom they choose to follow and share in his dominion over the earth. That agenda is clearly established in the Genesis 3:15 passage that removes man's dominion over the earth and assigns it to Satan. Satan's power will end if the seed of the woman comes into His fullness. Simply stated, if the seed line of Messiah could be destroyed, then Yeshua/Jesus would never be born, and Satan would rule and reign as the prince of this earth for eternity.

A People Set Apart

Since, even after the Flood, all of humanity continued in depravity and idol worship, the seed line of Messiah had to be established through a people set apart by God. Thus, we see the selection of Abram,[44] an idol-maker's son chosen by God to establish a covenant relationship with Him. No criteria are given as to why God selected Abram; however, the Bible implies that God's choice of the Jews was random; later traditions made the Jews seem deserving of this privilege.

Jewish history, as the Bible tells it, began when God singled out Abram (Abraham) with the command, "Get thee out of thy country, and from thy kindred, and from thy father's house, unto a land that I will show thee" (Genesis 12:1), and with the subsequent promise to bless Abram and his descendants. This blessing, reiterated several times throughout the Bible, became the basis for the idea that the Jewish people have a relationship with God unlike that of any other nation.

In the medieval period, Christian theologians pointed to the political domination of the Holy Roman Empire as proof that the Christians, not the Jews, were God's chosen people. However, God not only chose the Jewish people to be set apart unto Himself, He established them as the seed line of Messiah and the ones chosen to call for His return.

Genesis 15 not only opens the door to the confirmation that Abram would become the father of a great nation, but it establishes the inheritance of the land that both the natural-born Jews before Yeshua and the Jewish and Gentile believers after Yeshua would receive. This is the

—————✦—————

There are only two people groups in the Bible: Jews and Gentiles.

—————————

foundation for the ultimate tearing down of the division between Jew and Gentile, and also negates the need for one to replace the other.

As God confirmed His covenant with Abram in Genesis 15, He spoke a prophetic word over his descendants, as we read in Genesis 15:13–14:

And he said unto Abram, Know of a surety that thy seed shall be a stranger in a land that is not theirs, and shall serve them; and they shall afflict them four hundred years;

And also that nation, whom they shall serve, will I judge: and afterward shall they come out with great substance.

Ishmael vs. Messiah's Seed Line: Two Prophecies

Abram's first son, Ishmael,[45] was not the son of the promise, as the covenant between God and the boy's father had not yet been established at the time of Ishmael's birth. However, God did speak two distinct prophecies regarding Ishmael that we see being fulfilled in the world today.

Here is the first prophecy from Genesis 16:11–12 spoken to Hagar[46] about the child she now carried:

And the angel of the LORD said unto her, Behold, thou art with child, and shalt bear a son, and shalt call his name Ishmael; because the LORD hath heard thy affliction.

And he will be a wild man; his hand will be against every man, and every man's hand against him; and he shall dwell in the presence of all his brethren.

Ishmael's adversarial role against the seed line of Messiah would culminate in an unholy alliance whose sole purpose would be the annihilation of the Jews, thus thwarting the very ones who will call for Messiah's return. This was another added to Satan's army to thwart the birth of the seed of the woman who would crush his head.

It is the passages of Genesis 17 and 18 that establish God's covenant with Abram and his sign of the covenant, circumcision.[47] It is within this same text that we find the second prophecy over Ishmael.

Genesis 17:1–18:10:

And when Abram was ninety years old and nine, the LORD appeared to Abram, and said unto him, I am the Almighty God; walk before me, and be thou perfect.

And I will make my covenant between me and thee, and will multiply thee exceedingly.

And Abram fell on his face: and God talked with him, saying,

As for me, behold, my covenant is with thee, and thou shalt be a father of many nations.

Neither shall thy name any more be called Abram, but thy name shall be Abraham; for a father of many nations have I made thee.

And I will make thee exceeding fruitful, and I will make nations of thee, and kings shall come out of thee.

And I will establish my covenant between me and thee and thy seed after thee in their generations for an everlasting covenant, to be a God unto thee, and to thy seed after thee.

And I will give unto thee, and to thy seed after thee, the land wherein thou art a stranger, all the land of Canaan, for an everlasting possession; and I will be their God.

And God said unto Abraham, Thou shalt keep my covenant therefore, thou, and thy seed after thee in their generations.

This is my covenant, which ye shall keep, between me and you and thy seed after thee; Every man child among you shall be circumcised.

And ye shall circumcise the flesh of your foreskin; and it shall be a token of the covenant betwixt me and you.

And he that is eight days old shall be circumcised among you, every man child in your generations, he that is born in the house, or bought with money of any stranger, which is not of thy seed.

He that is born in thy house, and he that is bought with thy money, must needs be circumcised: and my covenant shall be in your flesh for an everlasting covenant.

And the uncircumcised man child whose flesh of his foreskin is not circumcised, that soul shall be cut off from his people; he hath broken my covenant.

And God said unto Abraham, As for Sarai thy wife, thou shalt not call her name Sarai, but Sarah shall her name be.

And I will bless her, and give thee a son also of her: yea, I will bless her, and she shall be a mother of nations; kings of people shall be of her.

Then Abraham fell upon his face, and laughed, and said in his heart, Shall a child be born unto him that is an hundred years old? and shall Sarah, that is ninety years old, bear?

And Abraham said unto God, O that Ishmael might live before thee!

And God said, Sarah thy wife shall bear thee a son indeed; and thou shalt call his name Isaac: and I will establish my covenant with him for an everlasting covenant, and with his seed after him.

And as for Ishmael, I have heard thee: Behold, I have blessed him, and will make him fruitful, and will multiply him exceedingly; twelve princes shall he beget, and I will make him a great nation.

But my covenant will I establish with Isaac, which Sarah shall bear unto thee at this set time in the next year.

And he left off talking with him, and God went up from Abraham.

And Abraham took Ishmael his son, and all that were born in his house, and all that were bought with his money, every male among the men of Abraham's house; and circumcised the flesh of their foreskin in the selfsame day, as God had said unto him.

And Abraham was ninety years old and nine, when he was circumcised in the flesh of his foreskin.

And Ishmael his son was thirteen years old, when he was circumcised in the flesh of his foreskin.

In the selfsame day was Abraham circumcised, and Ishmael his son.

And all the men of his house, born in the house, and bought with money of the stranger, were circumcised with him.

And the LORD appeared unto him in the plains of Mamre: and he sat in the tent door in the heat of the day;

And he lift up his eyes and looked, and, lo, three men stood by him: and when he saw them, he ran to meet them from the tent door, and bowed himself toward the ground,

And said, My Lord, if now I have found favour in thy sight, pass not away, I pray thee, from thy servant:

Let a little water, I pray you, be fetched, and wash your feet, and rest yourselves under the tree:

And I will fetch a morsel of bread, and comfort ye your hearts; after that ye shall pass on: for therefore are ye come to your servant. And they said, So do, as thou hast said.

And Abraham hastened into the tent unto Sarah, and said, Make ready quickly three measures of fine meal, knead it, and make cakes upon the hearth.

And Abraham ran unto the herd, and fetch a calf tender and good, and gave it unto a young man; and he hasted to dress it.

And he took butter, and milk, and the calf which he had dressed, and set it before them; and he stood by them under the tree, and they did eat.

And they said unto him, Where is Sarah thy wife? And he said, Behold, in the tent.

And he said, I will certainly return unto thee according to the time of life; and, lo, Sarah thy wife shall have a son. And Sarah heard it in the tent door, which was behind him.

Establishing the Covenant

In the same way that the Lord, as recorded in Genesis 15, made His covenant with Abram by passing through the cut animals, Isaac was the first child whose seed passed through the cut—circumcision. The sign of the covenant promise that established Isaac as the son of the promise was fulfilled during his conception, thus establishing the lineage of the seed of the woman prophesied in Genesis 3:15.

Although Christianity does not embrace physical circumcision as being necessary, the concept of the covenant being confirmed by the passing through the divide, or cut, is evident in both the construction of a church and a ceremony performed there. Many churches are intentionally built with a center aisle. Ask your pastor, and you might be surprised that he or she does not know why. When planning for a wedding, there is a bride's side and a groom's side. Thus, the families are divided. Traditional wedding ceremonies often feature different nuances, but traditionally, the groom and the officiate enter and pass through the divided families. The groom pays special attention to those sitting on "his" side. Without his knowledge, he is actually sending them a signal: "This is the last time you will see me." And to his parents, he is saying, "This is the last time I belong to you." As the groom waits to receive his bride, he watches as she makes the same journey he made as she walks through the separated families and friends. She is sending the same messages: "This is the last time you will see me as this single person" and, to her parents, "This is the last time I belong to you."

After the ceremony, the return journey is made through the divided families and friends, but this time, the bride and groom walk together, confirming their covenant to each other and illustrating that they no longer belong to either side.

This reenactment of God passing through the divided animals to confirm His covenant with Abraham and his descendants and the act of circumcision creating a cut that the seed must pass through are both a demonstration of God creating a oneness between Himself and the descendants of Abraham and the confirmation of the covenant of marriage as the two become one.

Tracking the Seed Line

Isaac married Rebecca, who bore twins Esau and Jacob, the eldest of whom was Esau. Again, it was not the firstborn who would secure the seed of the woman; Esau sold his birthright and fathered the Edomites, who would become enemies of the seed line of Messiah. And the enmity between the seed of the serpent and the seed of the woman grew stronger as Satan further divided brother against brother.

Over the course of time, the lineage of Abraham to Isaac and Isaac to Jacob was secured when Jacob married Leah and their son Judah was born. It was through Judah that the seed line of Messiah would pass. Ultimately, Jacob took four wives and, to his beloved Rachel, Joseph was born.

Joseph: Prophetic Roles

Of Jacob's twelve sons, Joseph was destined by God to be rejected by his family in order to fulfill two important prophetic roles. The first was after he had gained favor with Pharaoh. His family had been reduced to only seventy members, and it was on the verge of extinction due to the great famine. Joseph was able to bring his family to Egypt, where Pharaoh gave them the rich grazing fields of Goshen to replenish their dwindling numbers. For thirty years, they enjoyed the favor of Pharaoh, but, as God had prophesied to Abram in Genesis 15, they would be afflicted for four hundred years.

The second important prophetic role Joseph played was archetypal. During the twenty-five-year period between Joseph being given the dream by God and the dream's actual fulfillment as recorded in Genesis 50:20, Joseph became a poster child for suffering. He was rejected by his family, sold into bondage, falsely imprisoned, and served the dreams of the cupbearer and the baker, but was forgotten for the two years he spent in prison as punishment for a crime he did not commit.

Much can and has been said about the strength of Joseph's faith, and at no time did he speak out against God. Truly, Joseph was a model for suffering, giving us a glimpse into the character of Messiah, who came as the Suffering Servant.

These represent the more obvious attributes shared by Joseph and Jesus, but, as we examine the birth of Messiah, it's also important to note that God chose a man named Joseph to be His Son's earthly father. Certainly, God could have picked anyone with any Hebrew name, but He chose a man named Joseph so that Jesus would be known as "Yeshua ben Joseph." In this archetypal fulfillment, we can now read this as "Jesus, son of Suffering." And, equally as stunning will be His return when He comes as Jesus, Son of David. David is the archetype of Israel's long-awaited, victorious King.

Pharaoh's Efforts Thwarted

As a new Pharaoh who did not know Joseph rose to power, Satan's influence gripped the leader with a spirit of fear as he assessed the ever-increasing numbers of the Hebrew people. He unwittingly became a tool of Satan, ordering—in a diabolical attempt to cut off the seed line of Messiah—that boys born to Hebrew women should be killed. He increased his persecution of the Hebrew people until God sent a Redeemer, but that did not happen until near the very end of the prophesied four hundred years. At that time, in a stunning show of power, God delivered His people from centuries of slavery and defeated all of Pharaoh's armies. The seed line of Messiah remained intact; Satan's plan to destroy it failed.

2

Manifestations of
Satan's Influence

Old Testament

> Be sober, be vigilant; because your adversary the devil, as a roaring lion, walketh about, seeking whom he may devour: Whom resist stedfast in the faith, knowing that the same afflictions are accomplished in your brethren that are in the world.
>
> 1 PETER 5:8–9

Throughout Scripture, we see multiple manifestations of Satan's influence. In many cases, his attributes are seen without specific citation. However, as the "father of lies" who comes to lie, kill, and destroy, we see numerous examples of his influence on the character and behavior of many. Scripture establishes that God is light, and that every good gift comes from Him; therefore, it is safe to examine, in context, the numerous accounts of rebellion, pride, anger, envy, jealousy, rage, lies, and other behaviors that exhibit an evil agenda and attribute some of them to Satan's desire to eliminate the seed line of the woman. In other cases of man's avarice and sin that do not align with elimination of the seed line of the woman, Messiah, these are simply a reflection of the fallen state of man and the wickedness of our hearts.

The Divine Council

Satan is a member of God's divine council,[48] as described in *The Unseen Realm* by Dr. Michael Heiser:

> The contrasts of good versus evil and life versus death were never more pronounced than in Scripture's portrayal of the first defection from God's will. I speak here of the fall (Genesis 3).
>
> We tend to think of that episode primarily in human terms. That's understandable, since the fall affected the entirety of the human race.
>
> But behind the decisions of Adam and Eve to violate God's command about the tree of the knowledge of good and evil, there was another created being, supernatural in nature, who had decided his own will was preeminent.
>
> Most readers will acknowledge that the serpent (Heb. *nāḥāš*) was not simply a member of the animal kingdom. This conclusion seems obvious, since the New Testament identifies the serpent as Satan or the devil (Rev[elation] 12:9).
>
> The devil is certainly not a zoological specimen (2 Corinthians 11:14; cf. Matthew 4:1–11; John 8:44). Put simply, if we agree with the New Testament that a supernatural being (Satan) tempted Eve in Eden, then by definition the serpent must be more than a mere animal. We can only oppose this conclusion if we reject the New Testament assessment.
>
> Ancient readers—without the New Testament—would be able to draw the same conclusion, though they didn't necessarily use the same vocabulary. They of course knew that animals did not talk, and so when that sort of thing was encountered in storytelling, they knew supernatural power was at play or a divine presence had taken center stage.
>
> Ancient readers would have thought about Eden in such a

way that the supernatural nature of the serpent would have been conspicuous. We think of the garden of Eden like we think of earthly gardens. We know God was there, but a garden is a garden; Eden was a perfect garden, but, at the end of the day, it was just a garden.

People from the biblical period would have had a different perception, one that was more transcendent. They would have thought of Eden as a temple. After all, temples are where gods live. Eden was the abode of God, "an earthly archetype of the heavenly reality."

"Because Adam communed with God in Eden...the latter was the temporal analog for the celestial archetype."

The archetypal nature of Eden as the house-temple of God is why Eden is described as a well-watered garden (Genesis 2:6, 8–9, 10–16; Ezekiel 28:2, 13) and a holy mountain (Ezekiel 28:14). There is no contradiction. An ancient reader would have embraced both descriptions. Both were common characterizations for divine dwellings.

The motif of the garden as an abode of the gods is common in ancient Near Eastern literature.

Several Old Testament passages depict rivers flowing from God's dwelling in Jerusalem to water the desert (Ezekiel 47:1–12; Zechariah 14:8; Joel 3:18). Howard N. Wallace notes that "the main feature of the garden of God theme is the presence of the deity. The divine council meets there and decrees of cosmic importance are issued."

Wallace's observation that the cosmic dwelling (garden or mountain) was also home to the divine council would have been expected by an ancient reader. The scholarly literature on the divine council and its meeting place as a garden or a mountain is extensive.

The divine council, the assembly of the heavenly host, was perceived as an administrative bureaucracy. In biblical thought, the members of the divine council participate in issuing and executing divine decrees. Just as a king has a court, God was His own administration. Where He lives, He conducts business.

Genesis 2–3 portray[s] Eden as a divine garden and mountain. But what indication do we have from Genesis 3 that there is a group of divine beings (a council) in Eden? In Genesis 3:5, the serpent told Eve, "God knows that when you eat of it your eyes will be opened, and you will be like God ['elōhîm], knowing good and evil."

We discover that 'elōhîm in this verse should actually be read as a plural when we reach Genesis 3:22, where God—speaking not to Adam, Eve, or the serpent—says, "Behold, the man has become like one of us in knowing good and evil. Now, lest he reach out his hand and take also of the tree of life and eat, and live forever." The violation resulted in Adam and Eve becoming like "one of us," which obviously requires plurality.

The fact that their sin did indeed result in knowing good and evil tells us the serpent did not lie in that component of his deception. God Himself confirmed the result in verse 22. This means the 'elōhîm of verse 5 points to a group—God's heavenly council.

The implication of seeing Eden through ancient Near Eastern eyes is that God was not the only divine being.

God had created humankind as His imagers and tasked them with bringing the rest of the world outside Eden under control—in effect, expanding Eden through the rest of creation.

God's will was disrupted when an external supernatural tempter, acting autonomously against God's wishes, succeeded in deceiving Eve.[49]

Counterfeit Power Falls Short

In God's economy, wherever there is an authentic move of God, there will also be a counterfeit. Upon examination of the counterfeit, we see deception, lies, false manifestations, and convincing imitations that are similar to the authentic, but fall short. Most notable of these counterfeit manifestations are described in Exodus, as Pharaoh's magicians were able to imitate many of the signs God used to demonstrate His power. For example, when Moses threw down his rod and it turned into a snake, the magicians and priests did so as well; however, ultimately, Moses' snake consumed the snakes of the counterfeiters. In the same manner, the magicians were able to turn water into blood, but they lacked the power to turn the blood back to water. In every case, the authentic God of Abraham, Isaac, and Jacob was able to do exceedingly more than the false gods of Egypt.

Satan the Accuser

Although the book of Job clearly identifies Satan's access to God and includes accounts of direct interaction between Satan and Job, it does not fit into the narrative of impacting the seed line of the woman. What it does accomplish is establishing the fact of God's sovereignty over all things, both good and evil, and the truth that Satan is not God's enemy, but man's. His very name in Hebrew, *hasatan*, means "the adversary" or "accuser." As a divinely created entity,

Satan is not God's enemy, but man's.

his role and assignment are not independent of God's plan of redemption and salvation, but are clearly major tools in God's arsenal to bring

33

man to the crossroads of deciding whether to accept God's plan of salvation through Yeshua/Jesus or reject it and walk on the wide path that leads to destruction.

Breaking Birthright Traditions

Birthrights are traditionally passed to firstborn sons; however, upon examination of Scripture, this does not seem to be the pattern of God. The second Adam (Jesus) was chosen by God over the first Adam. Abel was chosen by God over the firstborn Cain. Isaac was chosen by God over the firstborn Ishmael. Jacob was chosen by God over the firstborn Esau. Rachel was Jacob's first choice, but God chose Leah to continue with the seed line of Messiah through her fourth son, Judah. However, God allowed Rachel's firstborn, Joseph, to endure great persecution and, through the trials of his life, gain favor with Pharaoh. Because of this, he was able to rescue the almost extinct remnant of seventy Hebrews to ultimately preserve the seed line of Messiah and secure a place for his sons Ephraim and Manasseh as half tribes to replace the disgraced firstborn of Leah, Reuben.

Inclination toward Evil

In our examination of whether or not human actions and characteristics are influenced by Satan to accomplish his purposes, we often find that the contrary nature that God implanted into both the created angels and man prevailed in various forms. None of these are impacted by Satan's agenda, but demonstrate man's evil inclination that sets the stage for our openness to be used by Satan to carry out his agenda.

We read of several instances in the Old Testament when deceptive practices were employed by the patriarchs. For example, Abraham passed

Sarah off as his sister twice in deliberate acts of deception motivated by fear. Isaac repeated the same lie regarding his own wife, and, in the pattern of generational behaviors, Jacob participated in deceiving Isaac to obtain the birthright.

Jacob and Esau

It is in this deception that we see the greatest long-term impact on the seed line of Messiah and the pattern set for the future role of the descendants of Jacob and Esau in the enmity between the seed of the woman and that of the serpent. Just as Cain's jealousy turned into a murderous plot to kill his brother, Abel, so too did Esau plot to kill Jacob, but without success. This struggle between the brothers did not suddenly appear; even in Rebecca's womb, the boys jostled with each other. When Rebecca sought wisdom from the Lord, He revealed a statement that continues to be truth to this day:

> And the LORD said unto her, Two nations are in thy womb, and two manner of people shall be separated from thy bowels; and the one people shall be stronger than the other people; and the elder shall serve the younger. (Genesis 25:23)

Much is revealed in the brothers' names, just as many names in the Bible carry significant prophetic meaning. The Jewish Virtual Library states the following about Esau (עֵשָׂו):

> Three popular etymologies are connected with Esau. In the description given of him at his birth—"red, like a hairy mantle all over" (Gen[esis] 25:25)—at most only the second part can have anything to do with the name Esau (Heb[rew] *Esav*, *'Esaw*), which may be related to the Arabic root ġšw, "to cover."

The redness, in contrast, can only explain his other name, Edom (Heb[rew] *'Edom*), connected with the word ' adom ("red"). In verse 30, the same name is explained by his impatient plea, when he came home hungry, for some of the "red stuff" (i.e., lentils) that Jacob was cooking. The red down ("hairy mantle," Heb[rew] ' adderet se ' ar) with which he is said to have been covered at birth may originally have served to explain the name Seir (Heb[rew] *se ' ir).* In essence Esau was described as hairy.[50]

God uses the things of the natural to reveal supernatural truths, and this description of Esau is integral to the parable of the sheep and goats, as goats are hairy. In Matthew 25:31–46, Yeshua/Jesus says:

When the Son of Man shall come in his glory, and all the holy angels with him, then shall he sit upon the throne of his glory.

And before him shall be gathered all nations: and he shall separate them one from another, as a shepherd divideth his sheep from the goats:

And he shall set the sheep on his righthand, but the goats on the left.

Then shall the King say unto them on his right hand, Come, ye blessed of my Father, inherit the kingdom prepared for you from the foundation of the world:

For I was an hungred, and ye gave me meat: I was thirsty, and ye gave me drink: I was a stranger, and ye took me in:

Naked, and ye clothed me: I was sick, and ye visited me: I was in prison, and ye came unto me.

Then shall the righteous answer him, saying, Lord, when saw we thee an hungred, and fed thee? Or thirsty, and gave thee drink?

When saw we a stranger, and took thee in? or naked, and clothed thee?

Or when saw we thee sick, or in prison, and came unto thee?

And the King shall answer and say unto them, Verily I saw unto you, Inasmuch as ye have done it unto one of the least of these my brethren, ye have done it unto me.

Then shall he say also unto them on the left hand, Depart from me, ye cursed, into everlasting fire, prepared for the devil and his angels:

For I was an hungred, and ye gave me no meat: I was thirsty, and ye gave me no drink:

I was a stranger, and ye took me not in: naked, and ye clothed me not: sick, and in prison, and ye visited me not.

Then shall they also answer him, saying, Lord, when saw we thee an hungred, or athirst, or a stranger, or naked, or sick, or in prison, and did not minister unto thee?

Then shall he answer them, saying, Verily I say unto you, Inasmuch as ye did it not to one of the least of these, ye did it not to me.

And these shall go away into everlasting punishment: but the righteous into life eternal.

As there was no New Testament at the time of Yeshua/Jesus, and His Jewish lineage is clearly established, the reference to "the least of His brothers" is a reference to the Jewish people. The condemnation of the goats hearkens back to the description of Esau and his ultimate enmity against the descendants of Jacob. Paul further expands on this in Romans 11:22 in his admonition to the new Gentile believers regarding how they treat the Jews:

Behold therefore the goodness and severity of God: on them which fell, severity; but toward thee, goodness, if thou continue in his goodness: otherwise thou also shalt be cut off.

When Jacob was born, his parents called him "Yaakov," derived from *akev* ('heel') because he emerged from his mother's womb holding on to the heel of his older brother Esau (Genesis 25:26; 27:36). The name "Israel" was bestowed on Jacob many years later, by a mysterious "divine being" after a night long struggle between the two (Genesis 32:25–29). The name "Jacob" has negative connotations in his relationship to his twin, Esau, and the deceit of his father, Isaac, but "Israel" marks the beginning of the Israelite peoplehood.[51]

The generations of Abraham to Isaac to Jacob are steeped in the conflict between the seed lines of the serpent and of the woman.

Rabbis over the centuries have compared the jealous, hate-filled character of Esau to the perpetual struggle between the descendants of both brothers. Jacob's descendants were birthed out of obedience to Isaac, who told him not to marry a Canaanite woman, and he did not. Esau, on the other hand, married two Canaanite women. One of Esau's Canaanite offspring was Amalek, who became an archenemy of pre-state Israel by attacking Moses and the Israelites while in the wilderness (Exodus 17). They also invaded Israel during the time of the judges:

> And so it was, when Israel had sown, that the Midianites came up, and Amalekites, and the children of the east, even they came up against them. (Judges 6:3)

Although one might look to Jacob as the deceiver, we must also examine the divided loyalties of Jacob and Rebecca. Jacob loved Esau, and Rebecca loved Jacob. Rebecca manipulated the situation when she disguised Jacob as Esau so that he would receive the patriarchal blessing. Yet, it was Esau who devalued his birthright and sold it for a meal. Jacob's willingness to go along with the ruse orchestrated by his mother follows the pattern of deception used by Abraham and Isaac. The root of dishonesty can be traced back to Abraham, who grew up in Terah's home surrounded by idols. Scripture does not tell us much more about Terah, but the pagan foundation of Abraham's earliest years apparently had some impact on his otherwise honorable character.

Sir Walter Scott is quoted as saying, "Oh what a tangled web we weave when first we practice to deceive." This tangled web of deception began with Abraham; it was repeated by Isaac and again by Jacob. What God allows and what He blesses are two different matters. The pattern here is indelibly connected to the duality of good and evil. From Abraham we have the line of Ishmael, who became an enemy of the seed line of Messiah, and Isaac, who became the son of the promise and carried the seed line. From Isaac, we have the same pattern of the duality of good and evil. In Esau, we see Satan's agenda being advanced as the Edomites became an enemy of the seed line that would run through Jacob's lineage. In fear, Jacob was sent by his mother to live with her brother Laban, who continued in the pattern of deception when he passed his daughter Leah off as Rachel. Although no citation of Satan's influence is stated, the generations of Abraham to Isaac to Jacob are steeped in the conflict between the seed lines of the serpent and of the woman.

Korah

Korah was a great-grandson of Levi, the third of Jacob's twelve sons, and a first cousin to Moses and Aaron, the Jewish leader and high priest, respectively. Korah was born in Egypt at the time when the Jews were enslaved to Pharaoh. He experienced the miraculous Exodus from Egypt and journey through the Red Sea on dry land, and he received the Torah at Mount Sinai along with the rest of his brethren. Korah was extremely wealthy, and was a clever and astute individual. His status as a member of the Levite tribe enabled him to participate in the service in the Mishkan (Tabernacle), the portable sanctuary the Jews carried with them throughout their journey to the Promised Land. Despite—and because of—his many qualities, Korah felt able to take a stance against Moses and Aaron, which ultimately led to his downfall.

Korah was jealous of the fact that Aaron had been chosen as high priest, to the exclusion of anyone else. Furthermore, his cousin Elitzafan had been appointed as head of the Levite family of Kehot, to which Korah belonged, and Korah felt this position was rightfully his.

These personal grievances led Korah to stage a full-blown rebellion. Accompanied by Dathan and Abiram, troublemakers since their early days in Egypt, he rallied an additional 250 community leaders to his cause. Together, they confronted Moses and Aaron and claimed that he had appointed his brother as high priest on his own accord, without being instructed to do so by God. They further demanded to all be allowed to serve as high priests.

Moses responded that this was impossible, as only one person could assume this sacred post. To demonstrate that Aaron was indeed heavenly ordained, he instructed them all to take pans the next day and offer *ketoret* (incense) before God, and God would accept the sacrifice of the one He deemed worthy.

Korah's group grew in size, as throughout the night he lured thousands to his side. The next day, the 250 men approached the sanctuary with their incense-filled pans. At this point, Moses warned the Jews to stay clear of the tents of Korah, Dathan, and Abiram. Addressing the crowd, he foretold of the punishment that would befall them: the earth would open its mouth and swallow them alive.

As Moses finished speaking, the earth indeed opened up and swallowed Korah and his two cohorts, along with their families and possessions—never to be seen again. At the same time, a heavenly fire went forth and consumed the 250 incense-bearers.

As a reminder to the nation of the calamitous outcome of the rebellion, Aaron's son Elazar was instructed to melt the pans and craft them as plates to cover the Tabernacle altar.

To further demonstrate that Aaron was divinely chosen, each tribe was instructed to give a staff to Moses, upon which was inscribed the name of the tribe's leader. On the staff of the tribe of Levi was Aaron's name. Moses placed the staffs in the sanctuary before the Ark of the Covenant, and the next morning, Aaron's was discovered to have miraculously flowered and produced almonds.

At first, Korah's three sons, Asir, Elkanah, and Aviasaf, joined in their father's quarrel. However, soon after, they regretted their actions and repented. As a result, they were spared their father's fate and survived. Indeed, Korah's descendants were among the Levites who sang in the Holy Temple, and a number of the Psalms were either composed or sung by them. Among Korah's descendants was the famed prophet Samuel, anointer of the first kings of Israel, Saul and David.[52]

The case can be made that the rebellion of Korah possesses all the attributes of being influenced by Satan without being specifically cited, and that the rebellion would have had a direct impact on the seed line of Messiah had Korah's three sons not repented. Samuel would not have been born. Although he is not in the seed line, his role in the lives of King Saul and King David had a direct impact on the preservation of the seed line of Messiah and was instrumental in God's covenant with David that Israel would always have a king in the line of David (Judah), which was Messiah's earthly lineage on both Joseph's and Mary's sides.

King Saul

After two hundred years under the leadership of the judges, Israel was not prospering in the Promised Land and demanded that God let them have a king like the surrounding nations. God did as they asked, establishing Saul as king. He is often referred to as the "head and shoulders king," as he was at least a head taller than the average Israelite, and in stature and appearance, he was much like the other kings. He, along with his son Jonathan, gained some notoriety for his campaign against the Philistines. However, he began to lose favor with God when He usurped the role of Samuel, high priest, in offering a sacrifice.

It was in Saul's next assignment that he ultimately put the seed line of Messiah in long-term jeopardy. Throughout Israel's history and during their entrance into the Promised Land, God's practice was to remove Israel's enemies that threatened the seed line of Messiah. Thus, He instructed Saul to annihilate the Amalekites, all their cattle, and everything connected to their existence. The instructions to Saul were clear; he was to carry out the assignment without exception. In God's economy, 99 percent obedient is the equivalent to 100 percent disobedient. Out of pride, Saul spared the life of Agag, king of the Amalekites. He also failed to kill the cattle, keeping it to feed his own army. He paraded Agag around the land as a symbol of his prowess, but God was so grieved by this display that He sent Samuel to chastise Saul and began to search for Saul's replacement. It was Samuel who completed the task of killing Agag, but not before the seed was planted that would blossom sixteen generations later. In addition, Saul became consumed with an obsessive jealousy over David's victory over Goliath and the people's response to the one who would ultimately replace him and cause him to take his own life out of complete despair.

How did Saul's error play out sixteen generations later? Israel was taken to the brink of annihilation by a man who was described as Haman the Agagagite. By virtue of his name and ancestral identity, he was clearly a descendant of the Amalekite king, Agag, whose life should have been taken by King Saul. But, by usurping God's plan to protect the seed line of Messiah, he was responsible for Agag's progeny, Haman, rising to power and serving as the chief minister of King Ahasuerus in Persia. By edict of the king, Haman ordered that, because of Mordechai's refusal to bow down to anyone but God alone, all the Jews were to be exterminated across the wide expanse of the Persian Empire, consisting of 127 provinces where all the Jews resided. Had it not been for the last-minute intercession of Esther, the entire Jewish population of the earth would have been annihilated, putting an end to the seed line of Messiah. Again, without it being specifically stated, we can see the influence of Satan's agenda manifested through Haman—all because of Saul's pride.

> *In God's economy, 99 percent obedient is the equivalent to 100 percent disobedient.*

Jezebel & Ahab

By every account in Scripture, Jezebel is depicted as a worshiper of Baal[53] and an enemy of the prophets of Israel. Through cunning and manipulation of her weak husband, King Ahab, she wreaked havoc upon Israel and the surrounding nations. When Ahab married Jezebel, he created an unholy alliance with the King of Sidon, Jezebel's father. Jezebel's country worshiped Baal and Ashera, and Israel was beginning to do the same. She persuaded Ahab to introduce the worship of the Tyrian god

Baal-Melkart,[54] a nature god. Baal was supposed to be a dominant god that controls storms and rain. Baal and Ashera,[55] his companion, were fertility gods.

Ahab and Jezebel were the most wicked and evil rulers Israel had ever known. They employed 850 prophets of Baal and his consort, Ashera, and were killing the prophets of Yahweh. Jezebel's relentless pursuit of God's prophets set the stage for the enmity she ultimately focused on His messenger, Elijah.

Because of their worship of Baal, God issued a stern rebuke through Elijah, demonstrating that He alone was the God of storms and rain:

> And Elijah the Tishbite, who was of the inhabitants of Gilead, said unto Ahab, As the LORD God of Israel liveth, before whom I stand, there shall not be dew nor rain these years, but according to my word.
>
> And the word of the LORD came to him, saying,
>
> Get thee hence, and turn thee eastward, and hide thyself by the brook Cherith, that is before Jordan.
>
> And it shall be, that thou shalt drink of the brook; and I have commanded the ravens to feed thee there.
>
> So he went and did according to the word of the LORD, for he went and dwelt by the brook Cherith, that is before Jordan.
>
> And the ravens brought him bread and flesh in the morning, and bread and meat in the evening; and he drank of the brook.
>
> And it came to pass after a while, that the brook dried up, because there had been no rain in the land. (1 Kings 17:1–7)

The following passage describes Elijah's confrontation with Ahab and the defeat of the prophets of Baal:

> And it came to pass, when Ahab saw Elijah, that Ahab said unto him, Art thou he that troubleth Israel?

And he answered, I have not troubled Israel; but thou, and thy father's house, in that ye have forsaken the commandments of the LORD, and thou hast followed Baalim.

Now therefore send, and gather to me all Israel unto mount Carmel, and the prophets of Baal four hundred and fifty, and the prophets of the groves four hundred, which eat at Jezebel's table.

So Ahab sent unto all the children of Israel, and gathered the prophets together unto mount Carmel.

And Elijah came unto all the people, and said, How long halt ye between two opinions? If the Lord be God, follow him: but if Baal, then follow him....And the people answered him not a word.

Then said Elijah unto the people, I, even I only, remain a prophet of the Lord; but Baal's prophets are four hundred and fifty men.

Let them therefore give us two bullocks; and let them choose one bullock for themselves, and cut it in pieces, and lay it on wood, and put no fire under: and I will dress the other bullock, and lay it on wood, and put no fire under:

And call ye on the name of your gods, and I will call on the name of the LORD: and the God that answereth by fire, let him be God. And all the people answered and said, It is well spoken.

And Elijah said unto the prophets of Baal, Choose you one bullock for yourselves, and dress it first; for ye are many; and call on the name of your gods, but put no fire under.

And they took the bullock which was given them, and they dressed it, and called on the name of Baal from morning even until noon, saying, O Baal, hear us. But there was no voice, nor any that answered. And they leaped upon the altar which was made.

And it came to pass at noon, that Elijah mocked them, and

said, Cry aloud: for he is a god; either he is talking, or he is pursuing, or he is in a journey, or peradventure he sleepeth, and must be awaked.

And they cried aloud, and cut themselves after their manner with knives and lancets, till the blood gushed out upon them.

And it came to pass, when midday was past, and they prophesied until the time of the offering of the evening sacrifice, that there was neither voice, nor any to answer, nor any that regarded.

And Elijah said unto all the people, Come near unto me. And all the people came near unto him. And he repaired the altar of the LORD that was broken down.

And Elijah took twelve stones, according to the number of the tribes of the sons of Jacob, unto whom the word of the LORD came, saying, Israel shall be thy name:

And with the stones he built an altar in the name of the LORD: and he made a trench about the altar, as great as would contain two measures of seed.

And he put the wood in order, and cut the bullock in pieces, and laid him on the wood, and said, Fill four barrels with water, and pour it on the burnt sacrifice, and on the wood.

And he said, Do it the second time. And they did it the second time.

And he said, Do it the third time. And they did it the third time.

And the water ran round about the altar; and he filled the trench also with water.

And it came to pass at the time of the offering of the evening sacrifice, that Elijah the prophet came near, and said, LORD God of Abraham, Isaac, and of Israel, let it be known this day that thou art God in Israel, and that I am thy servant, and that I have done all these things at thy word.

Hear me, O LORD, hear me, that this people may know that thou art the LORD God, and that thou hast turned their heart back again.

Then the fire of the LORD fell, and consumed the burnt sacrifice, and the wood, and the stones, and the dust, and licked up the water that was in the trench.

And when all the people saw it, they fell on their faces: and they said, The LORD, he is the God; the LORD, he is the God.

And Elijah said unto them, Take the prophets of Baal; let not one of them escape. And they took them: and Elijah brought them down to the brook Kishon, and slew them there.

And Elijah said unto Ahab, Get thee up, eat and drink; for there is a sound of abundance of rain. (1 Kings 18:17–41)

And Ahab told Jezebel all that Elijah had done, and withal how he had slain all the prophets with the sword.

Then Jezebel sent a messenger unto Elijah, saying, So let the gods do to me, and more also, if I make not thy life as the life of one of them by tomorrow about this time. (1 Kings 19:1–2)

Although Elijah is not in the seed line of Messiah, he plays a key role as foretold by the prophet Malachi:

For, behold, the day cometh, that shall burn as an oven; and all the proud, yea, and all that do wickedly, shall be stubble: and the day that cometh shall burn them up, saith the LORD of hosts, that it shall leave them neither root nor branch.

But unto you that fear my name shall the Sun of righteousness arise with healing in his wings; and ye shall go forth, and grow up as calves of the stall.

And ye shall tread down the wicked; for they shall be ashes

under the soles of your feet in the day that I shall do this, saith the LORD of hosts.

Remember ye the law of Moses my servant, which I commanded unto him in Horeb for all Israel, with the statutes and judgments.

Behold, I will send you Elijah the prophet before the coming of the great and dreadful day of the LORD:

And he shall turn the heart of the fathers to the children, and the heart of the children to their fathers, lest I come and smite the earth with a curse. (Malachi 4:1–6)

Had Jezebel succeeded in killing Elijah, this prophecy could not be fulfilled. Although Jezebel's actions are not said to have been directed by Satan, they did, in fact, fall into complete alignment with his agenda of disrupting the coming seed of the woman who will crush the serpent's head.

The great irony of Jezebel and Ahab's attempt to disrupt God's prophetic plan is that Jezebel, in fact, is in the lineage of Messiah. Matthew's genealogy concludes with the following statement:

So all the generations from Abraham to David are fourteen generations; and from David to the deportation to Babylon, fourteen generations; and from the deportation to Babylon to the Messiah, fourteen generations. (Matthew 1:17)

The genealogy of Yeshua/Jesus in Matthew is based on history, but it is not a complete genealogy. Matthew's genealogy is artificially divided into three sections, each containing fourteen generations: from Abraham to David, from David to the exile of Judah to Babylon, and from the exile to Jesus.

The evidence that Matthew's genealogy is artificial is found in the second section, from David to the Babylonian exile, where we find that three generations are omitted. Matthew writes that Asa was the father of Jehoshaphat, Jehoshaphat was the father of Joram, and Joram was the father of Uzziah (Matthew 1:8). However, according to the genealogy of David in 1 Chronicles 3, these are the descendants of David beginning with Solomon:

The descendants of Solomon: Rehoboam, Abijah his son, Asa his son, Jehoshaphat his son, Joram his son, Ahaziah his son, Joash his son, Amaziah his son, Azariah his son, Jotham his son. (1 Chronicles 3:10–12)

Thus we see that Matthew omitted three names: Ahaziah, Joash, and Amaziah, all of whom were kings of Judah and descendants of David.

The same thing occurs in the third group. Whereas Matthew says that Jechoniah (Jehoiachin) was deported to Babylon, and after the deportation there were fourteen generations until Yeshua/Jesus, if we count Salathiel as the first generation after the deportation to Joseph, the adoptive father of Jesus, there are only twelve names.

In the genealogy of Yeshua/Jesus in Luke, there are eighteen names from Zerubbabel to Joseph (Luke 3:23–27), while in the genealogy of Yeshua/Jesus in Matthew, there are only eleven names from Zerubbabel to Joseph.

There are several ways of understanding these omissions in Matthew's genealogy. When the evangelist says that "so and so was the father of so and so," it does not mean that he was the immediate father of the person named. Rather, it means that he was the ancestor or forefather of that person.

Jehoshaphat made a military alliance with Ahab to fight against the Arameans. This alliance was sealed with the marriage between Joram, Jehoshaphat's son, and Athaliah, the daughter of Ahab and Jezebel (2 Kings 8:18; 2 Chronicles 21:6). Joram and Athaliah had a son whose name was Ahaziah. Since Athaliah was the wife of the king of Judah and one of the great-grandmothers of Yeshua/Jesus, then Jezebel was also a great-grandmother of Yeshua/Jesus. Jezebel entered Yeshua/Jesus' family line because of her direct relationship with Athaliah. Jezebel was the grandmother of Ahaziah, Athaliah's son.[56]

In God's sovereignty, we see a pattern best expressed in Joseph's words to his brothers in Genesis 50:20: "What you meant for evil; God will work for good so that many may be saved" (paraphrased).[57]

3

Daniel

Daniel, in modern Jewish theology, is not considered a prophet, although Jesus refers to him this way. The reasoning behind this is explained in a number of Jewish texts.

The opinions stated in the cited article are different from those of venerated rabbinical scholars.

Rambam (Moreh Nevukhim 2:42[58]) argues that angels only appear to people in visions. Therefore, the story of Abraham and his three guests was a vision. Ramban (Genesis 18:1) strongly disagrees.

The Ramban says that any vision of an angel as an angel, rather than as a person, must take place in a vision. However, that vision does not have to constitute prophecy. For example, Hagar saw an angel (Genesis 16:7–12) and she was not a prophet. Daniel saw an angel (Daniel 9:21, 10:4) and he was not a prophet. As support, Ramban quotes the Gemara (Megillah 3a) that compares Daniel with Haggai, Zechariah, and Malachi; they were prophets, but he was not.

Rambam (Moreh Nevukhim 2:45) similarly writes that Daniel was not a prophet. He had *ru'ach ha-kodesh*, divine spirit.

Rambam adds that the Book of Daniel is included among Ketuvim (Writings), not Nevi'im (Prophets). Ramban echoes this point. According to the Rambam, a vision within a dream is not prophecy. A prophetic vision seems real, not like a dream.

However, Rashi (Megillah 3a sv. deinhu) says that Daniel was a prophet. When the Gemara declares the Daniel was not a prophet, according to Rashi it means that Daniel was not a prophet sent to the nation. In other words, he was a prophet but one who prophesied for his own benefit, not as a divine emissary.

Similarly, Abarbanel (Ma'ayanei Ha-Yeshu'ah 3:1–2) argues against the Rambam's view that Daniel was a prophet. Daniel saw a vision of the future, a prophecy of the rise and fall of future nations. He was privy to divine secrets. The prophecies in the book of Daniel are extremely important in rabbinic theology. How could he be anything other than a prophet?[59]

Although Daniel is referred to as one of the four major prophets in the Christian Bible, the Hebrew Bible does not recognize him as such, since he had no direct interaction with God except through the Holy Spirit. The qualifications for being included as a prophet in the section of the Hebrew Bible containing the prophets is that you must have heard directly from God, and the words spoken by God were to be conveyed to the people as, "Thus says the Lord God of Israel." The word "prophet" in Hebrew means "messenger of God."

It is for this reason the religious in Israel are so anxious to build the Third Temple without connecting Daniel's implications related to the Tribulation Temple that is defiled by the Antichrist:

And from the time that the daily sacrifice shall be taken away, and the abomination that maketh desolate set up, there shall be a thousand two hundred and ninety days. (Daniel 12:11)

Less credence is given to Daniel than to the major prophets, and this is a perfect example of how the Jewish religious scholars are still playing into the hands of the one who will command the armies that will attempt to annihilate the Jews and thwart the Second Coming of Messiah.

The expulsion of the Jews into Babylonian captivity represents a great victory for Satan and put the seed line of Messiah in jeopardy. In Jeremiah's letter to the exiles in Babylon, he wrote:

Now these are the words of the letter that Jeremiah the prophet sent from Jerusalem unto the residue of the elders which were carried away captives, and to the priests, and to the prophets, and to all the people whom Nebuchadnezzar had carried away captive from Jerusalem to Babylon;

(After that Jeconiah the king, and the queen, and the eunuchs, the princes of Judah and Jerusalem, and the carpenters, and the smiths, were departed from Jerusalem;)

By the hand of Elasah the son of Shaphan, and Gemariah the son of Hilkiah, (whom Zedekiah king of Judah sent unto Babylon to Nebuchadnezzar king of Babylon) saying,

Thus saith the LORD of hosts, the God of Israel, unto all that are carried away captives, whom I have caused to be carried away from Jerusalem unto Babylon;

Build ye houses, and dwell in them; and plant gardens, and eat the fruit of them;

Take ye wives, and beget sons and daughters; and take wives for your sons, and give your daughters to husbands, that they may bear sons and daughters; that ye may be increased there, and not diminished.

And seek the peace of the city whither I have caused you to be carried away captives, and pray unto the LORD for it: for in the peace thereof shall ye have peace.

For thus saith the LORD of hosts, the God of Israel; Let not your prophets and your diviners, that be in the midst of you, deceive you, neither hearken to your dreams which ye cause to be dreamed.

For they prophesy falsely unto you in my name: I have not sent them, saith the Lord. (Jeremiah 29:1–9)

Shifting ID of Jewish Lineage

For seventy years, God had instructed the Israelites to intermarry, and during this time there was a shift in the identification of Jewish lineage.

Prior to the time of Ezra and Nehemiah, Jewish lineage was attributed to the father, as referenced in Genesis 17:5. Until the time of the Babylonian captivity, intermarriage was prohibited and the Jewish lineage was paternal. After the Babylonian captivity, it became impossible to determine if the father was Jewish; therefore, the new basis for determining Jewish lineage was maternal. This is the source of Jewish identity for citizenship in Israel. However, tribal identity still remained paternal. Therefore, if a Levite male married a Judahite woman, their male child would be a Levite.

A Look at the Future

Much has been written in interpreting the visions of King Nebuchadnezzar II, King Belshazzar, King Darius I, and King Cyrus. The future configuration of the rising world powers coming together under the leadership of the Antichrist clearly advances Satan's agenda to rise up in authority to subjugate all who align themselves with him either out of belief or fear. Regardless, he directly impacts the seed line of the woman.

Daniel 12 opens the door to the time of the end (more clearly defined in the book of Revelation) and is the foundation of the opening of that which is sealed up until God is ready to unleash His power and fulfill what is written here:

> And at that time shall Michael stand up, the great prince which standeth for the children of thy people: and there shall be a time of trouble, such as never was since there was a nation even to that same time: and at that time thy people shall be delivered, every one that shall be found written in the book.
>
> And many of them that sleep in the dust of the earth shall awake, some to everlasting life, and some to shame and everlasting contempt.
>
> And they that be wise shall shine as the brightness of the firmament; and they that turn many to righteousness as the stars for ever and ever.
>
> But thou, O Daniel, shut up the words, and seal the book, even to the time of the end: many shall run to and fro, and knowledge shall be increased.
>
> Then I Daniel looked, and, behold, there stood other two, the one on this side of the bank of the river, and the other on that side of the bank of the river.

And one said to the man clothed in linen, which was upon the waters of the river, How long shall it be to the end of these wonders?

And I heard the man clothed in linen, which was upon the waters of the river, when he held up his right hand and his left hand unto heaven, and sware by him that liveth for ever that it shall be for a time, times, and an half; and when he shall have accomplished to scatter the power of the holy people, all these things shall be finished.

And I heard, but I understood not: then said I, O my Lord, what shall be the end of these things?

And he said, Go thy way, Daniel: for the words are closed up and sealed till the time of the end.

Many shall be purified, and made white, and tried; but the wicked shall do wickedly: and none of the wicked shall understand; but the wise shall understand.

And from the time that the daily sacrifice shall be taken away, and the abomination that maketh desolate set up, there shall be a thousand two hundred and ninety days.

Blessed is he that waiteth, and cometh to the thousand three hundred and five and thirty days.

But go thou thy way till the end be: for thou shalt rest, and stand in thy lot at the end of the days. (Daniel 12:1–13)

God always reserves a remnant to fulfill His purposes.

This timeline is often referred to as the seventieth week of Daniel, and is a future event that lasts for seven years. It is at the midpoint of three and a half years that the abomination that makes desolate will expose the true agenda of the Antichrist. In the battle that ensues in the campaign of Armageddon, two-thirds of the Jewish population will die. But God always reserves a remnant to fulfill His purposes, and although it will appear that the Antichrist is victorious and has cut off the seed of the woman, God has another plan.

Satan's Authority?

One point in Daniel that is not often explored is directly linked to a statement made by Satan during his temptation of Messiah. When we read the account from the book of Luke, we see words that do not appear in the other Gospels:

> And the devil said unto him, If thou be the Son of God, command this stone that it be made bread.
>
> And Jesus answered him, saying, It is written, That man shall not live by bread alone, but by every word of God.
>
> And the devil, taking him up into a high mountain, shewed unto him all the kingdoms of the world in a moment of time.
>
> And the devil said unto him, All this power will I give thee, and the glory of them: *for that is delivered unto me; and to whomsoever I will I give it.*
>
> If thou therefore wilt worship me, all shall be thine.
>
> And Jesus answered and said unto him, Get thee behind me, Satan: for it is written, Thou shalt worship the Lord thy God, and him only shalt thou serve. (Luke 4:3–8, emphasis added)

In Luke's account, Satan claims that he, in fact, has the authority to make this claim because it was "delivered"—given—to him.

Is this just the father of lies speaking, or is this something that Satan has the power to do? If such power did exist, then this particular promise, if accepted, would certainly ensure Satan's reign upon the earth and nullify the prophecy of Genesis 3:15. Does such a scriptural basis exist that would in any way imply that Satan could deliver on this promise?

In Daniel 4:17, such a statement is made by God:

This matter is by the decree of the watchers, and the demand by the word of the holy ones: to the intent that the living may know that the most High ruleth in the kingdom of men, and giveth it to whomsoever he will, and setteth up over it the basest of men.

This declaration is confirmed in Jeremiah 27:5:

I have made the earth, the man and the beast that are upon the ground, by my great power and by my outstretched arm, and have given it unto whom it seemed meet unto me.

In both cases, Satan believes that God has given him the authority to make such a promise and believes he can convince Jesus to yield to that authority. Jesus does not, but unfortunately many do, and align themselves with Satan's agenda to destroy the seed line of Messiah.

4

Ezekiel's Prophecy

Although Satan has a plan to cut off the seed line of Messiah, it is often no more diabolical than man's own predilection for sin. Satan still sits as a member of the council of Heaven and is a dissenting member; God has allowed him to advance evil upon the earth. There are times in Israel's history when it appeared that God had forgotten Israel and He sent reminders of His sovereignty through His prophets.

Israel had reached a point where the warnings of Jeremiah were being ignored and the kingdom of Judah had suffered greatly at the hands of victorious Babylon. Ezekiel's ministry position moved from being a priest to a prophet, and in that process, he encountered God in three dramatic experiences marked by the phrase "the Word of the Lord came" being used fifty times. Ezekiel is called "son of man" ninety-three times in this book.

Ezekiel was the "prophet of human responsibility," as described by Bible teacher and author Warren Wiersbe,[60] and he was called to remind the hard-hearted Jews headed toward Babylonian captivity that God was still sovereign and had not forsaken them. His message fell on deaf ears, however; the people of Israel continued in their sinful ways and God punished them openly as a warning to both the Jews and the Gentiles that the God of Israel was a God of justice. On August 14, 586 BC, the Babylonians set fire to the Temple in Jerusalem.

The book of Ezekiel begins with a vison from an open Heaven that only few in the Bible had ever encountered. The prophet's vision was illuminated by light emanating from the cherubim. The works of Satan are shrouded in darkness, but the work of the Lord is bathed in light. For the prophet, this vision was clearly from the Lord. Because Ezekiel recognized this was an encounter with God Himself, he fell prostrate before the Lord.

Ezekiel had his vision in Babylon as one of the captive exiles (Ezekiel 1:1–3). Comparing his vision to Babylonian iconography reveals that Ezekiel saw a divine "throne chariot" of the heavens—widely described in the ancient biblical world. Just as human kings had chariots, so did deities. A deity would traverse the heavens in his chariot throne, inspecting his domain and exercising authority over it. In Ezekiel's vision, this throne sits atop the "expanse" (רקיע, raqia', 1:26)—the same word used in Genesis 1:6–8 for the heavens (see also Psalms 29:10) and to describe God's abode (Psalm 150:1).

Wheels supported the chariot throne, along with four unusual creatures (identified as cherubim in Ezekiel 10:4). Each creature had four faces: human, lion, eagle, and ox (Ezekiel 1:10). Next to each cherub were four gleaming wheels (Ezekiel 1:15–16). These wheels were set on edge, since they are described as "tall" (Ezekiel 1:18). They had wheels within them—that is, each one had at least one concentric circle within it. The vision describes the outer edge, or "rim," of each wheel as having "eyes" (עַיִ, 'ayin). The prophet Daniel, who was also in Babylon, described the very same blazing throne with wheels (Daniel 7:9).

The four faces of the four animals or cherubim correspond to the iconography of the Babylonian zodiac. Each represents a seasonal constellation in Babylonian astrology, and each face or constellation also represented one of the four directions (N, S, E, W) or quadrants of the sky. Babylonians knew that the heavens were connected to what happened on earth (times, seasons, crops, weather, etc.), and they believed their gods controlled those functions. Information about the stars was laid out on Mesopotamian astrolabes, clay tablets whose concentric circles could well correspond to the "wheels within wheels" imagery.

English translations of Ezekiel's vision often break down at the point where the prophet describes "eyes" (עַיִן, 'ayin) on the rims of the wheels. 'Ayin occurs a number of places in the vision, but it is not always translated. Taking the ESV as an example, 'ayin occurs six times in chapter 1 (vv. 4, 7, 16, 18, 22, 27) but is left untranslated three times (vv. 4, 7, 27). In the vision's description of the wheels, the word 'ayin is translated once as "sparkling" (Ezekiel 10:9). Since ancient astronomical texts commonly describe shining stars as "eyes," 'ayin can refer to stars or their sparkling appearance. Many translators miss this possibility, failing to consider the astronomical context portrayed by the four faces.

During their time of exile, the Jewish captives might have easily believed Yahweh had abandoned them forever. Likewise, the Babylonians could have simply assumed their gods had defeated Yahweh and ruled the heavens and the earth unchallenged. But Ezekiel's imagery sends a message to the Jews in exile—and to their Babylonian captors: Both assumptions are flawed. Yahweh has not been defeated, nor has He turned away from His people, Israel. He remains seated in His chariot throne at the center of His domain—the entire cosmos. When we read Ezekiel through ancient eyes, we can feel the same hope today: Even in the midst of difficult circumstances, we can know that an all-powerful God is active and present in our lives.[61]

Rabbi Eric E. Walker

Armies of Antichrist Aligning against Israel

Preeminent among the prophecies that align the armies of the Antichrist against Israel are the ones contained in Ezekiel chapters 38 and 39. An unholy alliance is formed with the sole purpose of invading Israel and eliminating the Jewish people. However, according to Daniel 9:24–27:2, the nation of Israel will make an agreement with the head of a ten-nation European coalition to protect them for seven years so they can rebuild their Temple in Jerusalem. It's the signing of the covenant that triggers the start of the seven-year Tribulation period described in Matthew 24:1–28 and Revelation 6–19. After three and a half years, this European leader will emerge as the Antichrist (the Beast). He will break the covenant with Israel, set up his own image in the Jewish Temple, and try to force the world to worship and obey him (Daniel 9:27; 2 Thessalonians 2:1–12; Matthew 24:15; Revelation 13). During the last three and a half years of the Tribulation, the world will experience "the wrath of God," and the period will climax with the return of Messiah to the earth to defeat Satan and the Beast and establish His kingdom. That's when the Battle of Armageddon will be fought.

If this is the correct sequence of prophetic events, then, during the first half of the Tribulation period, Israel will be in its land, protected by the strongest political leader in the world. The nation will experience a time of peace and safety, unthreatened by the other nations (Ezekiel 38:8, 11, 14). It's possible that the Jews and the powerful European leader will complete their negotiations very soon after the saints have been taken out (if a pre-Tribulation Rapture should occur). We don't know how long it will take for Israel to rebuild the Temple, but it will be complete by the middle of this seven-year period. That's when the powerful European leader will break the covenant, reveal himself as the man of sin, and set up his own image in the Temple.

Rapture's Effect on Satan's Strategy

There are those who subscribe to a pre-Tribulation Rapture of the Church and others who subscribe to a mid-Tribulation Rapture. There are also those who subscribe to a post-Tribulation Rapture. In these three scenarios, the belief is that those who are taken up will not have to contend with taking the Mark of the Beast and enduring God's wrath.

One could argue that, in all three of these scenarios, God's greatest army for bringing salvation to the Jews and the rest of the world will be taken out of their role in the Great Commission. Isn't this the same question Paul raised in the following?

> How then shall they call on him in whom they have not believed? and how shall they believe in him of whom they have not heard? and how shall they hear without a preacher?
>
> And how shall they preach, except they be sent? as it is written, How beautiful are the feet of them that preach the gospel of peace, and bring glad tidings of good things! (Romans 10:14–15)

It is puzzling that the events describing the "catching away" would evoke a faith response as opposed to a fear response. Chaos would ensue and the setting would become ripe for a false leader to rise up to lead a dazed and confused remnant of nonbelievers on the earth. The description of people driving cars or flying planes simply disappearing into thin air would in no way create an atmosphere of security. Since people are subject to following the strongest spirit, as I experienced when I explored New Age practices, it would seem more logical to follow what you could see in the natural. Isn't that what clearly distinguished the Israelites from the pagans? The Israelites believed in a God they could not see, but could hear. The pagans believed in gods they could see, but could not hear.

Those remaining after the Rapture will be unbelieving Jews and Gentiles, or the "goat" believers whom Jesus has rejected. Those who are left behind will face taking the mark of the Beast and forgoing salvation, and will be aligned with Satan's plan to eliminate the seed line of Messiah. Since the breakdown of how many will be affected is not stated in Scripture, we have no way to measure how significantly this impacts Satan's plan.

Armageddon

In the description of the campaign of Armageddon, the Jews have fled to safety and God intervenes, causing an earthquake that will be felt around the world (Ezekiel 38:19–20). This drives panic into the invading armies, who turn on each other. In Ezekiel 39:12, God sends rain, hailstones, fire, and brimstone from Heaven to end the invasion.

Those who are left behind will face taking the mark of the Beast and forgoing salvation...

In order for the call of Matthew 23:37–39 for Messiah's return, it would appear that Israel is under siege and is a parallel to the Ezekiel 38–39 war that is not described in Revelation. The leadership of Israel must be the ones to cry out *Baruch haba B'Shem Adonai*—"Blessed is He who comes in the Name of the Lord." It is the final cry before their perceived imminent destruction.

Messiah Returns

In keeping with the theme of Ezekiel's scenario and his description of the Millennial Temple in the last eight chapters, the following passage from Isaiah makes more sense:

The reference to these words proclaimed two times in Matthew occur upon Jesus' entrance through the Eastern Gate when He is greeted by an adoring crowd and again upon His exit that same evening through the same gate on His way back to Bethany. The ones who proclaimed this blessing believed Jesus was the Son of David who had come to save them from the oppression of Roman rule. As triumphant an entry as this has been described, Jesus already knew that the Sanhedrin would reject Him and proclaimed over the city that He would return when the head of Israel called for Him, not the common man. Not only is this significant in understanding why it must be repeated by the leadership of Israel at a future point in time; it also explains why Ezekiel is shown this same gate in the vision that is now permanently closed that no man can open and no man can shut.

"Then he brought me back the way of the gate of the outward sanctuary which looketh toward the east; and it was shut.

"Then said the Lord unto me; This gate shall be shut, it shall not be opened, and no man shall enter in by it; because the Lord, the God of Israel, hath entered in by it, therefore it shall be shut.

"It is for the prince; the prince, he shall sit in it to eat bread before the Lord; he shall enter by the way of the porch of that gate, and shall go out by the way of the same." (Ezekiel 44:1–3)

How prophetic that Jesus would enter through this gate, have the Last Supper within the walls of Jerusalem, and that gate is now twenty feet below ground and the one that was built on top of it is sealed with stone that no man can open or shut.

Who is this that cometh from Edom, with dyed garments from Bozrah? this that is glorious in his apparel, travelling in the greatness of his strength? I that speak in righteousness, mighty to save.

Wherefore art thou red in thine apparel, and thy garments like him that treadeth in the winefat?

I have trodden the winepress alone; and of the people there was none with me: for I will tread them in mine anger, and trample them in my fury; and their blood shall be sprinkled upon my garments, and I will stain all my raiment.

For the day of vengeance is in mine heart, and the year of my redeemed is come.

And I looked, and there was none to help; and I wondered that there was none to uphold: therefore mine own arm brought salvation unto me; and my fury, it upheld me.

And I will tread down the people in mine anger, and make them drunk in my fury, and I will bring down their strength to the earth. (Isaiah 63:1–6)

If this portrays the return of Messiah, then Satan is bound along with his demons for one thousand years. Since no time is given as to when this will happen, Satan is aware that he must cut off the seed line of Messiah prior to this event.

Millennial Temple

In preparation for the return of Messiah, the conversation between God and Ezekiel regarding the construction of the Millennial Temple requires further examination. If the timing of Messiah's return is connected with the victory of Gog/Magog, then Messiah will have, as stated in Isaiah 63, defeated the armies of the Antichrist and will be in some way planting His feet on the Mount of Olives per Zechariah 14, bringing about the earthquake that will destroy the Third or Tribulation Temple that has been defiled by the Antichrist. This would call for the building of a Temple for Yeshua/Jesus to rule and reign from for one thousand years.

Major questions surface in the Zechariah 14 narrative and its implications related to the earthquake of such magnitude that it will split the mountain in half.

> And his feet shall stand in that day upon the mount of Olives, which is before Jerusalem on the east, and the mount of Olives shall cleave in the midst thereof toward the east and toward the west, and there shall be a very great valley; and half of the mountain shall remove toward the north, and half of it toward the south.
>
> And ye shall flee to the valley of the mountains; for the valley of the mountains shall reach unto Azal: yea, ye shall flee, like as ye fled from before the earthquake in the days of Uzziah king of Judah: and the LORD my God shall come, and all the saints with thee. (Zechariah 14:4–5)

The motivation of an alliance formed between the enemies of Israel involving a confederacy led by Iran, Turkey, Russia, Libya, Ethiopia, Gomer, and Beth-Togarmah is certainly inspired by the Antichrist to accomplish his plan to eliminate the seed line of Messiah, but in this case his plan fails, with the exception of those who take the mark. The result is that Messiah returns and faith in the God of Abraham, Isaac, and Jacob is restored.

5

Manifestations of Satan's Influence

New Testament

But thou, Bethlehem Ephrathah, though thou be little among the thousands of Judah, yet out of thee shall come forth to unto me that is to be ruler in Israel, whose goings forth have been from of old, from everlasting.

MICAH 5:2

Herod the Great

Generational sin is insidious and motivates many to act out of fear and instinct. Such is the case of Herod the Great. In the following account from Matthew 2, we once again see the assault on the seed of the woman who has now come to be born. This confirms that all prior attempts to keep the seed of the woman from being born had failed, and that Satan must deploy a new strategy to eliminate the child.

Now when Jesus was born in Bethlehem of Judaea in the days of Herod the king, behold, there came wise men from the east to Jerusalem,

Saying, Where is he that is born King of the Jews? for we have seen his star in the east, and are come to worship him.

When Herod the king had heard these things, he was troubled, and all Jerusalem with him.

And when he had gathered all the chief priests and scribes of the people together, he demanded of them where Christ should be born.

And they said unto him, In Bethlehem of Judaea: for thus it is written by the prophet,

And thou Bethlehem, in the land of Juda, art not the least among the princes of Juda: for out of thee shall come a Governor, that shall rule my people Israel.

Then Herod, when he had privily called the wise men, inquired of them diligently what time the star appeared.

And he sent them to Bethlehem, and said, Go and search diligently for the young child; and when ye have found him, bring me word again, that I may come and worship him also.

When they had heard the king, they departed; and, lo, the star, which they saw in the east, went before them, till it came and stood over where the young child was.

When they saw the star, they rejoiced with exceeding great joy.

And when they were come into the house, they saw the young child with Mary his mother, and fell down, and worshipped him: and when they had opened their treasures, they presented unto him gifts; gold, and frankincense, and myrrh.

And being warned of God in a dream that they should not return to Herod, they departed into their own country another way.

And when they were departed, behold, the angel of the Lord appeareth to Joseph in a dream, saying, Arise, and take the young child and his mother, and flee into Egypt, and be thou there until I bring thee word: for Herod will seek the young child to destroy him.

When he arose, he took the young child and his mother by night, and departed into Egypt:

And was there until the death of Herod: that it might be fulfilled which was spoken of the Lord by the prophet, saying, Out of Egypt have I called my son.

Then Herod, when he saw that he was mocked of the wise men, was exceeding wroth, and sent forth, and slew all the children that were in Bethlehem, and in all the coasts thereof, from two years old and under, according to the time which he had diligently inquired of the wise men.

Then was fulfilled that which was spoken by Jeremy the prophet, saying, In Rama was there a voice heard, lamentation, and weeping, and great mourning, Rachel weeping for her children, and would not be comforted, because they are not. (Matthew 2:1–18)

What possessed King Herod to act in the same manner as Pharaoh with a policy of infanticide and employ the same deceptive practices of the patriarchs? Could he really have been that threatened by a newborn baby being referred to as "King of the Jews"? Was this a display of paranoia, an unnatural fear of something that has not yet happened?

Herod eliminated all potential rivals to his power, and he personally knew the Roman commanders Mark Antony, Cleopatra, and Augustus.

Herod was a descendant of Esau, an Edomite, and wired into his DNA was the desire to follow in Esau's stated mission to kill Jacob ...

He had four wives, and he killed a few of his sons because he believed that they were trying to assassinate him. Herod supported the Olympic games, and he helped to avert food shortages in times of famine. Though he did some noble things during his reign, he was also remembered for his great cruelty.

We see no reference of Satan directly interacting with Herod, yet the king's agenda perfectly aligned with Satan's assault on this promised seed.

Who was Herod that he should be so motivated to kill the newborn child? Herod was a descendant of Esau, an Edomite, and wired into his DNA was the desire to follow in Esau's stated mission to kill Jacob and all his descendants, thus taking his place in attempting to end the life of the seed of the woman.

The Temptation of Messiah

One would be biblically uninformed to view Yeshua/Jesus' immersion by John and God's public proclamation of His Sonship as the setting for Yeshua/Jesus and Satan's first encounter. As far back as Genesis 1:1, we see Yeshua as a part of the compound unity of God in the plural form of the singular God referred to as Elohim. In the English, it states, "In the beginning God"; therefore, Yeshua was there at the start. Like the other members of the council of Heaven, Satan was there in the beginning as well. To further clarify Jesus' intimate knowledge of Satan, we read in Luke 10:18 that Jesus says, "I saw Satan fall like lightening from Heaven."

Upon examination of the full council of Heaven, we look for clarity in understanding who was gathered there in the beginning.

Dr. Michael Heiser has the following to say about Elohim as gods in the Old Testament:

The Hebrew word *elohim* lies behind the word "God" in the OT. Several instances of this word are plural, which may seem to indicate polytheism. For this reason, modern English translations often obscure the Hebrew text's references to plural *elohim*. For example, the NASB renders the second *elohim* in Psalm 82:1 as "rulers." Other translations—more faithful to the original Hebrew—opt for "gods" or "divine beings." However, this usage does not imply polytheism.

Several different entities are referred to as *elohim* in the OT. Considering this variety provides insight as to how the term should be understood. The Hebrew text of the OT refers to the following as *elohim*: Yahweh, the God of Israel (over 1000 times); the members of Yahweh's heavenly council (Psalms 82); the gods of foreign nations (1 Kings 11:33); demons, spirits of the human dead (1 Samuel] 28:13); and angels.

This variety demonstrates that the word should not be identified with one particular set of attributes: *elohim* is not a synonym for God. We reserve the English "g-o-d" for the God of Israel and His attributes. Despite their usage of *elohim*, the biblical writers do not qualitatively equate Yahweh with demons, angels, the human disembodied dead, the gods of the nations, or Yahweh's own council members. Yahweh is unique and above these entities--yet the same term can be used to refer to all of them.

All beings called *elohim* in the Hebrew Bible share a certain characteristic: they all inhabit the non- human realm. By nature, *elohim* are not part of the world of humankind, the world of ordinary embodiment. Elohim—as a term—indicates residence, not a set of attributes; it identifies the proper domain of the entity it describes. Yahweh, the lesser gods of His council, angels, demons, and the disembodied dead all inhabit the spiritual world. They may cross over into the human world—as the Bible informs us—and certain humans may be transported to the non-human realm (e.g., prophets; Enoch). But the proper domains of each are two separate and distinct places.

Within the spiritual world, as in the human world, entities are differentiated by rank and power. Yahweh is an *elohim*, but no other *elohim* is Yahweh. This is what an orthodox Israelite believed about Yahweh. He was not one among equals; He was unique. The belief that Yahweh is utterly and eternally unique—that there is none like Him—is not contradicted by plural *elohim* in the OT.[62]

Some have postulated that the command, "Let there be light," was a reference to Yeshua/Jesus, as He is later self-described as the "light of the world," and that the darkness was Satan. Regardless, they knew one another at the earliest past of Creation.

In the temptation of Messiah, the pattern is the same as it was in Genesis 1. In both cases, God did not speak until the Spirit fell. The account in Matthew 3:13–17 confirms this:

Then cometh Jesus from Galilee to the Jordan unto John, to be baptized of him.

But John forbad him, saying, I have need to be baptized of thee, and comest thou to me?

And Jesus answering said unto him, Suffer it to be so now: for thus it becometh us to fulfil all righteousness. Then he suffered him.

And Jesus, when he was baptized, went up straightway out of the water: and, lo, the heavens were opened unto him, and he saw the Spirit of God descending like a dove, and lighting upon him:

And lo a voice from heaven, This is my beloved Son, in whom I am well pleased.

This event was immediately met with a Spirit-led, forty-day and forty-night journey of fasting through the wilderness, setting the stage for the first cited face-to-face encounter between the seed of the woman and Satan, the devil.

Then Yeshua/Jesus was led up by the Spirit into the wilderness to be tempted by the devil. And when He had fasted forty days and forty nights, afterward He was hungry. Now when the tempter came to Him, he said, "If You are the Son of God, command that these stones become bread." But He answered and said, "It is written, 'Man shall not live by bread alone, but by every word that proceeds from the mouth of God.'"

Then was Jesus led up of the Spirit into the wilderness to be tempted of the devil

And when he had fasted forty days and forty nights, he was afterward an hungred.

And when the tempter came to him, he said, If thou be the Son of God, command that these stones be made bread.

But he answered and said, It is written, Man shall not live by bread alone, bt by every word that proceedeth out of the mouth of God.

Then the devil taketh him up into the holy city, and setteth him on a pinnacle of the temple,

And saith unto him, If thou be the Son of God, cast thyself down: for it is written, He shall give his angels charge concerning thee: and in their hands they shall bear thee up, lest at any time thou dash thy foot against a stone.

Jesus said unto him, It is written again, Thou shalt not tempt the Lord thy God.

Again, the devil taketh him up into an exceeding high mountain, and sheweth him all the kingdoms of the world, and the glory of them;

And saith unto him, All these things will I give thee, if thou wilt fall down and worship me.

Then saith Jesus unto him, Get thee hence, Satan: for it is

written, Thou shalt worship the Lord thy God, and him only shalt thou serve.

Then the devil leaveth him, and, behold, angels came and ministered unto him. (Matthew 4:1–11).

This face-to-face encounter was proof positive that Satan's prior efforts to keep the seed of the woman from coming into the world had failed and that the power and anointing of God Himself were enough to frustrate Satan and compel him to leave, defeated. Satan would need a new strategy if his plan to eliminate the seed of the woman was to prevail.

The Sanhedrin

Sanhedrin comes from the Greek term *sunedrion* (literally, "sitting together") meaning "council." The Sanhedrin is both a Jewish judicial and administrative body. The Sanhedrin was composed of local elites—including members of the high-priestly family, scribes (religious experts), and lay elders. The leader of the Sanhedrin was the high priest and the governing body was a diverse group of seventy others. The high priest was to be a direct descendant of Aaron; however, under the Greek rulership of Israel, this position became highly politicized and required an appointment by both the Greek and Roman rulers of Israel. Regarding the Sanhedrin in place that will call for Yeshua's return, the high priest will be a Levite in the line of Aaron.

Many connect the plot to kill Yeshua/Jesus by the Pharisees and teachers of the Law to His proclamation of condemnation found in Matthew 23:

Then spake Jesus to the multitude, and to his disciples,

Saying, "The scribes and the Pharisees sit in Moses' seat:

All therefore whatsoever they bid you observe, that observe and do; but do not ye after their works: for they say, and do not.

For they bind heavy burdens and grievous to be borne, and lay them on men's shoulders; but they themselves will not move them with one of their fingers.

But all their works they do for to be seen of men: they make broad their phylacteries, and enlarge the borders of their garments,

And love the uppermost rooms at feasts, and the chief seats in the synagogues,

And greetings in the markets, and to be called of men, Rabbi, Rabbi.

But be not ye called Rabbi: for one is your Master, even Christ; and all ye are brethren.

And call no man your father upon the earth: for one is your Father, which is in heaven.

Neither be ye called masters: for one is your Master, even Christ.

But he that is greatest among you shall be your servant.

And whosoever shall exalt himself shall be abased; and he that shall humble himself shall be exalted.

But woe unto you, scribes and Pharisees, hypocrites! for ye shut up the kingdom of heaven against men: for ye neither go in yourselves, neither suffer ye them that are entering to go in.

Woe unto you, scribes and Pharisees, hypocrites! for ye devour widows' houses, and for a pretense make long prayer: therefore ye shall receive the greater damnation.

Woe unto you, scribes and Pharisees, hypocrites! for ye compass sea and land to make one proselyte, and when he is made, ye make him twofold more the child of hell than yourselves.

Woe unto you, ye blind guides, which say, Whosoever shall swear by the temple, it is nothing; but whosoever shall swear by the gold of the temple, he is a debtor.

Ye fools and blind: for whether is greater, the gold, or the temple that sanctifieth the gold?

And, Whosoever shall swear by the altar, it is nothing; but whosoever sweareth by the gift that is upon it, he is guilty.

Ye fools and blind: for whether is greater, the gift, or the altar that sanctifieth the gift?

Whoso therefore shall swear by the altar, sweareth by it, and by all things thereon.

And whoso shall swear by the temple, sweareth by it, and by him that dwelleth therein.

And he that shall swear by heaven, sweareth by the throne of God, and by him that sitteth thereon.

Woe unto you, scribes and Pharisees, hypocrites! for ye pay tithe of mint and anise and cummin, and have omitted the weightier matters of the law, judgment, mercy, and faith: these ought ye to have done, and not to leave the other undone.

Ye blind guides, which strain at a gnat, and swallow a camel.

Woe unto you, scribes and Pharisees, hypocrites! for ye make clean the outside of the cup and of the platter, but within they are full of extortion and excess.

Thou blind Pharisee, cleanse first that which is within the cup and platter, that the outside of them may be clean also.

Woe unto you, scribes and Pharisees, hypocrites! for ye are like unto whited sepulchres, which indeed appear beautiful outward, but are within full of dead men's bones, and of all uncleanness.

Even so ye also outwardly appear righteous unto men, but within ye are full of hypocrisy and iniquity.

Woe unto you, scribes and Pharisees, hypocrites! because ye build the tombs of the prophets, and garnish the sepulchers of the righteous,

And say, If we had been in the days of our fathers, we would not have been partakers with them in the blood of the prophets.

Wherefore ye be witnesses unto yourselves, that ye are the children of them which killed the prophets.

Fill ye up then the measure of your fathers.

Ye serpents, ye generation of vipers, how can ye escape the damnation of hell?

Wherefore, behold, I send unto you prophets, and wise men, and scribes: and some of them ye shall kill and crucify; and some of them shall ye scourge in your synagogues, and persecute them from city to city:

That upon you may come all the righteous blood shed upon the earth, from the blood of righteous Abel unto the blood of Zacharias son of Barachiah, whom ye slew between the temple and the altar.

Verily I say unto you, All these things shall come upon this generation." (Matthew 23:1–36)

However, upon closer examination of the text, we find a much earlier encounter that puts the Pharisees on the path of being instruments of Satan's agenda to kill the seed of the woman. This account predates the events of Matthew 23 by almost a year and a half.

Then was brought unto him one possessed with a devil, blind, and dumb: and he healed him, insomuch that the blind and dumb both spake and saw.

And all the people were amazed, and said, Is not this the son of David?

But when the Pharisees heard it, they said, This fellow doth not cast out devils, but by Beelzebub the prince of the devils.

And Jesus knew their thoughts, and said unto them, Every

kingdom divided against itself is brought to desolation; and every city or house divided against itself shall not stand:

And if Satan cast out Satan, he is divided against himself; how shall then his kingdom stand?

And if I by Beelzebub cast out devils, by whom do your children cast them out? therefore they shall be your judges.

But if I cast out devils by the Spirit of God, then the kingdom of God is come unto you.

Or else how can one enter into a strong man's house, and spoil his goods, except he first bind the strong man? and then he will spoil his house.

He that is not with me is against me; and he that gathereth not with me scattereth abroad.

Wherefore I say unto you, All manner of sin and blasphemy shall be forgiven unto men: but the blasphemy against the Holy Ghost shall not be forgiven unto men.

And whosoever speaketh a word against the Son of man, it shall be forgiven him: but whosoever speaketh against the Holy Ghost, it shall not be forgiven him, neither in this world, neither in the world to come.

Either make the tree good, and his fruit good; or else make the tree corrupt, and his fruit corrupt: for the tree is known by his fruit.

O generation of vipers, how can ye, being evil, speak good things? for out of the abundance of the heart the mouth speaketh.

A good man out of the good treasure of the heart bringeth forth good things: and an evil man out of the evil treasure bringeth forth evil things.

But I say unto you, That every idle word that men shall speak, they shall give account thereof in the day of judgment.

For by thy words thou shalt be justified, and by thy words thou shalt be condemned. (Matthew 12:22–37)

Since Yeshua/Jesus was operating under the still enforceable Mosaic system, He was applying Leviticus 24:16, which states that the punishment for blasphemy is death. In Jewish law, the only form of blasphemy punishable by death is blaspheming the name of the Lord.

The Seven Laws of Noah, which Judaism see as applicable to all people, prohibit blasphemy. Also, the Third Commandment clearly states:

Thou shalt not take the name of the Lord thy God in vain; for the Lord will not hold him guiltless that taketh his name in vain. (Exodus 20:7).

This stern rebuke and condemnation of those who had violated their own commandments ignited the Pharisees, Sadducees, and teachers of the Law to begin to set traps for Jesus through multiple encounters in an attempt to catch Him in a punishable offense.

Throughout Yeshua/Jesus' ministry, He invoked the ire of the established leadership in six key areas:

1. They were provoked by the claims He made regarding His authority and ultimately His claim to be the Messiah.
2. They attributed His power to heal, deliver, and raise the dead not to God or the Holy Spirit, but to Beelzebub, Satan himself.
3. He challenged their religious system by overturning the money-changers' tables and drawing attention to their self-serving leadership.
4. He was a challenge to the balance they had struck with Rome, and they feared He would cause an uprising against Rome.
5. They were distressed by those whom Yeshua/Jesus associated with, as they took pride in not mixing with the sinners and tax collectors that Yeshua/Jesus kept company with.
6. He showed no respect for their restrictions on the Sabbath and other religious traditions.

For the Pharisees, the ultimate offense against them was Yeshua/Jesus healing on the Sabbath. Their response is found in Mark 3:6:

And the Pharisees went forth, and straightway took counsel with the Herodians against him, how they might destroy him.

Their plans intensified as we read the account found in John 11:45–57:

Then many of the Jews which came to Mary, and had seen the things which Jesus did, believed on him.

But some of them went their ways to the Pharisees, and told them what things Jesus had done.

Then gathered the chief priests and the Pharisees a council, and said, "What do we? for this man doeth many miracles.

If we let him thus alone, all men will believe on him: and the Romans shall come and take away both our place and nation.

And one of them, named Caiaphas, being the high priest that same year, said unto them, Ye know nothing at all,

Nor consider that it is expedient for us, that one man should die for the people, and that the whole nation perish not.

And this spake he not of himself: but being high priest that year, he prophesied that Jesus should die for that nation;

And not for that nation only, but that also he should gather together in one the children of God that were scattered abroad.

Then from that day forth they took counsel together for to put him to death.

Jesus therefore walked no more openly among the Jews; but went thence unto a country near to the wilderness, into a city called Ephraim, and there continued with his disciples.

And the Jews' Passover was nigh at hand: and many went

out of the country up to Jerusalem before the Passover, to purify themselves.

Then sought they for Jesus, and spake among themselves, as they stood in the temple, What think ye, that he will not come to the feast?

Now both the chief priests and the Pharisees had given a commandment, that, if any man knew where he were, he should shew it, that they might take him.

Once again, we see that, although there is no interaction between Satan and the Jewish leadership, they were fully aligned with his desire to kill the seed of the woman.

Yeshua/Jesus

Yeshua/Jesus was well aware of Satan's agenda, but because He and the Father are One, He also knew of His coming death, resurrection, and Second Coming. He did not keep this information to Himself, and on four occasions discussed it with His disciples.

Matthew 16:21:

From that time forth began Jesus to shew uno his disciples, how that he must go unto Jerusalem, and suffer many things of the elders and chief priests and scribes, and be killed, and be raised again the third day.

Matthew 17:22–23:

And while they abode in Galilee, Jesus said unto them, The sone of man shall be betrayed into the hands of men:

Matthew 20:17–19:

> And Jesus going up to Jerusalem took the twelve disciples apart
> in the way, and said unto them,
>
> Behold we go up to Jerusalem; and the Son of man shall be
> betrayed unto the chief priests and unto the scribes, and they
> shall condemn him to death,
>
> And shall deliver him to the Gentiles to mock, and to
> scourge, and to crucify him: and the third day he shall rise again.

Although He had foreknowledge of His death and resurrection,
after delivering the ultimate parable and judgment found in the parable
of the sheep and goats at the end of Matthew 25, we read in Matthew
26:1–2:

> And it came to pass, when Jesus had finished all these sayings, he
> said unto his disciples,
>
> Ye know that after two days is the feast of the Passover, and
> the Son of man is betrayed to be crucified.

Since Yeshua/Jesus had already directly encountered Satan and frustrated him with three passages from Deuteronomy and commanded
Him to leave, there was no concern that the Father's plan would not be
fulfilled. Armed with the resolve of, "Not my will be done, but Your will
be done," Yeshua/Jesus accepted a positive final outcome.

Judas Iscariot

Judas was the betrayer who was directly influenced by Satan to play a
key role in delivering Yeshua/Jesus into the hands of Rome. His role

was foreknown to Yeshua/Jesus, as He publicly declared at the Passover Seder/the Last Supper.

In John 13:1–30, we read several acknowledgments of Satan's role with Judas:

Now before the Feast of the Passover, when Jesus knew that his hour had come to depart out of this world to the Father, having loved his own who were in the world, he loved them to the end.

And supper being ended, the devil having now put into the heart of judas Iscariot, Simons son, to betray him;

Jesus knowing that the Father had given all things into his hands, and that was come from God, and went to God;

He riseth from supper, and laid aside his garments; and took a towel, and girded himself.

After that he poureth water into a basin, and began to wash the disciples' feet, and to wipe them with the towel wherewith he was girded.

Then cometh he to Simon Peter: and Peter saith unto him, Lord, dost thou wash my feet?

Jesus answered and said unto him, What I do thou knowest not now; but thou shalt know hereafter.

Peter saith unto him, Thou shalt never wash my feet. Jesus answered him, If I wash thee not, thou hast no part with me.

Simon Peter saith unto him, Lord, not my feet only, but also my hands and my head.

Jesus saith to him, He that is washed needeth not save to wash his feet, bu is clean every whit: and ye are clean, but not all.

For he knew who should betray him; therefore said he, Ye are not all clean.

So after he had washed their feet, and had taken his garments, and was set down again, he said unto them, Know ye what I have done to you?

Ye call me Master and Lord: and ye say well; for so I am.

If I then, your Lord and Mater, have washed your feet; ye also ought to wash one another's feet.

For I have given you an example, that ye should do as I have done to you.

Verily, verily, I say unto you, The servant is not greater than his lord; neither he that is sent greater than he that sent him.

If ye know these things, happy are ye if ye do them.

I speak not of you all: I know whom I have chosen: but that the scripture may be fulfilled, He that eateth bread with me hath lifted up his heel against me.

Now I tell you before it come, that, when it is come to pass, ye may believe that I am he.

Verily, verily, I saw unto you, He that receiveth whomsoever I send receiveth me; and he that receiveth me receiveth him that sent me.

When Jesus had thus said, he was troubled in spirit, and testified, and said, Verily, verily, I saw unto you, that one of you shall betray me.

Then the disciples looked one on another, doubting of whom he spake.

Now there was leaning on Jesus' bosom one of his disciples, whom Jesus loved.

Simon Peter therefore beckoned to him, that he should ask who it should be of whom he spake.

He then lying on Jesus' breast saith unto him, Lord, who is it?

Jesus answered, he it is, to whom I shall give a sop, when I have dipped it. And when he had dipped the sop, he gave it to Judas Iscariot, the son of Simon.

And after the sop Satan entered into him. Then said Jesus unto him, That thou doest, do quickly.

Now no man at the table knew for what intent he spake this unto him.

For some of them thought, because Judas had the bag, that Jesus had said unto him, Buy those things that we have need of against the feast; or that he should give something to the poor.

He then having received the sop went immediately out: and it was night.

After Judas departed, Yeshua/Jesus poured into His disciples and revealed to them many new truths and revelations. Many were confusing and mysterious, but would be understood once He returned.

In John 18:1–9, we read:

When Jesus had spoken these words, he went forth with his disciples over the brook Cedron, where was a garden, into the which he entered, and his disciples.

And Judas also, which betrayed him, knew the place: for Jesus ofttimes resorted hither with his disciples.

Judas then, having received a band of men and officers from the chief priests and Pharisees, cometh thither with lanterns and torches and weapons.

Jesus therefore, knowing all things that should come upon him, went forth, and said unto them, Whom seek ye?

They answered him, Jesus of Nazareth. Jesus saith unto them, I am he. And Judas also, which betrayed him, stood with them.

As soon then as he had said unto them, I am he, they went backward, and fell to the ground.

Then asked he them again, Whom seek ye? And they said, Jesus of Nazareth.

Jesus answered, I have told you that I am he: if therefore ye seek me, let these go their way:

That the saying might be fulfilled, which he spake, Of them which thou gavest me have I lost none.

This is the first account in the New Testament of Satan directly enlisting someone to assist him in his plan to kill the seed of the woman.

6

Second Chances

It was the tenth of Nisan, the day God established in Exodus 12 for the selection of the lambs for the Passover. On the morning of Yeshua/Jesus' entry into Jerusalem, Josephus, a first-century Jewish historian who served Rome to document their activity and portray them in the most positive light, reports that 256,500 lambs were entering the Sheep Gate for examination by the priests. Yeshua/Jesus entered through the Eastern Gate riding on a donkey to symbolize that He was entering in peace. (Had he been riding a horse, that would have symbolized that He was coming in war.)

Matthew 21:8–11:

And a very great multitude spread their garments in the way; others cut down branches from the trees, and strewed them in the way.

And the multitudes that went before, and that followed, cried, saying, "Hosanna to the Son of David: Blessed is he that cometh in the name of the Lord; Hosanna in the highest."

And when he was come into Jerusalem, all the city was moved, saying, "Who is this?"

And the multitude said, "This is Jesus the prophet of Nazareth of Galilee."

Satan's Second Chance

As prescribed in Exodus chapter 12, the sacrificial lambs were to be inspected for four days to determine if they were without blemish or spot. So, too, Yeshua/Jesus was questioned and challenged by Pharisees and teachers of the Law. Upon each examination, all concluded that they found no error in Him. His response is summarized as the "seven woes" in Matthew 23:1–36. After He had finished delivering this message and before leaving the Temple, Jesus declared in Matthew 23:37–39:

> O Jerusalem, Jerusalem, thou that killest the prophets, and stonest them which are sent unto thee, how often would I have gathered thy children together, even as a hen gathereth her chickens under her wings, and ye would not!
>
> Behold, your house is left unto you desolate.
>
> For I say unto you, Ye shall not see me henceforth, till ye shall say, Blessed is he that cometh in the name of the Lord.

This was Satan's second chance. Yeshua/Jesus was proclaiming that the condition upon which He would return would be for the Pharisees and scribes to call for His return. Oddly, these were the exact words that Yeshua/Jesus was greeted with upon His entrance into Jerusalem by the people gathered on the streets. It is clear from this that Yeshua/Jesus was addressing the leadership of Israel, not the Jewish people themselves. These are the same leaders He had previously condemned when they accused Him of casting out demons in the name of Beelzebub. He had now made it clear that the conditions surrounding the Second Coming were in the hands of those He was most critical of.

After leaving the Temple with His disciples, He stopped on the Mount of Olives to share a prophetic message describing the future destruction of the Second Temple and outlining the signs and conditions that will be in place at the time of His return.

Matthew 26:1–5:

And it came to pass, when Jesus had finished all these sayings, he said unto his disciples,

Ye know that after two days is the feast of the Passover, and the Son of man is betrayed to be crucified.

Then assembled together the chief priests, and the scribes, and the elders of the people, unto the palace of the high priest, who was called Caiaphas,

And consulted that they might take Jesus by subtilty, and kill him.

But they said, Not on the feast day, lest there be an uproar among the people.

If Satan had thought the crucifixion of Jesus would be the time to take a victory lap around Jerusalem, hearing that Yeshua/Jesus was going to be resurrected on the third day brought him no comfort. But something had changed among the people, and in this change, Satan saw that he would have a second chance to eliminate the seed line of Messiah. His focus must now be on eliminating the Jews to keep them from calling for the Messiah's return.

> *Satan began to plant seeds of rebellion into the Jewish hearts while empowering Rome to further subjugate the Jews.*

The Great Revolt

Since Rome was in power at the time of Jesus' crucifixion and was already looking for ways to control the Jews, Satan began to plant seeds of rebellion into the Jewish hearts while empowering Rome to further subjugate the Jews. The destruction of the Second Temple in AD 70 began a period of rebellion in which many Jewish lives were lost.

The Jews' Great Revolt against Rome in AD 66 led to one of the greatest catastrophes in Jewish life and, in retrospect, might well have been a terrible mistake. No one could argue with the Jews for wanting to throw off Roman rule. Since the Romans had first occupied Israel in 63 BC, their rule had grown more and more onerous. From almost the beginning of the Common Era, Judea was ruled by Roman procurators, whose chief responsibility was to collect and deliver an annual tax to the empire. Whatever the procurators raised beyond the quota assigned, they could keep. Not surprisingly, they often imposed confiscatory taxes. Equally infuriating to the Judeans, Rome took over the appointment of the high priest (a turn of events that the ancient Jews appreciated as much as modern Catholics would have appreciated Mussolini appointing the popes). As a result, the high priests, who represented the Jews before God on their most sacred occasions, increasingly came from the ranks of Jews who collaborated with Rome.

At the beginning of the Common Era, a new group arose among the Jews: the Zealots (in Hebrew, *Ka-na-im*). These anti-Roman rebels were active for more than six decades, and later instigated the Great Revolt. Their most basic belief was that all means were justified to attain political and religious liberty.

The Jews' anti-Roman feelings were seriously exacerbated during the reign of the half-crazed emperor Caligula, who in the year AD 39 declared himself to be a deity and ordered his statue to be set up at every temple in the Roman Empire. The Jews, alone in the empire, refused the command; they would not defile God's Temple with a statue of pagan Rome's newest deity. Caligula threatened to destroy the Temple, so a delegation of Jews was sent to pacify him—but their effort was to no avail. Caligula raged at them, "So you are the enemies of the gods, the only people who refuse to recognize my divinity." Only the emperor's sudden, violent death saved the Jews from wholesale massacre.

Caligula's action radicalized even the more moderate Jews. What assurance did they have, after all, that another Roman ruler would not arise and try to defile the Temple or destroy Judaism altogether? In addition, Caligula's sudden demise might also have been interpreted as confirming the Zealots' belief that God would fight alongside the Jews if only they would have the courage to confront Rome.

In the decades after Caligula's death, Jews found their religion subject to periodic gross indignities, with Roman soldiers exposing themselves in the Temple on one occasion and burning a Torah scroll on another.

Ultimately, the combination of financial exploitation, Rome's unbridled contempt for Judaism, and the unabashed favoritism that the Romans extended to Gentiles living in Israel brought about the revolt.

In the year AD 66, Florus, the last Roman procurator, stole vast quantities of silver from the Temple. The outraged Jewish masses rioted and wiped out the small Roman garrison stationed in Jerusalem. Cestius Gallus, the Roman ruler in neighboring Syria, sent in a larger force of soldiers. But the Jewish insurgents routed them as well.

This was a heartening victory that had a terrible consequence: Many Jews suddenly became convinced that they could defeat Rome, and the Zealots' ranks grew exponentially. Never again, however, did the Jews achieve so decisive a victory.

When the Romans returned, they had sixty thousand heavily armed and highly professional troops. They launched their first attack against the Jewish state's most radicalized area, the Galilee in the north. The Romans vanquished the Galilee, and an estimated one hundred thousand Jews were killed or sold into slavery.

Throughout the Roman conquest of this territory, the Jewish leadership in Jerusalem did almost nothing to help their beleaguered brothers. They apparently had concluded—too late, unfortunately—that the revolt could not be won, and wanted to hold down Jewish deaths as much as possible.

The highly embittered refugees who succeeded in escaping the Galilean massacres fled to the last major Jewish stronghold—Jerusalem. There, they killed anyone in the Jewish leadership who was not as radical as they. Thus, all the more moderate Jewish leaders who headed the Jewish government at the revolt's beginning in AD 66 were dead by AD 68—and not one died at the hands of a Roman. All were killed by fellow Jews.

The scene was now set for the revolt's final catastrophe. Outside Jerusalem, Roman troops prepared to besiege the city; inside the city, the Jews were engaged in a suicidal civil war. In later generations, the rabbis hyperbolically declared that the revolt's failure, and the Temple's destruction, was due not to Roman military superiority but to causeless hatred (*sinat khinam*) among the Jews *(Yoma* 9b). While the Romans would have won the war in any case, the Jewish civil war both hastened their victory and immensely increased the casualties. One horrendous example: In expectation of a Roman siege, Jerusalem's Jews had stockpiled a supply of dry food that could have fed the city for many years. But one of the warring Zealot factions burned the entire supply, apparently hoping that destroying this "security blanket" would compel everyone to participate in the revolt. The starvation resulting from this mad act caused suffering as great as any the Romans inflicted.

We do know that some great figures of ancient Israel opposed the revolt, most notably Rabbi Yochanan ben Zakkai. Since the Zealot leaders ordered the execution of anyone advocating surrender to Rome, Rabbi Yochanan arranged for his disciples to smuggle him out of Jerusalem disguised as a corpse. Once safe, he personally surrendered to the Roman general Vespasian, who granted him concessions that allowed Jewish communal life to continue.

During the summer of AD 70, the Romans breached the walls of Jerusalem and initiated an orgy of violence and destruction. Shortly thereafter, they destroyed the Second Temple. This was the final and most devastating Roman blow against Judea.

It is estimated that as many as one million Jews died in the Great Revolt against Rome. When people today speak of the almost two-thousand-year span of Jewish homelessness and exile, they are dating it from the failure of the revolt and the destruction of the Temple. Indeed, the Great Revolt of AD 66–70, followed some sixty years later by the Bar Kochba revolt, were the greatest calamities in Jewish history prior to the Holocaust. In addition to the more than one million Jews killed, these failed rebellions led to the total loss of Jewish political authority in Israel until 1948. This loss in itself exacerbated the magnitude of later Jewish catastrophes, since it precluded Israel from being used as a refuge for the large numbers of Jews fleeing persecutions elsewhere.[63]

In the spring of AD 70, Titus arrived outside Jerusalem. His army now numbered eight thousand or more. Titus breached the third wall near the end of May and slaughtered the people of that part of the city. Five days later, the second wall fell. Half of the city belonged to the Romans. In July, the Romans built a siege wall around the city to prevent escape and to starve the citizenry.

Unbelievably, the violence between Jewish factions continued. People murdered each other over scraps of food. Anyone suspected of contemplating surrender was killed. Because some Jews had swallowed gold coins before trying to escape, their fellow citizens began to disembowel those they caught, looking for money. In one night, two thousand people were ripped open. No one bothered to bury the dead. Many who did surrender were crucified just outside the walls so the hapless defenders could watch their agony. Josephus records that the Roman soldiers nailed people in various positions for their own amusement until they could not find enough crosses for the victims.

The famine took its toll as well. Josephus reports that six hundred thousand bodies were thrown out of the city. This may be an exaggeration, but it gives a sense of the carnage.

The Antonia fortress fell in mid-July. On August 6, the sacrifices ceased in the Temple. The Temple itself was burned and destroyed on the ninth of the Jewish month of Ab (the end of August), the same day it had been destroyed by the Babylonians more than six hundred years before. It has never been rebuilt.

On August 30, the lower city fell, and in September the upper did the same. Titus ordered all buildings leveled, except for three towers in Herod's palace, which were left as evidence of his former strength. All the citizens were executed, sold into slavery, or saved for the games in the arena. The slaughter was beyond description. Infants were thrown to their deaths from the tops of the city walls, and people were burned alive; the alleys of the city were choked with corpses. Eleven thousand prisoners died of starvation waiting for their execution. Josephus records that more than one million perished and nearly one hundred thousand were sold into slavery. The Jews' holy city was gone and their Temple destroyed.

A few Zealots took refuge at Herod's fortress of Masada. Here they hoped to outlast the Romans. One can only imagine the state of mind of these people, some of whom had seen Jerusalem fall. Titus left their fate in the hands of Silva, the new governor. The tenth legion laid siege to Masada in AD 72. A wall was built by Jewish slaves around the base of the enormous mountain plateau, six feet high and more than two miles in length. However, there was little chance of starving out the defenders because Herod's extensive storehouses were still filled with food and weapons and his cisterns with water. The Zealots apparently felt safe here.

Over the next seven months, the Romans built a siege ramp against the western side of the mountain. When the ramp was finished, a battering ram was winched to the top, and Roman soldiers smashed a hole in the fortress wall. The Zealots fortified their wall with timbers, but these were set on fire. That night the Zealots met. Their leader, Eleazar from Gamla, argued forcefully that suicide was the only honorable action. They had seen what the Romans would do to them, their wives, and their children. They had lived their lives for freedom and the opportunity to serve God alone. Now they must remove all possibility of serving anyone else.

Every man killed his family. Ten men were chosen to kill the Jewish soldiers; one killed the other nine and then committed suicide. In so doing, the Zealots stole the final victory from the Romans. However, the revolt was ended. Only two elderly women and five children survived to share the story with the world.

The Romans eventually built a temple to Jupiter on the Temple Mount. Emperor Hadrian (c. 117–138) desired to remake Jerusalem into a Roman city named Aelia Capitolina. The few Jews who remained held to their desire for freedom and their hopes of a conquering Messiah. When Simon Bar Kochba, a descendant of David and apparently a charismatic leader, began a new resistance, the religious community declared him Messiah. Open rebellion (the Second Jewish Revolt) began in AD 131 and the Jews rallied around his leadership.

The Romans were surprised and initially defeated, but their follow-up was swift and devastating. The Roman commander Julius Severus, and even Hadrian himself, responded with overwhelming force. Nearly a thousand villages were destroyed, and Bar Kochba was killed. In AD 135, the Second Jewish Revolt ended. Any Jews who had not fled the land were killed or enslaved. Jerusalem became Hadrian's Roman city, the Jewish religion was outlawed, and Judea became Palestine. The Jews were a people without a land.

Out of this disaster came two new religious movements: Christianity and rabbinic Judaism. The revolt drove Christianity to the ends of the earth, and it soon became a largely Gentile faith. Only today are its Jewish roots being recognized. Rabbinic Judaism became the Orthodox faith of the Jewish people of today, the descendants of the Pharisees. The Sadducees, the Essenes, and the Zealots are no more.

The First and Second Jewish Revolts were a disaster for God's people. The agony suffered over two millennia can be traced to those events. The same Romans crucified Jesus nearly forty years before the first revolt. Understanding the climate that led to the revolt and His anticipation of that event makes His teaching clearer.

Often people saw in Jesus a Davidic king, a military conqueror who would rescue them from the Romans (John 6:15; Acts 1:6). However, His kingdom was not the kingdom of the

Zealot or the sword (Matthew 26:51–52), though He had a Zealot disciple (Matthew 10:4). Jesus frequently commanded those He taught or healed not to tell anyone, possibly because they would misunderstand, given the political climate of the day (Mark 1:44, 7:36, 3:12, 5:43; Matthew 8:4, 9:30, 12:16; Luke 8:56). When we remember how many messiahs proclaimed their message during this time, we can understand the uniqueness of Christ's message and the reticence of His audience.

Jesus predicted the destruction that would result from the revolt (Matthew 24:1–2). It led Him to weep on one occasion as He described exactly what would happen (Luke 19:41–44). It seems that Jesus was saddened because His fellow Jews looked for military solutions to their problems rather than spiritual ones, and to a political messiah rather than the Lamb of God. Jesus warned His followers not to take part in that method of bringing in God's Kingdom. The coming destruction was not God's judgment as much as it was the natural result of human beings seeking salvation through their own political and military might. Jesus' method was the opposite of such an approach.

While we cannot fully understand God's reasons for shaping history the way He has, we must be able to weep with Jesus because the destruction wrought by the two Jewish revolts resulted from people seeking God in the wrong places and ways. We must be devoted to Jesus the Messiah's message, for He truly is God's hope of peace (Luke 2:14).[64]

Without knowing at what point in the future Yeshua/Jesus would return, Satan had to employ an indiscriminate strategy to enlist as many as he could to eliminate the seed line of Messiah. Without the ability to determine who would comprise the future leadership that would call for Messiah's return, his only option was to embark on a campaign to totally annihilate all the Jews.

7

The Rise of the
Counterfeit Seed

Jesus was well aware of the coming Antichrist, who, as the seed of the serpent, would deceive many and become the catalyst for a war that would exact a high cost on the population of the Jewish people. Knowing this was a future event, He warned the people not to fall prey to it. This event—foretold in Daniel and confirmed by Yeshua/Jesus—is pivotal to Satan's attack on the seed line of Messiah. Although Yeshua/Jesus is addressing Jewish believers, He clearly understands the implications to the nonbelieving Jewish population. The focus of mainstream Judaism is the restoration of Jewish worship on the Temple Mount. Since one of the main tactics of the Antichrist will advance this cause, the Jews will be blinded by this singular issue to the point of agreeing to almost anything to rebuild the Temple.

The scenes from Jerusalem at the Kotel (Western Wall) show everyone dressed in black. This is symbolic of wearing a mourning garment for the destruction of the Second Temple. They gather daily to pray, and in their prayers are the hopes of a new Temple and the coming of Messiah.

Biblical Mandate

The Temple Institute in Jerusalem believes there is a biblical mandate to build the Temple and states these foundational principles on their website:

> The Torah teaches that the positive commandment to build the Temple was given by G-d to the Jewish people at Mount Sinai, the day following Yom Kippur. It is counted as one of the 613 mitzvot, the commandments that Israel is perpetually obligated to fulfill.

—————— ✴ ——————

The focus of mainstream Judaism is the restoration of Jewish worship on the Temple Mount.

——————————————

> In his classic work *The Book of the Commandments*, the great authority Maimonides explains the details of each one of the Torah's commandments. Here, he explains G-d's instructions to build the Temple as follows:

> The Creator commanded us to erect a chosen House for His service, where the sacrificial offerings will be brought for all time. And the processionals and festive pilgrimages will be conducted there three times a year.

> The verse states: "And they shall make for Me a sanctuary, and I will dwell amongst them" (Exodus 25:8).... this commandment is general and includes many details: the menorah, the table, the altar, etc. These are all intrinsic parts of the Temple and all of the detailed ordinances of this commandment including the construction and its design are all explained in the tractate that was compiled for this purpose, Tractate Middot.

> There are three major points that Maimonides teaches us here:

1. The purpose of the commandment of building the Temple is in order to offer the sacrifices, and it is a perpetual commandment that is binding upon every successive generation.
2. The vessels of the Temple are an intrinsic part of the commandment and constitute a portion of the Temple structure, and all the units, separately and together, are considered as one precept.
3. The accepted design of the Holy Temple is that which is described in Tractate Middot of the Babylonian Talmud. These principles are universally accepted as legally binding by the great Torah scholars throughout the generations.[65]

Daniel's Prophecy

By the time that three and a half years will have passed, the Antichrist will defile the Temple and reveal his true agenda. Jewish worship will cease, and the Antichrist will unleash his plan to deploy the ten kings to subjugate the world to his New World Order.

In Orthodox Judaism, the "o" is omitted from the spelling of "God" as their very legalistic way of avoiding even the appearance of using God's name in vain. This is prevalent in all Jewish writings in the ultra-religious world. As believers, we are set free from this practice.

Daniel writes:

And arms shall stand on his part, and they shall pollute the sanctuary of strength, and shall take away the daily sacrifice, and they shall place the abomination that maketh desolate.

And such as do wickedly against the covenant shall he corrupt by flatteries: but the people that do know their God shall be strong, and do exploits.

And they that understand among the people shall instruct many: yet they shall fall by the sword, and by flame, by captivity, and by spoil, many days.

Now when they shall fall, they shall be holpen with a little help: but many shall cleave to them with flatteries.

And some of them of understanding shall fall, to try them, and to purge, and to make them white, even to the time of the end: because it is yet for a time appointed.

And the king shall do according to his will; and he shall exalt himself, and magnify himself above every god, and shall speak marvelous things against the God of gods, and shall prosper till the indignation be accomplished: for that that is determined shall be done.

Neither shall he regard the God of his fathers, nor the desire of women, nor regard any god: for he shall magnify himself above all.

But in his estate shall he honour the God of forces: and a god whom his fathers knew not shall he honour with gold, and silver, and with precious stones, and pleasant things.

Thus shall he do in the most strong holds with a strange god, whom he shall acknowledge and increase with glory: and he shall cause them to rule over many, and shall divide the land for gain.

And at the time of the end shall the king of the south push

at him: and the king of the north shall come against him like a whirlwind, with chariots, and with horsemen, and with many ships; and he shall enter into the countries, and shall overflow and pass over.

He shall enter also into the glorious land, and many countries shall be overthrown: but these shall escape out of his hand, even Edom, and Moab, and the chief of the children of Ammon.

He shall stretch forth his hand also upon the countries: and the land of Egypt shall not escape.

But he shall have power over the treasures of gold and of silver, and over all the precious things of Egypt: and the Libyans and the Ethiopians shall be at his steps.

But tidings out of the east and out of the north shall trouble him: therefore he shall go forth with great fury to destroy, and utterly to make away many.

And he shall plant the tabernacles of his palace between the seas in the glorious holy mountain; yet he shall come to his end, and none shall help him. (Daniel 11:31–45)

Jesus' Warning

Yeshua/Jesus issues a warning as a sign of the times that will usher in His return. His warning is to the believers, but He also knows the toll on the nonbelieving Jewish population who will be deceived. They will be counted as serving the seed of the serpent and advancing his agenda to eliminate those who would call for Yeshua/Jesus' return.

When ye therefore shall see the abomination of desolation, spoken of by Daniel the prophet, stand in the holy place, (whoso readeth, let him understand:)

Then let them which be in Judaea flee into the mountains:

Let him which is on the housetop not come down to take any thing out of his house:

Neither let him which is in the field return back to take his clothes.

And woe unto them that are with child, and to them that give suck in those days!

But pray ye that your flight be not in the winter, neither on the sabbath day:

For then shall be great tribulation, such as was not since the beginning of the world to this time, no, nor ever shall be.

And except those days should be shortened, there should no flesh be saved: but for the elect's sake those days shall be shortened.

Then if any man shall say unto you, Lo, here is Christ, or there; believe it not.

For there shall arise false Christs, and false prophets, and shall shew great signs and wonders; insomuch that, if it were possible, they shall deceive the very elect.

Behold, I have told you before.

Wherefore if they shall say unto you, Behold, he is in the desert; go not forth: behold, he is in the secret chambers; believe it not.

For as the lightning cometh out of the east, and shineth even unto the west; so shall also the coming of the Son of man be.

For wheresoever the carcase is, there will the eagles be gathered together. (Matthew 24:15–28)

And I beheld another beast coming up out of the earth; and he had two horns like a lamb, and he spake as a dragon.

And he exerciseth all the power of the first beast before him, and causeth the earth and them which dwell therein to worship the first beast, whose deadly wound was healed.

And he doeth great wonders, so that he maketh fire come down from heaven on the earth in the sight of men,

And deceiveth them that dwell on the earth by the means of those miracles which he had power to do in the sight of the beast; saying to them that dwell on the earth, that they should make an image to the beast, which had the wound by a sword, and did live.

And he had power to give life unto the image of the beast, that the image of the beast should both speak, and cause that as many as would not worship the image of the beast should be killed.

And he causeth all, both small and great, rich and poor, free and bond, to receive a mark in their right hand, or in their foreheads:

And that no man might buy or sell, save he that had the mark, or the name of the beast, or the number of his name.

Here is wisdom. Let him that hath understanding count the number of the beast: for it is the number of a man; and his number is Six hundred threescore and six. (Revelation 13:11–18)

For the believer, taking the mark will mean forfeiting one's salvation, but to the nonbeliever, it will mean he or she now belongs to the seed of the serpent and joins his army to annihilate the remnant of the seed line of the woman. This is a significant escalation of global proportion as the ten kingdoms align behind the agenda of the Antichrist and begin their campaign of recruitment.

8

The Roman Catholic Church as Satan's Army

The Pre-Constantine Years

The following pages outline a clear picture of the oath that has been chosen for most Christians. You may not have made the decisions that are chronicled here, but you do live under them. The research here was done with a KJV Bible in one hand and the hundreds of resources used to tell you this story. If I offend, I offend with the truth of God's Word in my hand. I reached a point in my life when man's answers were no longer satisfying or even true. I had only one place to turn. If you are shocked by these revelations and biblical facts, you are not alone. But, you cannot read them and not make a decision to do something about what you have read. That's what our ministry is for, and you are welcome to embrace the fullness of what God's Word says is yours.

From a Jewish perspective, it is a paradox to see the worship of the Jewish Messiah, yet create doctrine and traditions that remove the Jewishness of Jesus and raise up an army that would so grossly misunderstand the parable of the sheep and the goats and Paul's strongly worded admonition to the church in Romans 11.

The expectation of the Jews at the time of Jesus had already been established by God through the prophet Isaiah:

And he said, Go, and tell this people, Hear ye indeed, but understand not; and see ye indeed, but perceive not.

Make the heart of this people fat, and make their ears heavy, and shut their eyes; lest they see with their eyes, and hear with their ears, and understand with their heart, and convert, and be healed. (Isaiah 6:9–10)

These words were confirmed by Yeshua/Jesus in Matthew 13:10–17:

And the disciples came, and said unto him, Why speakest thou unto them in parables?

He answered and said unto them, Because it is given unto you to know the mysteries of the kingdom of heaven, but to them it is not given.

For whosoever hath, to him shall be given, and he shall have more abundance: but whosoever hath not, from him shall be taken away even that he hath.

Therefore speak I to them in parables: because they seeing see not; and hearing they hear not, neither do they understand.

And in them is fulfilled the prophecy of Esaias, which saith, By hearing ye shall hear, and shall not understand; and seeing ye shall see, and shall not perceive:

For this people's heart is waxed gross, and their ears are dull of hearing, and their eyes they have closed; lest at any time they should see with their eyes, and hear with their ears, and should understand with their heart, and should be converted, and I should heal them.

But blessed are your eyes, for they see: and your ears, for they hear.

For verily I say unto you, That many prophets and righteous men have desired to see those things which ye see, and have not seen them; and to hear those things which ye hear, and have not heard them.

As the Gentile church rose to power, the Jews were blamed for their rejection of Jesus. This blame continued as the official position until the Catholic Church issued its most authoritative teaching on the issue in its 1965 Second Vatican Council document, *Nostra Aetate*, which revolutionized the Church's relations with Jews by stating the following:

> True, the Jewish authorities and those who followed their lead pressed for the death of Christ; still, what happened in His passion cannot be charged against all the Jews, without distinction, then alive, nor against the Jews of today. Although the Church is the new People of God, the Jews should not be presented as rejected or accursed by God, as if this followed from the Holy Scriptures.[66]

What this statement says, in essence, is that the Catholic Church had been blaming the Jews for killing Jesus for almost two millennia.

Few, if any, have asked the eye-opening question, "Where would the Gentiles be today if all the Jews had accepted Jesus two thousand years ago?" God revealed that this would not be the case, as previously referenced in Isaiah 6:9–10 and confirmed by Jesus in Matthew 13:10–17. If this was God's plan all along to open the door for the redemption of sin to all who would believe, then why would there be such wholesale persecution and

> *...it is a paradox to see the worship of the Jewish Messiah, yet create doctrine and traditions that remove the Jewishness of Jesus.*

blame aimed at the Jews? If it does not line up with Scripture, then it doesn't line up. If it wasn't God's intention for "the Church" to persecute the Jews for His sacrifice of Jesus, then whose agenda was being followed?

Stripping away Jewish Identity

History has shown that one of the most effective ways to conquer a people or a nation is to strip away their identity. The elimination of the Jewish identity of the followers of the Jewish Messiah played right into the hands of Satan. The systematic approach over the span of almost two thousand years either subjugated Jews to either take on a "Christian" identity and abandon their Jewish heritage—or lose their lives. The theology of this new "Christianity" required the abandonment of all connection to the Old Testament and forced anyone who was not willing to give up their Jewish practices to either convert or die.

Over time, the deification of Mary and the elevation of men and women throughout the ages as saints to be prayed to blurred the lines of monotheism. The inerrant Word of God was being rewritten to support the elimination of all Jewish identity, and ultimately, catechism was written and applied, and was inherently different than anything even remotely recognizable compared to the original text of both the Old and New Testaments. Yeshua/Jesus as our intercessor was being replaced by the pope as the highest representative of God on earth. The elevation of priests as mediators was secured by addressing them as "Father" and nuns as "Mother" ("Superior"), further distancing all from having a direct personal relationship with God. This was not about salvation, redemption, or atonement through the shed blood of the Jewish Messiah. This was a new wall of partition that replaced the one God Himself tore down, once again separating Jew and Gentile and creating a new path to God through a man-made system that would promote conversion and the abandonment of all Jewish identity. The Roman Catholic Church became Satan's army and aligned perfectly with his agenda to eliminate the seed line of Messiah.

Ignatius and Barnabus

Early into the second century, Ignatius, bishop of Antioch,[67] taught in his epistle to the Philippians that whoever "celebrates the Passover along with the Jews, or receives emblems of their feast, he is a partaker with those who killed the Lord and His apostles."[68] In addition, the epistle of Barnabas states that "Jewish fasts are no longer acceptable to God" and that "Christians are the heirs of God's covenant with Abraham."[69] It goes on to state that the covenant was meant for Jews and Christians, but that the Jews lost it.[70] Now that all of the apostles were dead, signs began to appear indicating that Gentile believers were losing sight of their identity with the Jewish people. Forces were set in motion for the Gentiles to begin the process of divorcing themselves from their Jewish roots.

Marcion

It wasn't long before the heretic Marcion[71] appeared and began to teach that the Hebrew Scriptures "have no value or authority for the Church."[72] Marcion believed that the grace of God as taught by Sha'ul (Paul)[73] had replaced the Old Covenant. He maintained that the old legalism of the Bible had been fulfilled, and a new dispensation of grace had been inaugurated. In his opinion, Paul taught a more excellent way of grace. Moses brought condemnation, but Paul enabled men and women to discover God's grace. Marcion was aware of Yeshua's statement in Matthew 5:17: "I did not come to destroy the Torah but to fulfill." The disciples of Marcion were rumored to be so troubled by this verse that they changed the words to read, "Think not that I have come to fulfill the law but to destroy it." They simply inverted the words "fulfill" and "destroy" to suit their opinion. Marcion taught that "the God of the Old Testament was cruel and a totally different God from the one revealed in the New Testament."[74] He "founded his own church which merged Gnosticism with orthodox Christianity, creating a theology that was sharply dualistic, violently antagonistic toward Judaism, strictly ascetic and celibate, and wielded a wide and destructive influence throughout Christendom. Unfortunately, some modern Christians have unknowingly endorsed his ideas." His "theology was so contrary to God's word that Polycarp[75] called him the 'first-born of Satan.'"[76]

Years after Marcion's death, Tertullian[77] stated that Marcion "mutilated the Gospel according to Luke, removing all the narratives of the Lord's birth, and also removing much of the teaching of the discourses of the Lord wherein he is most manifestly described as acknowledging the maker of this universe to be his father."[78] He did the same to the letters of the Apostle Paul.[79] His flawed logic required him to do so. Otherwise, how could the God of the Old Covenant, a supposedly different God than the one revealed in the New Covenant, be his father?

Even though Marcion was declared a heretic, his dualistic concept of grace versus law was later accepted as truth. From this evidence, we can see that the rift between Jewish and Gentile believers began to widen. The Gentiles gained momentum in their efforts to separate themselves from their Jewish brethren. A Gentilized Church began to emerge.

Bar Kochba Revolt

A second war, the Bar Kochba war, broke out between Israel and Rome in AD 132. In this conflict, one of the generals, Bar Kosiba,[80] displayed great valor and military genius. Rabbi Akiva[81] changed his name to Bar Kochba ("son of a star"),[82] alluding to the verse in Numbers 24:17, "A star shall go forth from Jacob." The "star," in Jewish thought, was understood to be the Messiah. The Jewish believers of that day understood

Rabbi Akiva to be calling Bar Kochba the Messiah Himself. These Jewish disciples of Yeshua could not accept him as such. They once again fled to Pella, and once again they were "branded as deserters and destroyers." This time they remained in Pella, soon to become isolated from the rest of the Jewish community.

Once the war was over in 135, the Roman Emperor Hadrian[83] renamed the city of Jerusalem to *Aelia Capitolina* (*Aelia* in honor of his own name, Publius Aelius Hadrianus, and *Capitolina* in honor of Jupiter, whose temple in Rome was on the Capitoline Hill) and forbade

There is no linguistic basis for English Bibles to use the name "James." In the Greek New Testament the name of the disciple "James" is Yakobos, which is a Hellenized form of the Hebrew name Ya'akov ("Jacob"). When the NT refers to the patriarch Jacob, it uses the older Septuagint Greek spelling Yakob, without the later "-os" ending (Mt. 22:32; John 4:6; Rom. 11:26). The Hebrew and Greek forms of Ya'akov and Yakob(os) do not have an "m" or "e" in them. So the English "James" is not a transliteration of the originals. Thus, it is not etymologically or linguistically related at all. Translators could just as legitimately substitute "Henry" for Yakobos.

There is long history of anti-Judaism in the medieval English church. Since the man Jacob is frequently depicted negatively in Christian sermons and writings, it's easy to see why a key "Christian" apostle—brother of Jesus and author of a NT epistle—would never be allowed to bear the name "Jacob" in the pages of an English Bible.[86]

all Jews from entering it for one hundred years. He also renamed the territories of Judea and Samaria to "Palestine," a Romanized term for "Philistine," the name of Israel's ancient enemy. The result of the Bar Kochba war was a further rift between the Jewish believers and the rest of the Jewish community.

Gentile Christianity Expresses Its Own Identity

After Rome's victory over this revolt, the first Gentile bishop was appointed to preside over the congregation in Jerusalem since practically all Jewish believers had long ago vacated the city. This marked the end of an era for Jewish bishops. Following Jacob,[84] the brother of Yeshua, ancient church historian Eusebius[85] recorded another fourteen Jewish bishops presiding over the Jewish believers' community in Jerusalem since the beginning of the Renewed Covenant until this time. Reportedly, they were all direct descendants of David and blood relatives of Yeshua. As a result of Hadrian's decree, the believers who had resided in Jerusalem and the bishops of Jerusalem now became totally assimilated into a Gentile identity.

Following the Second Jewish Revolt against Rome, the Gentile believers throughout the Roman Empire "could not be expected to sympathize with the national aspirations of the Nazarenes. For them the destruction of Jerusalem and the cessation of the temple services meant the end of the Law. It came to them as a happy release from the incubus of Judaism and left them free to develop a Christian philosophy of their own better suited to the Gentile temperament."[87]

Ancient church historian Hegesippus[88] observed that as long as the apostles and the generation they taught were alive, the Jewish believers' community remained pure. But as soon as they passed away, false teachers arose who shamelessly taught false doctrine against the true gospel. This was less than one hundred years after Rav Sha'ul (the Apostle Paul) had warned of such errant leaders (Acts 20:29–30).

Over the next five years, writings from those assumed to represent the Gentile leadership within the Jewish believers' community began to move away from the original Jewishness of the faith.

In the mid-second century CE, Christianity began a gradual process of identity-formation that would lead to the creation of a separate, independent religion from Judaism. Initially, Christians were one of many groups of Jews found throughout the Roman Empire. The second century CE experienced a change in the demographics, the introduction of institutional hierarchy, and the creation of Christian dogma.[89]

Gentile Christianity had begun to express its own identity.

Justin Martyr[90] claimed that he met Trypho,[91] a Jewish refugee who had fled to Rome after the revolt. We cannot historically ascertain the existence of this individual; Trypho's responses and arguments may reflect some early Rabbinic views at the time. Justin's dialogue with Trypho became one of the most important of the Adversos texts in defining Christianity against Judaism. He proceeded to teach Trypho the true meaning of the Jewish Scriptures through allegory and exegesis. With the correct allegorical interpretation of the Jewish Scriptures, everywhere that "God" appeared in the texts, it was in fact, the "pre-existent Christ." It was Christ who spoke to Abraham, and when Moses heard the voice from the burning bush, this was Christ in an earlier manifestation of God on earth. Through his methods, he demonstrated that all the Prophets of Israel had predicted the coming of Christ as the savior. God sent Christ into the world to undo the corrupt practices of the Jews, and as proof, he pointed to the fact that God had permitted Rome to defeat the Jews twice. Added to their corruption, the Jews were now charged with the crime of deicide (the killing of God). Justin declared Christians as "versus Israel" and so Christians had usurped the place of the Jews as God's chosen. Because of this, Jews no longer had the capacity to correctly interpret their own Scriptures. This is when the Old Testament became joined to the New Testament (the Christians' sacred texts) as the complete understanding of God's divine plan. From this moment in time, Christians promoted supersession or replacement theology. God had replaced his protection and favor of the Jews with the Christians.[92]

Modern-day historian Jakob Jocz[93] concludes that there were four classes of Jewish believers by the middle of the second century:

1) Jews who were a part of the Gentilized Church; 2) Jewish believers who taught that the Torah of Moses was binding upon all men, Jew and Gentile; 3) Jewish believers who kept the Torah of Moses but did not demand that Gentile Christians do the same; and 4) secret Jewish believers who remained in the synagogues.[94]

From this observation, we can begin to obtain a clearer picture of how rapidly the Jewish believers' community was changing from a Jewish-centered faith to one that was Gentile. The idea of a Jewish believers' community was being replaced by the concept of a Gentile church.

Covenants, Controversy, Changes, and Compromise

About this time, a group of heretical Jewish believers appeared on the scene in the region of modern-day Jordan. This was the area where the Jewish believers had fled at the time of the Bar Kochba rebellion. This new group sprang up from the midst of the community of Jewish believers in that region. The Ebionites,[95] as they were called, denied the virgin birth and Messiah's deity. Irenaeus,[96] a late second-century patristic writer (church father), said concerning them:

Those who are called Ebionites…use only the Gospel according to Matthew; they reject the Apostle Paul, calling him an apostate from the law. The prophetic writings they strive to expound with especial exactness; they are circumcised, and persevere in the customs according to the Law, and in the Jewish mode of life, even to the extent of worshipping Jerusalem, as if it were the abode of God.[97]

Twenty-five years later, "Irenaeus was the first to apply the term New Testament to sacred scriptures." Similarly, "Milito of Sardis [was] credited for the first use of the term Old Covenant or Old Testament to refer to the [Hebrew Scriptures]." These terms actually refer to two different covenants God made with Israel—the Mosaic covenant and the renewed covenant. "These covenants are particular agreements, not designations for the two major parts of the Bible." By coining these terms, these individuals confused the distinction between the covenants and the Scriptures. For example, when the writer of the book of Hebrews speaks of the first covenant becoming obsolete (Hebrews 8:13), he refers to a change in the Mosaic covenant, not a passing away of the Scriptures, as some people now assert. This new labeling also led "to the erroneous belief that the 'Old Testament' was for the Jews, and the 'New Testament' is for the Church." Likewise, it also led to the old Marcionite heresy "that 'the God of the Old Testament' is a God of wrath, and 'the God of the New Testament' is a God of mercy." However, Scripture tells us that God is one (Deuteronomy 6:4) and that He never changes (Exodus 3:15; Deuteronomy 32:40).

Passover Observance

During the same period, a controversy arose between the bishop of Rome and those of Asia concerning when the Passover should be celebrated. In the beginning, the whole community of believers among the

Gentiles celebrated Passover at the same time and in the same manner as the Jews. Later on, the Gentile congregations in parts of the Roman Empire began to change the nature of Passover to commemorate the resurrection of Jesus. They also began to restrict the celebration to a single day rather than the entire week of Unleavened Bread, according to the biblical commandment found in Leviticus 23.

Contrary to the modern-day label that Leviticus 23 includes the "Jewish holidays," it clearly states these are God's appointed times and are not specifically and exclusively Jewish observances. As these congregations evolved further with their version of Passover, they moved their single day of Passover to Sunday. To them, Passover had become Resurrection Day—what we think of today as Easter. This consolidation into a single day of observance disconnected Yeshua from Exodus chapter 12, which chronicles the day of the selection of the lambs on the 10th of Nisan (Palm Sunday), the four days of inspection, the sacrifice of the Passover Lamb on the 14th of Nisan (crucifixion), and then the Feast of First Fruits from Leviticus 23, three days after the Passover (Resurrection Day).

Towards the end of the second century, these congregations, led by the bishops of Rome, Caesarea, and Jerusalem (where the bishops had been of Gentile origin since AD 135), began to push for unity so that all the congregations everywhere should keep the Passover on their single day of Sunday, rather than on Nisan 14, according to the biblical date set in Exodus 12. They had also begun to use the Roman calendar rather than the Jewish calendar for determining the date of Passover. This calendar was solar rather than lunar, thus changing the thirteen months of the Hebrew calendar into the twelve months of the Roman calendar. Today, the celebration of Easter is the first Sunday after the full moon that occurs on or after the spring equinox. If the full moon falls on a Sunday, then Easter is the next Sunday.

As Christians from the province of Asia, where the feast was kept according to the custom of the Jews who had migrated to Rome, controversy erupted. Victor,[98] the bishop of Rome, decided to bring about unity in the observance of the festival. He wrote to all the bishops of the congregations he apparently viewed as allies, including those of Caesarea, Jerusalem, and Pontus. They wrote back unanimously endorsing the observance of Passover/Easter on Sunday. Victor now called upon the bishops of the province of Asia to abandon their custom and to accept the now "universally" prevailing practice of always celebrating Passover/Easter on Sunday. In case they refused to comply, he declared they would be excluded from the fellowship of the Church.

He wrote Polycrates, the bishop of Ephesus, and urged him to call together the bishops of the province of Asia in order to discuss the matter with them. Polycrates did so and responded to the Roman bishop by letter, stating the following:

> We observe the exact day; neither adding, nor taking away. For in Asia also great lights have fallen asleep, which shall rise again on the day of the Lord's coming, when he shall come with glory from heaven, and shall seek out all the saints. Among these are Philip, one of the twelve apostles, who fell asleep in Hierapolis; and his two aged virgin daughters, and another daughter, who lived in the Holy Spirit and now rests at Ephesus; and, moreover, John, who was both a witness and a teacher, who reclined upon the bosom of the Lord, and, being a priest, wore the sacerdotal plate. He fell asleep at Ephesus. And Polycarp in Smyrna, who was a Bishop and martyr; and Thraseas, Bishop and martyr from Eumenia, who fell asleep in Smyrna.... All these observed the fourteenth day of Nisan in accordance with God's timeline for the Passover according to the Gospel, deviating in no respect, but following the rule of faith.
>
> And I also, Polycrates, the least of you all, do according to the tradition of my relatives, some of whom I have closely followed.

For seven of my relatives were Bishops; and I am the eighth. And my relatives always observed the day when the people [i.e., the Jews] put away the leaven. I, therefore, brethren, who have lived sixty-five years in the Lord, and have met with the brethren throughout the world, and have gone through every Holy Scripture, am not at all afraid of those things with which I am now threatened. For those greater than I have said "We ought to obey God rather than man" [Acts 5:29].[99]

Victor immediately attempted to cut off from the common unity the parishes of all Asia, and he wrote letters and declared all the brethren there wholly excommunicated. But this did not please all the bishops who kept Passover on Sunday. Among them was Irenaeus, bishop of Gaul. He convinced Victor that he should not cut off whole churches of God simply because they observed the tradition of an ancient custom. Though wisdom prevailed this time, it would not be accepted 135 years later at the Council of Nicea.[100]

A council was held in Caesarea in AD 196 and was attended entirely by Gentile Christian leaders. They decided that Passover (Resurrection Day) should be observed on Sunday, not the 14th day of Nisan as instructed by the emissaries. Apparently, what we think of as Easter, the Gentiles at that time still referred to as "Passover." Only later did they change the name to "Easter." Labeling it as "Passover" confuses its identity with the biblical holiday itself.

History is not clear on the subject, but it appears that the Gentile believers saw Passover as only commemorating Messiah's death, burial, and resurrection, and chose to recognize a single day during Passover week to observe these events, rather than observe the entire week. Jewish believers, on the other hand, would have also recognized these events, but would have kept the feast for the entire seven days beginning on Nisan 14, according to the biblical commandment (Leviticus 23:5–8;

Number 28:16–25). Passover, being the first spring feast appointed by God, was now becoming a wedge between the Gentile observance of the connection to the fullness of the Passover experience and the combination of all that it stood for into a one-day observance.

They may have even recognized a day during this seven-day period for commemorating Messiah's resurrection. If so, they likely observed it on Nisan 16, not Sunday. Nisan 16 was considered the Day of First Fruits during Passover and foreshadows Messiah's resurrection as "the firstfruits of those who have fallen asleep [i.e., died]" (1 Corinthians 15:20).

To the Jewish believers, Passover represented more than the sacrifice and subsequent resurrection of Yeshua. To them it also called to mind God's deliverance of Israel from Egypt, their redemption from slavery, and death of the firstborn. It further reminded them of the fact that God brought them out with great signs and wonders and that He brought them near to be His own special treasure. To them, Yeshua's righteous act gave new meaning to these events. Gentile Christians, many of whom were now estranged from their Jewish brothers, lost sight of these meanings. Even though some communities, both Christian and Jewish believers, did not accept the council's decision, we can now see that Gentile believers took the next step in the separation process. They were able to change the date and purpose of the biblical holiday.

Changing the day and name of the Passover served one purpose and one purpose only. History has shown us that when you strip away a people group's traditions and force them to comply with another set of customs and traditions, you ultimately blur the former identity. This assimilation into a new cultural norm also brings about intermarriage and the loss of a unique bloodline. The Torah specifically instructs the Jewish people to not assimilate and intermarry. By design, God intended to protect the seed line of Messiah and for it to remain intact.

Biblical Feasts

What's even more stunning is the rejection of God's command for Jews from all over the Diaspora to make pilgrimages to Jerusalem three times annually. These Moadim (appointed times) were set by God, and for God to be glorified in each of these remembrances. The Jewish people have kept many of the biblical feasts through the centuries. God established the biblical feasts, and they continue today. And since Israel became an independent nation in 1948, some of the feasts became official holidays in Israel.

What we commonly refer to as the "Jewish feasts" should more appropriately be called "biblical feasts or "feasts of the Lord," especially since, in the Bible, God calls these festivals simply His own. Just look at how many times that phrase is repeated in a single chapter of Leviticus:

- "These are the Feasts of the Lord, holy convocations which you shall proclaim at their appointed times" (23:4).
- "These are the Feasts of the Lord which you shall proclaim to be holy convocations" (23:37).
- "You shall keep it as a Feast to the Lord…" (23:41).
- "So Moses declared to the children of Israel the Feasts of the Lord" (23:44).

Sabbath

Since the elimination or alteration of these appointed times set in place by God seemed to be negotiable, why not aim for the single most holy observance commanded by God? So holy, in fact, it was included in the Ten Commandments. Few realize that the Sabbath is more than just an observance of the seventh day. It applied to every one of God's appointed times where He states, "Hold a sacred assembly and do no regular work."

This translates to no less than sixty-four Sabbaths in the calendar year! God had set the Sabbath apart and established its dates and times, all the while warning us to not add or take away any word from His instruction. These same feasts apply before the incarnate Messiah, during Messiah's life, and are partially fulfilled in sequence, as He was the Passover Lamb, He was our Unleavened Bread, He rose on the third day, He was our First Fruits, and He sent the Holy Spirit fifty days after His resurrection. Zechariah 14 instructs the nations to make these same pilgrimages in observance of God's appointed times beginning with the fall Feast of Tabernacles. Altering God's Word to deprive His chosen people would only launch an all-out attack on those who did not bend the knee to the rising power of Rome and face death. As this process unfolds, we see an even clearer alignment with Satan's agenda to eliminate the seed line of Messiah. In the simplest terms: NO Jews, no Second Coming of Jesus?

At the beginning of the third century, Tertullian spoke of keeping Sunday as the Lord's Day and of tracing the sign of the cross on the forehead. This is believed by some historians to be the first mention in history of Gentile Christians treating Sunday like the Sabbath, as a day of rest.

Assuming this observation is correct, we can conclude that sometime during the latter half of the second century (probably in keeping with the Roman practice mentioned earlier), the Gentile Christian leadership, in many places, began to teach that the Sabbath was changed to Sunday. Their reasons for doing so were likely tied to Yeshua's resurrection on the first day of the week (Matthew 28:1; Luke 24:1). Sadly, Tertullian acknowledged that in his day, Sunday was counted a pagan festival day by the heathens, and Christians who observed Sunday as a day of worship were thought to be sun-worshippers by the pagans around them. Although their intentions may have been noble, the advocates of change erred in their thinking. Scripture states that the Sabbath was given to the children of Israel as an everlasting covenant (Exodus 31:13–17).

Nowhere in Scripture do we find even a hint that God would one day change the nature or occurrence of the Sabbath in any way. Sixty years earlier, the Church at Rome began to honor Sunday as a day of worship. Now it was becoming a replacement for the Sabbath in many Gentile Christian communities.

Tertullian lamented that Gentile Christians compromised their faith with the pagans by joining them in their festival of the Saturnalia and other pagan cultural events. The Saturnalia was a Roman pagan holiday commencing on December 17 and concluding on December 23, in conjunction with the winter solstice. Our modern-day Christmas celebration comes from the early Gentile Church's embracing of this festival and calling it the season of the birth of Christ. Apparently, as late as Tertullian's day, the Christian communities did not observe a day in the year to honor the birth of the Messiah, at least not on December 25. From Tertullian's comment, the sentiment seems to be that to do so would have been considered idolatrous. Nevertheless, what was idolatrous in his day became accepted as divine in origin within two hundred years.

Heresy

Around AD 231, Origen[101] appeared on the scene. He was considered a heretic by some of the church leaders of his day. Origen said that keeping the Sabbath was meant to be interpreted mystically or spiritually, not literally. Not surprisingly, he is considered the father of the allegorical method of interpreting Scripture. In his book, *The Church and the Jews*, author Daniel Gruber[102] says of Origen:

> Origen is credited with being the father of the allegorical method of interpretation. The reason for this is that Origen, in a comprehensive system, made allegory the only way to truly understand the scriptures. In Origen's system of interpretation,

he often denied the ordinary sense of the text, and replaced it with allegories which he made up. These allegories then became the real meaning of the text. There was no way to challenge the allegories on the basis of the text, since what the text actually said was no longer what it meant. In this allegorical system, when the text said "Israel," it meant "the Church" and not the Jews, so long as the promise or comment was good. If the promise or comment was not good, then "Israel" still meant "the Jews," and not "The Church."[103]

Gruber goes on to say:

For some of the doctrines which he believed and taught, Origen was considered by many to be a heretic. During his lifetime, he was excommunicated by two church councils held in Alexandria in 231 and 232 A.D.[104]

However, the churches in Palestine did not recognize his excommunication and even "established a theological school and library dedicated to establishing Origen's views as the true orthodoxy throughout the entire Church."

After his death, some of the leaders in the Gentile Church regarded his views as heretical. Even today, some of his views would be considered too heretical for most of the modern Church. Nevertheless, Gruber says:

Most of the Greek fathers of the third and fourth centuries stood more or less under the influence of the spirit and the works of Origen, without adopting all his peculiar speculative views [including the well-known early church historian, Eusebius]. Though the third and fourth century church fathers "did not accept all the teachings which Origen's system of interpretation generated, they did accept the system itself." His system of interpretation is credited with producing the anti-Judaic "New Israel" theology where the Church replaces the Jews in the plan and purpose of God.[105]

Gruber continues:

Anyone who did not accept [Origen's] allegorical system of interpretation was nothing more than a "Jew," and really did not belong in the Church. Origen maintained, "If anyone wishes to hear and understand these words literally, he ought to gather with the Jews rather than with the Christians. But if he wishes to be a Christian and a disciple of Paul, let him hear Paul saying that 'the Law is spiritual' [and] declaring that these words are 'allegorical' when the Law speaks of Abraham and his wife and sons."[106]

Church historian, Dr. Hugh Schonfield "notes that the name of 'Nazarene,' which had previously referred to early Jewish followers of the man of Nazareth, now became a title of scorn." It now denoted the "heresy" espoused by those who believed in Yeshua, yet clung to the Torah of Moses.[107]

By this point, the separation of Gentile Christianity from its Jewish heritage was almost complete. What started out as the accepted, and even expected, way of life for first-century believers now became heretical.

The Great Persecution

The Roman Emperor Diocletian[108] began what is known as the Great Persecution in AD 303.[109] All Christian synagogues and churches were to be destroyed, all Bibles were to be confiscated, all clergy were to be put in prison, Christian expressions of worship were strictly forbidden, and every citizen was to sacrifice to pagan gods or else be put to death. This persecution lasted until 313, when the next Roman emperor, Constantine[110] restored all rights of citizenship to Christians. His action laid the groundwork that would ultimately lead to "an apostasy that would envelop Christendom for more than a millennium." Messiah's Bride would soon become wedded to paganism.

9

The Roman Catholic Church as Satan's Army

The Constantine Years

Constantine, emperor of Rome from AD 306–337, became a so-called follower of Messiah after having had a vision of himself being victorious in battle under the sign of the cross. We know from history, however, that Constantine never truly repented of his sins. He continued to serve as the high priest of the pagan priestly cult. He later had his own son, wife, and brother-in-law killed. As leader of the Roman Empire, he later forced the marriage of church and state. Constantine made a law for the whole Roman Empire to rest on Sunday in all cities and towns. This act officially sanctioned Sunday (known by the pagans as the venerable day of the sun) as the Sabbath for Christians. Until this time, they observed the Jewish Sabbath as well as Sunday. However, Sunday had not previously been an official day of abstinence from work.

In response to Constantine's edict, Sylvester,[111] the bishop of Rome, changed the name of the day (the venerable day of the sun at that time) to "Lord's Day." As bishop of Rome (not yet known as the pope), his office carried much authority. The following day, Constantine issued another decree stating that if any royal edifice should be struck by lightning, the ancient ceremonies propitiating the pagan deity should be practiced and the haruspices (a religious official who interpreted omens by inspecting the entrails of sacrificial animals) were to be consulted to learn the meaning of the misfortune. Such a decree could hardly be issued by someone of a regenerate heart.

In AD 323, Eusebius,[112] the authoritative writer of early church history, completed the ninth of his ten-volume work entitled *Ecclesiastical History.*[113] Most of what we know about early church history comes from him. He completed this work in 325. In broad terms, Eusebius was a disciple of third-century heretic, Origen, and sought to convince everyone that he was not a heretic. Origen taught Pamphilus,[114] "Pamphilus taught Eusebius, and Eusebius wholeheartedly gave himself to the task of defending the views of Origen." As Origen's views spread throughout the Church through men like Pamphilus and Eusebius, an anti-Judaic, "new Israel" philosophy began to take over.

> Eusebius firmly believed, in the fourth century, that the Church was the "new Israel," replacing the Jews. He firmly believed that there was no distinct future for the Jews in the plan of God. Wherever he discusses the issue of a physical millennium, he treats it as a heretical view. ("Millennium" comes from the Latin *mille annum*, a "thousand years.") Following Origen, Eusebius rejected the normal meaning of the Scriptures that promise restoration to the Jewish people. Or he ignored these scriptures altogether. The belief in the restoration of the Jewish people and the establishment in Israel of a millennial kingdom was not an [sic] heretical view, as we shall see. It had been the prevailing view. In fact, it had been the established orthodoxy. In the first and second centuries, it was the view that Eusebius chose to champion that the early Church had considered heresy.[115]

In contrast to Eusebius, the renewed covenant Scriptures plus two writings from the second century reveal a widely accepted view at that time of a literal thousand-year reign of Messiah in a restored Israel. These include the *Revelation of Peter* and Justin Martyr's *Dialogue with Trypho*. In addition, Eusebius admits that Papias,[116] a disciple of the Apostle John[117] credited with writing the fourth gospel at the apostle's dictation, Irenaeus, a disciple of Polycarp, and most of the first- and second-century writers were of a similar opinion. "In writing any book, an author chooses what to include and what to leave out. In writing history, a faithful historian will make those choices so as to present and accurate picture of the past. Eusebius was intentionally inaccurate. He had his own agenda."[118]

Nicean Council

Dealing with Arianism

The Roman Emperor, Constantine (now reigning from Constantinople, his new capital), called together a council to be held in the city of Nicea in AD 325. The purpose of the meeting was primarily to deal with a heresy called Arianism[119] that began to flourish. Arianism denies the deity of Yeshua. In response to this heresy, the doctrine of the Trinity[120] was formalized at this council. The introduction of three separate "people" of the Godhead was a direct repudiation of "the Shema" from Deuteronomy 6:4. This is known as the watchword of the Jewish people and states, "Hear, O Israel: The LORD our God is one LORD." Although argued by the Gentile Church that three in one is monotheistic based on the Hebrew word *echad* (אֶחָד), which means "one," but is a compound unity, it has an unexpected consequence that distinctly separates

Christians and Jews. Through the identification as God in three persons, many Christians and Catholic adherents now pray to God the Father, Yeshua/Jesus, and the Holy Spirit, even though the Lord's Prayer is addressed exclusively to the Father. Added to the practice of praying to Mary and a litany of saints, including statuary, medallions, and other "graven images," this has created a chasm between the Roman Catholic Church and the Jewish people that can never be crossed. In every definition of the practices of the pagans, divine power was an attribute of the inanimate objects they prayed to. Knowing that Abraham was called out of Terah the idol maker's home to become a "people set apart" is the foundation of Judaism and the lineage of Messiah.

Settling the Date for Passover

A secondary and lesser-known purpose for the meeting was to settle the date for Passover. Those on one side of this issue claimed that "the Jewish custom should be adhered to, [while] the other affirmed that the exact recurrence of the period should be observed, without following the authority of those who were in error, and strangers to gospel grace." A total of 318 bishops, plus a vast number of lesser clergymen, attended the council. Unfortunately, none of those invited were Jewish. Through the efforts of Constantine to achieve unity among all the bishops over this matter, the council decided that all the churches should celebrate Passover on the Sunday following the first full moon that occurs after the Spring equinox. We need to keep in mind that the nature of Passover had been redefined by this point to be a commemoration of the death, burial, and resurrection of Jesus. In other words, it had become like modern-day Easter. We also

> *Unity was a greater priority to Constantine and the Nicean Council than obeying the Word of God.*

need to realize that unity was the order of the day. Unity was a greater priority to Constantine and the council than obeying the Word of God. Constantine was not interested in the truth of the gospel, but in unifying the empire. As such, he was the first ecumenist and introduced that error into the now Gentilized church.

Constantine sent letters to all the churches in the Roman Empire encouraging them to follow the decision of the council. One might ask why the churches were so willing to follow his decree. Daniel Gruber answers:

What the Emperor said had great weight. After all, Constantine was the one who had ended the persecution of the churches. He was the founder of the Holy Roman Empire. He openly, personally professed the Christian faith. He had convened the council. The churches, therefore, were more than willing to hear whatever he had to say to them.[121]

According to Scripture, unity is a good thing. Psalm 133:1 says, "Behold how good and how pleasant it is for brothers to dwell together in unity." However, unity simply for the sake of unity is quite a different matter. The key to Psalm 133 is that "brothers" are the ones who "dwell together in unity." The unity brought about by the council's action was not between "brothers," but rather between believers and pagans. Such "unity" cannot exist. Scripture declares, "How can righteousness and lawlessness be partners? What fellowship does light have with darkness?" (2 Corinthians 6:14).

In his letter to the Gentile churches, Constantine wrote:

At this meeting the question concerning the most holy day of
Easter was discussed, and it was resolved by the united judgment
of all present, that this feast ought to be kept by all and in every
place on one and the same day. For what can be more becoming
or honorable to us than that this feast from which we date our
hopes of immortality, should be observed unfailingly by all alike,
according to one ascertained order and arrangement? And first
of all, it appeared an unworthy thing that in the celebration of
this most holy feast we should follow the practice of the Jews,
who have impiously defiled their hands with enormous sin, and
are, therefore, deservedly afflicted with blindness of soul. For we
have it in our power, if we abandon their custom, to prolong the
due observance of this ordinance to future ages, by a truer order,
which we have preserved from the very day of the passion until
the present time. Let us then have nothing in common with the
detestable Jewish crowd; for we have received from our Saviour
a different way. A course at once legitimate and honorable lies
open to our most holy religion. Beloved brethren, let us with
one consent adopt this course, and withdraw ourselves from all
participation in their baseness. For their boast is absurd indeed,
that it is not in our power without instruction from them to
observe these things. For how should they be capable of forming
a sound judgment, who, since their parricidal guilt in slaying
their Lord, have been subject to the direction, not of reason, but
of ungoverned passion, and are swayed by every impulse of the
mad spirit that is in them? Hence it is that on this point as well
as others they have no perception of the truth, so that, being
altogether ignorant of the true adjustment of this question, they
sometimes celebrate Easter twice in the same year. Why then
should we follow those who are confessedly in grievous error?

Surely, we shall never consent to keep this feast a second time in the same year. But supposing these reasons were not of sufficient weight, still it would be incumbent on your Sagacities to strive and pray continually that the purity of your souls may not seem in anything to be sullied by fellowship with the customs of these most wicked men. We must consider, too, that a discordant judgment in a case of such importance, and respecting such religious festival, is wrong. For our Saviour has left us one feast in commemoration of the day of our deliverance, I mean the day of his most holy passion; and he has willed that his Catholic Church should be one, the members of which, however scattered in many and diverse places, are yet cherished by one pervading spirit, that is, by the will of God. And let your Holinesses' sagacity reflect how grievous and scandalous it is that on the self-same days some should be engaged in fasting, others in festive enjoyment; and again, that after the days of Easter some should be present at banquets and amusements, while others are fulfilling the appointed fasts. It is, then, plainly the will of Divine Providence (as I suppose you all clearly see), that this usage should receive fitting correction, and be reduced to one uniform rule.[122]

After the council concluded its business, Constantine held a great feast in honor of the bishops who attended in order to demonstrate his victory and authority over the church. Eusebius recounts the event by writing:

About this time, he completed the twentieth year of his reign. On this occasion public festivals were celebrated by the people of the provinces generally, but the emperor himself invited and feasted with those ministers of God whom he had reconciled, and thus offered as it were through them a suitable sacrifice to God. Not one of the bishops was wanting at the imperial banquet, the circumstances of which were splendid beyond description. Detachments of the body-guard and other troops surrounded the entrance of the palace with drawn swords, and through the midst of these the men of God proceeded without fear into the innermost of the imperial apartments, in which some were the emperor's own companions at table, while others reclined on couches arranged on either side. One might have thought that a picture of Christ's kingdom was thus shadowed forth, and a dream rather than reality.[123]

In response, Daniel Gruber writes:

Eusebius is somewhat misleading. It is true that some of the Church leaders were brought into close relationship to the emperor, his private apartments, and his table—in time, such privileges became a measure of religious success—but it is highly doubtful that all the men of God walked through the circle of guards and soldiers without fear. The emperor intended the drawn swords to teach a lesson. On the Passover controversy, the Council of Nicea had chosen an anti-Biblical course and demanded conformity to it. The swords were a way of indicating the necessity of conforming to the official decree.[124]

Gruber continues:

But notwithstanding the decision of the council here were some *quartodecimans* [from Latin for fourteenth], as they were termed, who remained pertinaciously attached to the celebration of Easter on the 14th day of the moon, and among others the Audeans, schismatics of Mesopotamia. They found fault with the council, reproachfully remarking, that this was the first time that the ancient tradition, through complaisance for Constantine, had been departed from. In convening the council, Constantine had already declared that whoever would disturb the unity of the Church was a "malignant foe" motivated by a "malevolent demon," exposing God's law to "slander and detraction." ... Constantine had achieved political victory, in the name of the Lord, by the sword. He was not about to trade in his weapons.... From that point on, Church doctrine was to be enforced by the sword of the State. Those who would not conform were to be exiled or put to death. The books of heretics—those who taught what was contrary to the accepted teaching—were to be burned and exterminated from the earth.... The Church ceased to be the Church of Jesus, and became the Church of Constantine. It was no longer the bride of Messiah. It had become the bride of Caesar.... The Church was now officially Contra Judeos and Adversus Judeos—set against and set in opposition to the Jews. Thus, was established the anti-Judaic foundation on which both doctrine and practice were then built. The historical and theological eradication of the Jews prepared the way for the "lawful" attempts to physically eradicate them. The Church made a significant official change both in doctrine and in the way doctrine was to be established.... God's truth was to be determined by Church councils, and not by the Word of God. Consequently, the teaching which was a blasphemous heresy to Justin Martyr [AD 140–160] became the new, unchallengeable orthodoxy.[125]

As a result of this marriage of the bride of Messiah to paganism, all sorts of idolatry would soon creep in. One church historian writes:

An intimate and trustful worship of saints replaced the cult of pagan gods.... Statues of Isis and Horus were renamed Mary and Jesus; the Roman Lupercalia and the feast of purification of Isis became the Feast of the Nativity; the Saturnalia were replaced by [the] Christmas celebration...an ancient festival of the dead by All Souls Day, rededicated to Christian heroes; incense, lights, flowers, processions, vestments, hymns which had pleased the people in older cults were domesticated and cleansed in the ritual of the Church...soon people and priests would use the sign of the cross as a magic incantation to expel or drive away demons.[126]

A Great Divide

In a word, the Gentile Christians seceded from the commonwealth of Israel and formed their own nation.

At this time, the Jewish believers in Messiah were faced with a dilemma. They found themselves long ago excluded from the Jewish community for their faith in Yeshua. Now they found themselves excluded from the officially Gentilized Christian community.

...most of church history is a record of anti-Judaic decrees, doctrines, and practices.

The cracks that had begun to develop in the early second century had now become a great divide. The Gentilized Church had totally separated itself from its Jewish roots. The Church attempted to cut down God's "olive tree" (Romans 2:17–21) and plant itself as another.

When Satan took Yeshua up on a high mountain and offered Him all the kingdoms of the world (Matthew 4:8), saying, "All these things I will give You if You will fall down and worship me" (verse 9), we know, of course, that Yeshua refused. Tragically, the Gentile Church fell for the same offer when it was made through Constantine.

Constantine, the so-called believer, ordered his son Crispus to be put to death, suffocated his wife, Fausta, in an overheated bath, and had his sister's husband strangled. From this point in AD 326 forward, most of church history is a record of anti-Judaic decrees, doctrines, and practices. In addition, we find many compromises with paganism along with persecution of those who remained faithful to the true gospel. No longer would faith in Yeshua be viewed as an expression of Judaism, but rather as a separate religion altogether.

10

The Roman Catholic Church as Satan's Army

The Post-Constantine Years

nti-Jewish sentiment became the law of the Church. In AD 329, regulations were passed forbidding Jews to circumcise their children. The death penalty was imposed on anyone who embraced the Jewish faith. In addition, marriage between Jews and Christians was forbidden. Anyone found transgressing this law was to be put to death. In AD 341, the Council of Antioch[127] enjoined Gentile Christians from keeping Passover on the 14th day of Nisan. The penalty for doing so was excommunication. It also forbade them from keeping it with the Jews and barred them from keeping the biblical Sabbath. The decision of this council provides some of the first evidence we have that not all Christians complied with the decree of the Council of Nicea sixteen years earlier. Apparently, the number of dissenters proved great enough that another council met to discuss and decide on the matter.

During the fourth century, various councils met to discuss matters of church doctrine. From one of these councils emerged the so-called Apostolic Canons.[128] They decreed:

If any clergyman shall enter into a synagogue of Jews or heretics [Nazarenes] to pray, let him be deposed. If a layman does so, let him be excommunicated. If any Bishop, presbyter or deacon, or anyone of the list of the clergy, keeps fast or festival with the Jews, or receives from them any of the gifts of their feasts, as unleavened bread, or any such things, let him be deposed. If he be a layman, let him be excommunicated. If any Christian brings oil into a temple of the heathen, or into a synagogue of the Jews, or lights lamps, let him be excommunicated.[129]

Epiphanius and Jerome

Late into the fourth century, we begin to see the rise of two more so-called patristic writers, or church fathers—Epiphanius[130] and Jerome.[131] Jerome is known for translating the Bible into Latin around AD 400. His translation is known as the Vulgate.

Epiphanius and Jerome were both familiar with the Jewish believers of their day, both those who were considered orthodox in their beliefs and those considered heretical. However, these writers, particularly Epiphanius, lumped together both orthodox Jewish believers and heretical Ebionites[132] and Elkasites,[133] thereby obscuring the differences between the two groups. "This lumping together…reflects a patristic view that to live Jewishly as a believer was in itself heretical." We should not be surprised at such a theological position given the Council of Nicea's anti-Judaic outcome.

Christianity: Rome's Official Religion

In 380 CE, the emperor Theodosius[134] issued the Edict of Thessalonica,[135] which made Christianity, specifically Nicene Christianity, the official religion of the Roman Empire. Most other Christian sects were deemed heretical, lost their legal status, and had their properties confiscated by the Roman state. In Antioch in AD 387, John Chrysostom[136] delivered eight unrestrained sermons[137] that demonstrated his utter contempt of Jews. His purpose was to cause Gentile Christians to terminate all contact with Jewish believers. Examples of his statements include: "[The Jews] really are pitiable and miserable"; "the Jews are worse than wild beasts and are murderers"; "their synagogue is not only a brothel and a theater; it is also a den of robbers and a lodging for wild beasts"; and "no Jew adores God." His only proof offered for these diatribes was that "the Son of God says so." In his attempts to totally separate the Gentilized Christian faith from what little remained of its Jewish heritage, he asked his audience in one of his sermons, "If the ceremonies of the Jews move you to admiration, what do you have in common with us [true followers]?" In another sermon, he continued his attack:

Faith in Yeshua was no longer viewed as an expression of Judaism.

> Let me, too, now say this against these Judaizing Christians. If you judge that Judaism is the true religion, why are you causing trouble to the church? But if Christianity is the true faith, as it really is, stay in it and follow it. Tell me this. Do you share with us the mysteries, do you worship Christ as a Christian, do you ask him for blessings, and do you then celebrate the festival with his foes? With what purpose, then, do you come to the church?[138]

Upon close examination, one can see that the term "Christianity" had come into vogue by this time, signifying that faith in Yeshua was no longer viewed as an expression of Judaism. Rather, it was seen as an entirely different religion. By extension, no longer did the community of believers see themselves as a part of the Jewish nation, Israel. Instead, they saw themselves as the Church, the New Israel.

By the end of the fourth century, the process of Gentilization of the faith was complete. Jewish believers were caught between two opposing groups: the traditional Jews who excommunicated them, and the Gentile Christians who rejected them. Their numbers and influence shrank to a level of insignificance. By the seventh century, it went into exile.

Augustine

Sadly, at the turn of the century, Augustine[139]—the bishop of Hippo, a city in northern Africa, who is revered by modern-day Catholics (Roman and Eastern) and Protestants alike and whose writings had a major influence on such men as Martin Luther[140] and John Calvin,[141] the fathers of the Christian Reformation—wrote that, in the churches in his time, one would see "many drunkards, covetous men, deceivers, gamesters, adulterers, fornicators, men who bind upon their persons sacrilegious charms and others given up to sorcerers and astrologers, and diviners practiced in all kinds of impious arts." He further stated that these same individuals would "fill the theaters on the festival days of the pagans." In his writings, we see the fruits of the "unity" sought by the Council of Nicea seventy-five years earlier. We should not be surprised, for the "unity" spoken of was really nothing more than compromise—compromise with the pagans around them in order to achieve the "unity" of the empire required by Constantine.

Augustine completed his treatise, entitled *Concerning the City of God Against the Pagans,*[142] in AD 426. One writer[143] declared Augustine "deserves to be named the Doctor of the Church as well as the Doctor of Grace."[144] Another wrote, "For depth of feeling and power of conception nothing written on the Church since St. Paul's time, is comparable to the works of St. Augustine."[145]

On the contrary, one might expect such a well-respected theologian to adhere to sound doctrine. Augustine adopted Origen's allegorical system of interpretation, "at least as far as it defined the Church as Israel." His work, *City of God*,[146] provides "the framework for almost all Church theology down to this day." In it, he defined the Church as having replaced Israel. He also denied a literal thousand-year reign of Messiah at the end of days. Augustine believed that, during his own time, the devil had already begun to be bound for a thousand years (Revelation 20:2–3) and the saints were reigning with Messiah, in a spiritual sense. At the end of that period, Messiah would return to earth and the saints would reign with him here in a greater way.

Daniel Gruber points out all sorts of problems with such an interpretation. He says:

If the thousand years begins with "Christ's first coming," then whatever happens before the thousand years begins must have happened before "Christ's first coming." These things would include the marriage supper of the Lamb [Revelation 19:7–9]; the return of Jesus with the Church to the earth for battle against the *goyim* ["nations"—Revelation 19:11–21]; the destruction in the lake of fire of the beast, the false prophet, and those who received the mark of the beast or worshipped his image [Revelation 19:20–21]; and the beheading of those who, for the testimony of Jesus (who had not yet come and died), did not receive the mark of the beast or worship his image [Revelation 20:4]. It also would mean that before "Christ's first coming," the Devil was bound with a great chain, thrown into the abyss, which is then shut and sealed over him so that he cannot deceive the Gentiles any more [Revelation 20:1–3]. When did these things happen before "Christ's first coming"? The words must have some meaning. To what events do they refer? For Augustine's explanation to be an actual interpretation, there must be some way in which all these things happened before "Christ's first coming." But all of these are unanswered questions for Augustine. In fact, they do not even arise, because he ignores the words of the text.[147]

Others see the ideas of second-century heretic Marcion as a major part of Augustine's theology. Marcion taught that God's grace was opposed to His Torah. With the separation of the Church from natural Israel in AD 325 and its self-declaration as the New Israel, the new, post-Nicene breed of biblical scholars, Augustine included, was left with no other choice than to allegorize their interpretations of Scripture. To do otherwise would undermine the new orthodoxy the Council of Nicea had established.

Second-Chance Theology

Pope Gregory I,[148] bishop of Rome from AD 590–604, proposed the idea of a place called "purgatory." This was believed to be a place where "the spirits of the dead suffered in order to be purged of their sins and fully delivered from the 'debt of eternal punishment.'" The Roman Catholic Church accepted this idea as church doctrine. Once again, a foundation stone of the Catholic Church had been laid that was in complete opposition to the text of the Bible. This "second-chance" theology blurs the message of Messiah, who said in John 14:6, "Jesus saith unto him, I am the way, the truth, and the life: no man cometh unto the Father, but by me."

Further Exclusion of Jews and
Requirements of Renouncement

In AD 637, the Muslims conquered the Gentile Christians and took over occupation of the land of Israel. With the rise of Islam, Messianic Judaism (Jewish believers) in the Near East ceased. From the seventh century until the mid-twentieth century, the history of Messianic Judaism is mostly a record of individual Jews who accepted Yeshua as the Messiah and who expressed their faith as Christians, not as Jewish believers. By now, Jews who accepted Yeshua/Jesus were excluded from the Jewish community from which they came and were forced to renounce their Jewish upbringing by their Gentile "brothers and sisters," if they could be called that at all.

The late historian Dr. Hugh Schonfield provides several examples of different confessions that Jewish converts were required to make upon acceptance of Yeshua. One will suffice. In front of the entire church, the convert would recite:

> I renounce all customs, rites, legalisms, unleavened breads and sacrifice of lambs of the Hebrews, and all the other feasts of the Hebrews, sacrifices, prayers, aspersions, purifications, sanctifications and propitiations, and fasts, and new moons, and Sabbaths, and superstitions, and hymns and chants and observances and synagogues, and the food and drink of the Hebrews; in one word, I renounce absolutely everything Jewish, every law, rite and custom, and above all I renounce Antichrist, whom all the Jews await in the figure and form of Christ; and I join myself to the true Christ and God.[149]

Roman Catholic Church in the West and Greek Orthodox in the East

By the middle of the eleventh century, the bishop of Rome began to exert authority over the rest of the Gentile Church in the Roman Empire, claiming that he was the sole representative "of Christ on earth." He forbade all other bishops throughout the Roman Empire to be called "papa" or "pope," and took upon himself the three titles formerly reserved for the Roman emperors since the time of Constantine: "Pontifex Maximus," "Vicar of Christ," and "Bishop of Bishops." The popes have retained these titles down to our day. As a result of the Roman bishop's declaration, Michael Cerularius, the patriarch of Constantinople, excommunicated the bishop of Rome, Pope Leo IX. The first pope of the now Roman Catholic Church likewise excommunicated the patriarch of Constantinople. Thus began the Roman Catholic Church in the West and the Greek Orthodox (also known as Eastern Orthodox) Church in the East. To this day, the two have been at odds with one another. Their animosity has played a major role in European wars, including some of the Crusades and even the war in Bosnia.

Since the Roman emperor had long since left Rome for Constantinople and the Roman Empire by now had fallen, the bishop probably made a power play to fill the vacuum being felt in that part of the Mediterranean. The bishop of Rome soon took on the titles of "Vicar" and "Pontiff," titles previously reserved for the emperor. Through this, we can see that the bishop was in actuality attempting to become king. As history shows, that is precisely what happened. The term "Vicar of Christ," a title first originated by Constantine, then later by the popes, is a Latin term that means "anti-Christ" when translated to Greek.

First Crusade

Pope Urban II[150] initiated the first crusade, or holy war, in AD 1090, when he rallied the Roman Catholic faithful from all over Europe to liberate the Holy Land from the Muslims and the Jews. He decreed that all heretics (Muslims and Jews) were to be tortured and killed. As they marched across Europe on their way to the Holy Land, the Crusaders gave the Jews the choice of being baptized, i.e., converting to Roman Catholicism, or being killed. After capturing Jerusalem, the crusaders herded the Jews into the synagogue and set it on fire. As the soldiers marched around it led by a priest, they sang "Christ We Adore Thee."

The Waldenses

Late in the twelfth century, a group known as the Waldenses[151] appeared on the scene in southern France, although many scholars believe their origin is much older, at least seventh century. They were known as the "Poor Men of Lyons," from the city on the Rhone River where they originated. They rejected the authority and practices of the Roman Catholic Church, and were known to go about preaching and teaching in pairs of two. They were also called, "The Israel of the Alps." This group placed great emphasis on following the practice of the apostles and obeying Yeshua's teachings in the Sermon on the Mount; they also kept the Sabbath and proclaimed the Bible as the final authority on matters of life and faith. They later embraced the Reformation movement. Some eventually emigrated to the U.S. in the nineteenth century. A small remnant remains to this day, mostly in northern Italy and in Valdese, North Carolina.

Passiginians

Arising out of the Waldenses came a group known as the Passaginians.[152] They were referred to by Cardinal Humbert[153] as "Nazarenes." Neander, a German church historian of the early 1800s, said that the origin of the word "Passaginian" pointed to Palestine; he believed them to be a surviving remnant of Judaizing Christians. The word comes from the Latin *passagium*, meaning "passage." Some say it referred to the mountain passes where they lived, and therefore associate them with the Waldenses. Others say it referred to their wandering, unsettled lifestyle as a result of the persecution they suffered. Some authorities claimed that the Passaginians taught believers to keep the Law of Moses, including keeping the Sabbath and circumcision. The Passigianians remained a movement until they were persecuted out of existence in the early 1500s.

Heresy Hunting

In 1208, Pope Innocent III[154] instituted the Office of the Inquisition.[155] Its stated purpose was to keep the Church free from heresies. Regarding the Inquisition, William Lecky,[156] a nineteenth-century historian, wrote:

> Almost all Europe, for many centuries, was inundated with blood, which was shed at the direct instigation or with the full approval of the ecclesiastical authorities…. That the Church of Rome has shed more innocent blood than any other institution that has ever existed among mankind, will be questioned by no Protestant who has a competent knowledge of history. The memorials…of many of her persecutions are now so scanty, that it is impossible to form a complete conception of the multitude

of her victims, and it is quite certain that no powers of imagination can adequately realize their sufferings. [157]

Juan Antonio Llorente, [158] who (as one-time secretary in the Office of the Inquisition) had free access to the archives of the Spanish Inquisition, assures us that, by that tribunal alone, of the more than 3 million tried, more than 300,000 persons were burnt, and more than 290,000 were condemned to punishments less severe than death. Overall estimates of the numbers of those killed during the Rome's 700 years of terror exceeded 50 million. [159]

Since the time of Lecky, we have seen the twentieth-century horrors of the Russian pogroms, the Holocaust, and even other attempts at "ethnic cleansing." These events claimed the lives of millions of Jews and people of other faiths considered harmful to the human race by those in power. Even though these numbers seem to outweigh those of the Roman Catholic Church, one must realize that the centuries of anti-Judaic teaching of both Roman and Eastern Catholics, as well as some of the Protestant denominations, played a major role in these events. This is another direct assault on the seed line of Messiah.

Forcing Jews to Convert

By this point in history, early into the thirteenth century, the Roman Catholic Church had a practice of periodically forcing Jews to convert. In some countries, Jews were deprived of all their possessions upon being baptized. The reason was that, as Roman Catholic Christians, they ceased to be the lawful prey of the king. The practice supposedly served as a test of their sincerity to convert.

Pope Innocent III brought together the Fourth Lateran Council in 1215. [160] The council decreed that Jews were to wear a special piece of clothing (believed to be a badge). On Good Friday, Jews were to remain indoors in order not to cause riots through their alleged mockery of the Christians' lamentations of the death of their Savior. Jews and pagans were forbidden to be elected or appointed to a public office. The logic of that day was that those who blaspheme Christ should not be allowed to hold authority over His followers.

The Inquisition

Fifteen years later, Pope Gregory IX[161] began what is known today as the Inquisition. He "declared that the duty of every [Roman] Catholic is 'to persecute heretics,'" meaning "anyone who did not give complete allegiance to the Roman Catholic Church. Such persons were to be tortured, imprisoned, and slain." The pope required the civil authorities in each Catholic country to carry out the punishments. The reason he held such sway over kings was that "the keys of heaven" belonged to him, according to their understanding. "The most powerful civil rulers trembled when threatened with excommunication, for it was almost universally believed that outside the [Roman Catholic] Church there was no salvation."[162] Furthermore, if they refused to comply with the pope's demands, they could "be brought before the Tribunal and consigned to the flames." Such was the authority of the pope over the kings of Europe. Every citizen of the Holy Roman Empire was required to be a Roman Catholic. Anyone not giving complete obedience to the pope was considered guilty of treason and became subject to the death penalty. The Office of the Inquisition sought out such heretics, "found them guilty, and handed them over to the civil authorities for execution."

Whenever the inquisitors swept into a town, an "Edict of Faith"[163] was issued requiring everyone to reveal any heresy of which they had knowledge. Those who concealed a heretic came under the curse of the Church and the inquisitors' wrath. Informants would approach the inquisitors' lodgings under cover of night and were rewarded for information. No one arrested was ever acquitted. "Heretics" were committed to the flames, because the popes believed that the Bible forbade Christians to shed blood. The victims of the Inquisition exceeded by hundreds of thousands the number of Christians and Jews who had suffered under pagan Roman emperors. The Inquisition…was the perfect setup for bigots, villains, enemies, and crazies with overworked imaginations to seek revenge, rid themselves of a rival, or gain personal satisfaction of having become important to the Church…. The property of heretics was confiscated and divided between the inquisitors and the popes.

In keeping with the practice of forced conversions, a decree of James II of Aragon[164] in 1297 reads:

We also desire and ordain, that the brethren of the Order of Preachers (the Dominicans) do offer the Word of God to the Jews and Saracens of both sexes, by preaching, arguments, conversations, or declaration of the Christian faith. These shall assemble at their call, and listen without interruption to the preaching. Also, to avoid the possibility of their suppressing the conviction of truth by stubborn silence, they shall reverently answer to the interrogations or objections of the said brethren; they shall also be compelled, when desired, to give access to their books for the investigation of any matters, that so the truth may be the better sifted by a mutual exhibition and collation of writings, and thus be brought to more open light.[165]

At the Council of Vienne[166] in 1311, the Roman Catholic Church restricted social interaction between Christians and Jews. Two years later, the Council of Zamora[167] ruled that Jews must be kept in strict servitude and subjection.

The Council of Basel[168] in 1431 renewed canonical decrees forbidding Christians to associate with Jews. It further required civil governments to confine Jews in separate quarters (ghettos), compel them to wear a distinguishing badge, and ensure their attendance at sermons aimed to convert them. Forced conversions of Jews in Spain and Portugal had grown so numerous that they formed a distinct class of citizens known as the Marranos[169] and Conversos.[170] Some believe that Christopher Columbus[171] may have been among this group. Many of these converted Jews continued to secretly practice their Judaism. For this "crime," the Office of the Inquisition was set up in Spain about fifty years later, unleashing a reign of terror against all Spanish citizens, both Jew and non-Jew alike.

Gutenberg's Effect

Gutenberg[172] invented the printing press in 1450, thereby making the printed word available to the masses. Many historians and others agree that this tool has done more to bring about increases in knowledge and science than any other human invention. It more than likely made possible the Reformation,[173] which took place seventy years later. Prior to the printing press, common people were kept from reading the Scriptures. Only those "properly" trained could do so. From this point forward, that would forever change. This was a jewel in the crown of the Jews, as Paul wrote in Romans 3:1–2:

> What advantage then hath the Jew? or what profit is there of circumcision? Much every way: chiefly, because that unto them were committed the oracles of God.

The Spanish Inquisition

Some thirty years later, in response to assertions of the Dominicans[174] to root out the evil of the converted Jews of Spain who continued to practice Judaism, King Ferdinand[175] and Queen Isabella[176] requested that the pope set up the Office of the Inquisition. In response, the Holy Office was established in Seville and run by Thomas de Torquemada[177] as the inquisitor-general. The stated objective of the Inquisition was the purification of the Roman Catholic Church from heresy, and in particular, from the dangers of Judaism. Thus began the infamous Spanish Inquisition. No one was safe—from the highest ranking in the land to the lowest. Historian Dr. Hugh Schonfield, author of *The History of Jewish Christianity*, records that:

> One of the earliest decrees of the Inquisition provided that no Bishop or other priest of Jewish descent should have a seat in the court. Twenty-seven indications of secret Judaism were drawn up, including the following: expecting the Messiah; hoping for justification by the Law of Moses; keeping the Sabbath by wearing better clothes or not lighting fires on that day; ...celebrating the Jewish festivals or fasting on Jewish fast days; ...bewailing the destruction of Jerusalem on [Tisha B'av (the Ninth day of Av)]; performing any Jewish rites such as circumcision; retaining Jewish marriage or burial customs.[178]

An edict was issued in 1492[179] ordering all unbaptized Jews to be expelled from Spain in four months' time. When Christopher Columbus set sail on his famous voyage, boatloads of Jewish refugees were in the harbor, and Jewish believers were among the members of his crew. Jews were given the choice of converting or leaving the country. Those who chose to convert had to face the wrath of the Inquisition should they be suspected or accused of practicing their Judaism in secret. Columbus may have been a Passaginian (see AD 1179). The evidence strongly points to this belief. His personal physician was Jewish, as was his mapmaker. The mapmaker supplied Columbus with astronomical tables in Hebrew. On his voyage in 1492, Columbus took with him a Jew who spoke Hebrew and Chaldean,[180] just in case they came upon any "lost tribes" of Israel. He set the date for his voyage on August 3, 1492, the day after the Jews were ordered to leave Spain. Perhaps he intended to try and rescue some of the Jews who had been set adrift the day before, in boats with no oars, anchors, sails, food, or water. Columbus mentions the exodus in his diary and connected it with Tisha B'Av,[181] the date on which the two previous Jewish Temples were destroyed by the Babylonians[182] and again by the Romans. Columbus also understood Hebrew and the Scriptures, a rare trait for Catholics.

In 1514, John Wycliffe[183] and Miles Coverdale[184] worked to translate the Bible into English. These men were heavily influenced by fifth-century theologian, Augustine, who in turn was influenced by second-century heretic, Marcion. Like Augustine and Marcion, these men taught that grace was in opposition to Law.

Martin Luther and the Reformation

The second decade of the sixteenth century introduces us to the character of Martin Luther,[185] considered the father of the Reformation. Luther was a Roman Catholic monk of the Augustinian[186] order, having entered the monastery in 1505 after surviving a lightning strike. Several years later, he gained revelation knowledge of the meaning of the first chapter of Romans. Verse 17 of this chapter says, "the righteous shall live by his faith." Luther suddenly realized that all of his years of fasting and penance as a monk counted for nothing, and the only thing that could save him was simple faith in the Messiah Yeshua. This understanding became a fundamental doctrine of Protestantism[187] and is often referred to as "justification by faith." He also came to understand that anyone could obtain forgiveness from God independent of any priest.

In the year 1515, the Roman Church was presumably in need of funds, so Pope Leo X[188] commissioned Friar Tetzel,[189] of the Dominican order, to sell indulgences that would totally remit sins forever. Anyone who bought these indulgences supposedly would bypass purgatory upon death and go immediately to Heaven without having to first repent. Tetzel proclaimed his famous sales pitch in appealing for funds. When he came to Wittenberg in 1517, Luther was so outraged that he nailed his famous ninety-five theses[190] onto the Wittenberg castle door (the community bulletin board of that day) challenging the scriptural basis of indulgences. This act is considered by many to be the start of the Reformation in Europe.

Over the next three years, Luther further developed his doctrinal position so that by 1520 he argued that the pope had no special powers and that the doctrine of apostolic succession of the popes was blatantly false. He taught that only Church councils, not popes, could decide matters of doctrine, and that laymen could participate in those councils. As laymen, the governing authorities were considered just as valid a leader as any priest. He even stated that the emperor had an obligation to call a general council.

Until Luther, the kings of Europe trembled before the Church of Rome. The popes were believed to hold the power to give or withhold salvation from anyone, including monarchs. Outside the church, many believed that they could not be saved from their sins. Through his teaching, Luther broke that power. He encouraged the German ruling class "to throw off the yoke of Rome." Luther did not let go of some of the erroneous doctrines handed down to him from the writings of Augustine and Thomas Aquinas,[191] considered by some to be the theologian of the Inquisition. In 1265 Aquinas began work on his theological treatise, *Sumna Theologicae.*[192] Daniel Gruber "states that his teaching is based on philosophy, not Scripture, but that it calls upon Scripture intermittently to support a chosen philosophical or traditional view."[193] Luther claimed that much of what Aquinas wrote was heretical. In his work, Aquinas claimed that dissenters from the Catholic Church (i.e., "heretics") could be physically punished or even put to death, providing justification for the Inquisition. Hence, many people see him as the theologian of the Inquisition.

Luther's Replacement Theology

For instance, in his letter to Philip of Hesse,[194] he asserted the right of civil magistrates to punish heresy—i.e., anyone holding a contrary doctrinal view. Luther also believed that the Gentile Church replaced Israel as God's elect. His commentary on the New Covenant book of Romans begins with a chapter-by-chapter summary of its contents. While he wrote much on other chapters, he devoted a mere three paragraphs to chapters 9, 10, and 11—without once mentioning Israel or the Jewish people. In these chapters, Rav Sha'ul (Paul) explained why only a remnant of Israel had accepted the message of Yeshua. The apostle further explained that the remainder, even though they had rejected Yeshua, had not been cast away but continued to be God's chosen people. Finally, he instructed the Gentiles on how they fit into the nation of Israel as grafted-in branches, and provided a warning not to be boastful against the natural branches lest they be cut off. How Luther can write a summary on these chapters without mentioning these things is a mystery.

In commenting on Romans 11:28, Luther says:

As concerning the gospel, they are enemies for your sakes. The word "enemies" must here be taken in a passive sense; that is, they deserve to be hated. God hates them, and so they are hated by the Apostles and all who are of God.

Luther ignores the rest of this verse and the next, which say, "but concerning the election they are beloved for the sake of the fathers. For the gifts and calling of God are irrevocable."

Romans 11:5 implies that, throughout history, God has maintained a remnant of those who would adhere to His calling, including those in every generation who would accept Yeshua as Messiah. Luther claimed that "Jews and heretics are incapable" of "seeking to obtain only the righteousness of [Messiah]."

For Luther, a Jew who follows Yeshua is no longer a Jew. He drew his conclusion from Galatians 3:28, which states, "there is neither Jew nor Greek…slave nor free…male nor female; for you are all one in Messiah Yeshua." The context of the verse shows that the writer, Rav Sha'ul, does not mean to imply that these distinctions have been done away with. For example, we still have separate bathrooms, showers, and changing rooms for men and women. Rav Sha'ul is simply telling us that, in God's eyes, we who are in Messiah are all equal.

Luther says of this verse (Galatians 3:28):

The Apostle speaks not here of the Jew according to his nature and substance: but he calls him a Jew, who is the disciple of Moses, is subject to the law, is circumcised, and with all his endeavor keeps the ceremonies commanded by the law. For [Messiah] has abolished all the laws of Moses that ever were. Wherefore, the conscience believing in [Messiah] must be so surely persuaded that the law is abolished, with its terrors and threatenings, that it should be utterly ignorant whether there were ever any Moses, any law, or any Jew. For [Messiah] and Moses can in no wise agree. Moses came with the law, with works, and with ceremonies; but [Messiah] came without law, or works, or ceremonies, giving grace and righteousness, remission of sins and eternal life: "For the law was given by Moses, but grace and truth came by [Yeshua Messiah]" (John 1:17).

In defense of the apostle, Gruber points out several errors in Luther's conclusions. He writes:

Luther makes five serious errors in this one comment. First, he says, "The Apostle speaks not here of the Jew according to his nature and substance," but that is exactly what the apostle is speaking of. As Paul [Rav Sha'ul] notes earlier in Galatians 2:15–16, he had said to Peter, "We are Jews by nature...even we have believed in Messiah [Yeshua], that we may be justified by faith in Messiah..." Paul and Peter are believers, but they are still Jews by nature. Second, Luther asserts that "[Messiah] has abolished all the laws of Moses that ever were." But [Yeshua] said, "Do not think that I came to abolish the Law or the Prophets; I did not come to abolish, but to fulfill" (Matthew 5: 17). Third, Luther says that "the conscience believing in [Messiah] must be so surely persuaded that the law is abolished, with its terrors and threatenings, that it should be utterly ignorant whether there were ever any Moses, any law, or any Jew." But Paul's conscience did not operate that way. By Moses and the law, he was led to Messiah (Galatians 3:24). In Messiah he became fully Jewish (Romans 2:28–29).... Fourth, Luther claims that, "[Messiah] and Moses can in no wise agree." But [Yeshua] said, "For if you believed Moses, you would believe Me; for he wrote of Me" (John 5:46).... Fifth, Luther maintains that, "[Messiah] came without law or works, or ceremonies." [Yeshua] said, "...the works which the Father has given Me to accomplish, the very works that I do, bear witness of Me, that the Father has sent Me.... For if you believed Moses, you would believe Me; for he wrote of Me..." (John 5:36, 46). [Yeshua] came as a Jew, did the works of the Law, and observed the ceremonies which God had prepared before the foundation of the world.[195]

On the one hand, Luther seemed to be friendly toward the Jews. For instance, in a pamphlet entitled *Jesus Christ Was Born a Jew,*[196] he writes:

> If the apostles, who were also Jews, had dealt with us Gentiles as we Gentiles have dealt with the Jews, no Christians would ever have emerged from among the Gentiles. For our fools, the popes, Bishops, sophists, and monks—the gross asses' heads—have treated the Jews to date in such fashion that he who would be a good Christian might almost have to become a Jew. And if I had been a Jew and had seen such oafs and numskulls governing and teaching the Christian faith, I would have rather become a sow than a Christian.[197]

Many believe that he wrote this pamphlet in the early years of the Reformation. Later on, however, he seemed to change his position toward the Jews. He later wrote:

> Everything concurs with [Messiah's] judgement that the Jews are venomous, bitter, vengeful, slimy snakes, assassins and devil's children, who steal and wreak havoc on the sly because they cannot afford to do so in the open. A Christian has, next to the devil, no more venomous, bitter enemy than the Jew.... (The Jews ought to convert,) but if they refuse, we should neither tolerate nor suffer their presence in our midst![198]

Though modern Christians can look back in appreciation for what Martin Luther did to bring about the radical changes of the Reformation, we can see from his writings that he was by no means infallible. The reforms introduced by Luther and others were an attempt to return to the biblical gospel. Yet they were only a beginning. Certainly, more reforms are needed to return the believing community back to the Jewish heritage from which it came.

Anabaptists

In Zurich, Switzerland, a separate group of reformers began to organize, holding to the teaching that in order for a Christian baptism to be valid, one must do so upon confession of faith in Yeshua. Accordingly, anyone not baptized, or immersed, in this manner, though he may belong to some (Catholic or Reformed) church, must be baptized according to Scripture before he can be scripturally received into fellowship. All people holding to this belief were known as "Anabaptists"[199]—from Latin, meaning "to baptize again." This teaching became a radical departure from the status quo of that day. The accepted practice among Catholics was to baptize an infant as soon as he or she was healthy enough. In the minds of Catholics, this act removed the stain of original sin and initiated the child into the Kingdom of God.

By 1524, these reformers began to disagree with the practice of infant baptism, claiming they could find no scriptural basis for it. Some began to refuse baptism for their infant children, an act deemed treasonous by the Church at Rome. In 1525, the Zurich City Council[200] ordered them to do so or face exile from the city. A group of these reformers rebelled against the government's demands and soon after formed a small community of believers. By 1527, this group was persecuted out of existence in Zurich. Some of these early Anabaptists escaped and eventually came to Moravia.[201] Over the next few years, Anabaptists spread along the Rhine River in Germany, to the city of Munster,[202] and into Holland. In Holland, a Dutch Catholic priest named Menno Simons[203] took hold of the doctrine of the Anabaptists and began to teach others the same. His followers, and Anabaptists in general, became known as Mennonites[204] and exist to this

More reforms are needed to return the believing community back to the Jewish heritage from which it came.

day. When the Roman Catholic Inquisition spread to Holland, where most of these Anabaptists/Mennonites were found, tens of thousands of them were burned at the stake for espousing the baptism of adults who had come to faith (in Messiah). Over thirty thousand Anabaptists were put to death in Holland and Friesland between 1535 and 1545. Not only the Roman Catholics, but also Lutherans and Calvinists of that day hated the Anabaptists. In some regions of Europe, they sought to purge this radical group from their territories.

Anabaptists were by no means monolithic in their beliefs. Not all of them formed communities. However, they did share a core set of doctrines. The first and foremost of these is believer's baptism. They also held to a separation of true Christians from the state, freedom of conscience and worship, pacifism, voluntary church attendance, the teachings of the Sermon on the Mount, refusal to take oaths, mutual help, and instructing others in the community of believers. All of these beliefs were at odds with the Roman Catholic Church, and to some extent with Lutherans and Calvinists.

John Calvin

In 1541, John Calvin,[205] yet another former Catholic priest, published his revised version of the *Institutes of the Christian Religion*[206] in France. The book has since become "the definitive statement of Calvinism." Like Luther before him, Calvin was one of the leaders of the Reformation sweeping across Europe at that time. Calvin was another who rejected the authority of Rome. He accepted "the Bible as the ultimate standard of truth." This was a radical change to what had been the status quo until that time. Many of the mainline Protestant denominations today are descended from his many followers. Among them include Huguenots, Puritans, Presbyterians, and Dutch Reformers. In spite of all the corrections that Calvin brought about in the Reformation, he was heavily influenced by the writings of Augustine and Marcion, which teach that God's grace is opposed to His Law. Like Augustine, Calvin taught that the Church had replaced Israel as God's chosen people. Like Luther, he also believed that persecution of heretics was a lawful practice, an obvious carryover from his Catholic background.

Calvin is known for his "Five Points (of Calvinism)." Playing on this theme, Gruber points out "Five Errors of Calvin." The first of these is that the covenant of Law brings condemnation to all men. Concerning this belief, Daniel Gruber writes:

> The Covenant of the Law was not made with "the whole human race," or with "all sons of Adam," but with Israel alone. Therefore, neither "the whole human race" nor "all the sons of Adam" can break the Covenant of the Law or be condemned by it.... The Old Covenant cannot bring condemnation for those with whom it was not made.

The second error Gruber points out is that the faithful in any particular time are the Church. He continues:

> Calvin asserts that the Covenant of the Law applies to all men so that he can eliminate the difference between Israel and the Church. Without doing this, he cannot establish his point that the faithful in any particular time are the Church. His ENTIRE theology depends upon this point.... [Calvin writes,] "In Isaiah's day, there was a church in Jerusalem which God had not yet forsaken.... The church also endured to the time of Jeremiah." This is critical for Calvin, because he intends to show that the New Covenant is made with the Church. If previous believers in Israel are identified as the Church, then he can take the promise made to Israel of a New Covenant and transfer it to the Church.

The third error Gruber points out is that the New Covenant is made with the Church. He states:

First, Calvin calls the people whom God brought out of Egypt "the church." Then he refers to Jeremiah's prophecy concerning the New Covenant. Since the New Covenant is promised to the people whom God brought out of Egypt, Calvin is then able to speak of the New Covenant as being made with the Church.

The fourth point Gruber maintains Calvin is in error is that individuals are grafted into the Church. He writes:

Calvin maintains the olive tree in various ways: "Christ," "the body of Christ," "the church," "the people of God," etc....

In his commentary on Romans, Calvin says, "It follows that the calling of the Gentiles resembled an engrafting, and that they grew together into the people of God only as they struck root in the stock of Abraham."... [Calvin says] that individuals are grafted into the Church [not into Israel, as Scripture states]. ...He replaces Israel's olive tree with the Church. He replaces "Christ" with "the body of Christ." The two are closely related, but they are not the same.... Calvin repeats the point: "For Paul tells the Gentiles, whom he is teaching, not to vaunt it proudly and inhumanly over the Jews because they have been introduced in place of the latter who have defected (cf. Rom. 11:18ff.).... Paul warned the Gentiles, who were put in the place of a peculiar and holy people.

The fifth error introduced by Calvin, according to Gruber, is that there is no future restoration of the Jews or any millennial kingdom. He says:

When it comes to commenting on the verse itself ([Romans] 11:26), where the Apostle Paul writes, "and thus all Israel will be saved…," Calvin cannot accept the only and obvious meaning of Paul's words. He writes, "and so all Israel shall be saved." Many understand this of the Jewish people, as if Paul were saying that religion was to be restored to them again as before. But I extend the word Israel to include all the people of God. Calvin rejects the millennial reign of Messiah, so he has to change Paul's meaning by "extend[ing] the word Israel to include all the people of God." …did not…believe in a thousand-year reign of any kind. He believed that the return of the Lord would be followed by an eternal reign on the earth.

There is the inescapable historical fact that those who wrote the New Covenant Scriptures believed in and taught a thousand-year corporeal reign of Messiah on this earth in a restored Jerusalem and Israel. No matter how people in the intervening centuries or people today interpret these Scriptures, what the biblical authors believed and meant is indisputable…a denial of the millennial reign of Messiah is a denial of the apostolic New Covenant teaching.

In spite of the errors introduced by Calvin, we must not underestimate the benefits to our generation of the Reformation. The movement brought about sweeping political and social changes. Men began to think freely and to be self-governed. Nevertheless, in many ways the Reformation was only a beginning. Necessary doctrinal changes were made in critical areas. Yet in other areas, the Reformers did not return to biblical teaching, but instead accepted the Catholic tradition handed down to them. That's why Daniel Gruber calls it the "Partial Reformation."[207]

Most mainline denominations today either descended from or have been heavily influenced by these three men: Martin Luther, John Calvin, and Menno Simmons. All three were former Roman Catholic priests who held on to some of the Catholic teachings. That is why we still see elements of Roman Catholicism in Protestant denominations today.

Martin Luther, father of the Reformation movement, became frustrated in his attempts to win Jewish people to Messiah. He therefore published a book in 1544 entitled, *Of the Jews and Their Lies*, in which he vents his anger upon them. He states, "doubt not, beloved in Christ, that after the Devil you have no more bitter, venomous, violent enemy, than the real Jew, the Jew in earnest in his belief." Tragically, he urged his followers:

> (i) burn their synagogues and schools..., (ii) break into and destroy their houses, (iii) take away all their prayer books and talmuds, in which are nothing but godlessness, lies, cursing, and swearing, (iv) forbid their rabbis to teach on pain of life and limb.

Four hundred years later, Adolf Hitler[208] pointed to these writings of Luther to justify his policy of Jewish extermination. For this reason, Luther is viewed by many as the theologian of the Holocaust, the largest single attempt by Satan to eliminate the seed line of Messiah through the extermination of six million Jews.

Council of Trent

The Council of Trent[209] began in 1545 and lasted eighteen years. It was the nineteenth ecumenical council held by the Roman Catholic Church. This council "denounced the Reformation and damned evangelicals' beliefs with more than 100 anathemas." Pope Paul III,[210] who convened the council, offered the Holy Roman Emperor, Charles V of Spain,[211] great riches if he would use his army to force the Protestant kings of Germany into subjection under the pope once again and put an end to

Protestantism. The result of Charles' action was to bring about almost ten years of war. The Protestants remained too strong for Charles and forced a compromise. One church historian explained the peace arrangement:

> In order to permit peace among and within the states each prince was to choose between Roman Catholicism and Lutheranism; all his subjects were to accept "his religion whose realm" it was; and those who did not like it were to emigrate. There was no pretense on either side to toleration; the principle which the Reformation had upheld in the youth of its rebellion—the right of private judgement—was as completely rejected by the Protestant leaders as by the Catholics....
>
> The Protestants now agreed with Charles and the popes that unity of religious belief was indispensable to social order and peace...the princes [were to] banish dissenters instead of burning them.... Each became, like Henry VIII of England, the supreme head of the Church in his territory, with the exclusive right to appoint the clergy and the men who should define the obligatory faith.[212]

The "Erastian"[213] principle—that the state should rule the Church—was definitely established. As it was the princes, not the theologians, who had led Protestantism to its triumph, they naturally assumed the fruits of victory—their territorial supremacy over the emperor, their ecclesiastical supremacy over the Church.

In 1555, Pope Paul IV[214] issued a papal bull that returned Jews to the "ghettos,"[215] forced them to sell their properties at huge losses, and reduced them to the status of slaves and rag merchants." Marriage between Jews and Christians became forbidden on threat of death. Only one synagogue per city was allowed within the Holy Roman Empire. Keep in mind that, as a result of the Reformation, the decree was now ignored in Protestant countries.

Publication of the KJV

The English version of the Bible was published in England in 1611.[216] It became known as the authorized King James Version and incorporated terminology foreign to the language of Scripture. For example, the names given to biblical characters were often Anglicized. For example, as addressed earlier, Jacob, the brother of Yeshua and writer of one of the books of the Bible, was given the name James. Miriam's name was changed to Mary. We also find the term "Easter" in place of Passover. The King James Bible also changed the order of the books and used the Greek titles for many of the books in place of the Hebrew titles. For example, *Bereshit* ("In the Beginning") became Genesis; *Shemot* ("Names") became Exodus; *Vayikra* ("And He Called") became Leviticus; *Bamidbar* ("In the Wilderness") became Numbers; and *Devarim* ("Words") became Deuteronomy. The translation, though commissioned by King James, was based largely on the work of John Wycliffe and Miles Coverdale from the previous century. Coverdale was a Catholic monk. As a result, the King James translation, as well as most other Gentile-published English translations, contain some of the ideas of Marcion and Augustine.

The Rise of Messianic Expectations

Messianic expectations among Jews and even some Christians arose about this time in anticipation of the year 1666—a year mistakenly believed to be the year of the apocalypse. In response to the worldwide Jewish hope, a man named Shabbetai Zevi[217] arose. Born on the Hebrew calendar on the 9th of Av, the date that both the First and Second Temples were destroyed, he:

> ...gained a broader and more devoted following than any Messianic claimant since the Bar Kochba rebellion against Rome.

Jews from around the world, including many learned rabbis, announced that Shabbetai Zevi was authentic. Jews from all over Europe and the Turkish empire abandoned their work and their worldly goods and prepared to follow Shabbetai Zevi to the Holy Land.

Unlike Bar Kochba, a man of war, "Zevi was a mystic, a kabbalistic visionary." By the middle of 1666, he proclaimed to the Jewish world that he was heading to Constantinople to "knock the turban off the head of the Turkish sultan and re-establish sovereignty in the Land of Israel." Upon his arrival to the city, the sultan arrested Zevi, then gave him the choice of being put to death or converting to Islam. He chose the latter, bringing great sorrow and disappointment to the worldwide Jewish community.

John Toland

The eighteenth century ushered in a Gentile voice that began "crying in the wilderness," encouraging Jews who accepted Yeshua to remain Jews. His name was John Toland,[218] an Irish minister. In his work, *Nazarenus*, he declared:

> From this doctrine it follows that Jesus did not take away or cancel the Jewish Law in any sense whatsoever, sacrifices only excepted.[219]

He believed that Gentiles who taught that the Law was eradicated by Jesus and was no longer applicable to Jewish believers who "err not knowing the Scriptures" and did "almost wholly subvert the True Christianity."

Until this point in history, official church doctrine had been that

God had completely abolished the Torah of Moses. Toland's views, however, were not widely accepted. One senses from his writings that he was 250 years ahead of his time.

Jewish Revival and Return to the Holy Land

After a lapse of several hundred years of silence, Jewish people began once again accepting the good news of Yeshua. The nineteenth century brought about a Renaissance period of Jewish revival. Reportedly, at least a quarter of a million Jews accepted Yeshua as Messiah during this century.

In 1881, the first of three waves of Jewish immigration back to the Holy Land occurred. The second and third waves occurred in the twentieth century. God was raising up the remnant and began to return the Jews to Israel. He would first gather them in unbelief and begin the preparations for Messiah's return.

Church history records that, beginning in AD 326, Constantine started construction of the Church of the Holy Sepulcher. This began the process of building churches all throughout Israel commemorating significant New Testament events. In 1948, at the time of Israel's birth as the Jewish State, it was decided that no churches or mosques would be destroyed and the ownership of the property would remain with the previous owners. This was done to demonstrate that, although Jewish holy sites and synagogues had been destroyed around the world, Israel would not repay evil for evil.

The Roman Catholic Church, from its very beginnings, persecuted, converted, and killed countless millions of Jews. During this process, Jewish identity was stripped away and the seed line of Messiah was attacked from within the single most powerful organized body that worshiped the Jewish Messiah. In war, these casualties would be classified as "death by friendly fire." Of the estimated 2.5 billion Christians around the world, approximately 1.5 billion are a part of the Roman Catholic Church. There is no greater example of the creation of a global entity forcing absolute adherence to an ideology that strips away all Jewish identity. In so doing, they have become one of the strongest weapons in Satan's arsenal to eliminate the seed line of the woman. It is no wonder that many eschatologists identify the Roman Catholic Church as the "little horn" of the Beast of Daniel and Revelation.

The Protestant Church as Satan's Army

Today in the U.S. alone, there are more than one thousand different Christian branches professing many diverse and conflicting beliefs. It would be an understatement to say that Christianity is a severely divided faith.

What Is a Denomination in Christianity?

A denomination in Christianity is a religious organization (an association or fellowship) that unites local congregations in a single legal and administrative body. Members of a denominational family share the same beliefs or creed, participate in similar worship practices, and cooperate to develop and preserve shared enterprises.

The word "denomination" comes from the Latin *denominare*, meaning "to name."

Initially, Christianity was considered a sect of Judaism (Acts 24:5). Denominations began to develop as the history of Christianity progressed and adapted to the differences of race, nationality, and theological interpretation.

As of 1980, British statistical researcher David B. Barrett[220] identified 20,800 Christian denominations in the world. He classified them into seven major alliances and 156 ecclesiastical traditions.

Examples of Christian Denominations

Some of the oldest denominations in church history are the Coptic Orthodox Church,[221] Eastern Orthodox Church,[222] and the Roman Catholic Church.[223] A few newer denominations, by comparison, are the Salvation Army,[224] the Assemblies of God Church,[225] and the Calvary Chapel Movement.[226]

Many Denominations, One Body

There are many denominations, but one Body of Christ. Ideally, the Church on earth—the Body of Christ—would be universally united in doctrine and organization. However, departures from Scripture in doctrine, revivals, reformations, and various spiritual movements have forced believers to form distinct and separate bodies.

Every believer today would benefit from reflecting on this sentiment found in *Foundations of Pentecostal Theology*:

> Denominations may have been God's way of preserving revival and missionary fervor. The members of denominational churches, however, must keep in mind that the Church which is the Body of Christ is composed of all true believers, and that true believers must be united in spirit to carry forward the Gospel of Christ in the world, for all will be caught up together

at the Coming of the Lord. That local churches should band together for fellowship and missions is certainly a Bible truth.

Evolution of Christianity

Seventy-five percent of all North Americans identify themselves as Christian, with the United States being one of the most religiously diverse countries in the world. Most of the Christians in America belong to either a mainline denomination or the Roman Catholic Church.

There are numerous ways to dissect the many Christian faith groups. They can be separated into fundamentalist or conservative, mainline and liberal groups. They can be characterized by theological belief systems such as Calvinism and Arminianism. And lastly, Christians can be categorized into a vast number of denominations.

Fundamentalist / Conservative / Evangelical Christian groups can generally be characterized as believing that salvation is a free gift of God. It is received by repenting and asking for forgiveness of sin and trusting Jesus as Lord and Savior. They define Christianity as a personal and living relationship with Jesus Christ. They believe the Bible is God's inspired Word and is the basis of all truth. Most conservative Christians believe that hell is a real place that awaits anyone who does not repent of their sins and trust Jesus as Lord.

Mainline Christian groups are more accepting of other beliefs and faiths. They usually define a Christian as anyone who follows the teachings of and about Jesus Christ. Most mainline Christians will consider the contributions of non-Christian religions and give value or merit to their teaching. For the most part, mainline Christians believe that salvation comes through faith in Jesus, however, they vary widely in their emphasis on good works and the effect of these good works on determining their eternal destination.

Liberal Christian groups agree with most mainline Christians and are even more accepting of other beliefs and faiths. Religious liberals generally interpret hell symbolically, not as an actual place. They reject the concept of a loving God who would create a place of eternal torment for unredeemed humans. Some liberal theologians have abandoned or completely reinterpreted most of the traditional Christian beliefs.

For a general definition, and to establish common ground, we will maintain that most members of Christian groups will agree on the following things: Christians follow the teachings of Jesus Christ, the Jewish Messiah, who was born in Bethlehem and executed by Roman crucifixion (death on a cross).

Most Christians regard Jesus as the Son of God, and believe that He is God, the Second Person of the Trinity. Most Christians believe the Trinity consists of the Father, Son and Holy Spirit—three separate persons, all-eternal, all-present, all-powerful, all-knowing. They form a single, unified deity. Most Christians believe that Jesus coexisted with God before the foundation of the world, that He was born to a virgin named Mary, that He was resurrected in bodily form three days after His death, and that He later ascended into Heaven.

Brief History of the Church

To try to understand why and how so many different denominations developed, let's take a very brief look at the history of the church.

After Jesus died, Simon Peter, one of Jesus' disciples, became a strong leader in the Jewish Christian movement. Later, James,

(Jacob) most likely Jesus' brother, took over leadership. These followers of Christ viewed themselves as a reform movement within Judaism, yet they continued to follow many of the Jewish laws.

At this time, Saul, originally one of the strongest persecutors of the early Jewish Christians, had a blinding vision of Jesus Christ on the road to Damascus and became a Christian. Adopting the name "Paul," he became the greatest evangelist of the early Christian church. Paul's ministry, also called "Pauline Christianity," was directed mainly to Gentiles rather than Jews. In subtle ways, the early church was already becoming divided.

Another belief system at this time was Gnostic Christianity, with adherents believing they had received a "higher knowledge" and teaching that Jesus was a spirit being, sent by God to impart knowledge to humans so that they could escape the miseries of life on earth.

In addition to Gnostic, Jewish, and Pauline Christianity, there were already many other versions of Christianity being taught. After the fall of Jerusalem in AD 70, the Jewish Christian movement was scattered. Pauline and Gnostic Christianity were left as the dominant groups.

The Roman Empire recognized Pauline Christianity as a valid religion in AD 313. Later in that century, it became the official religion of the Empire, and during the following one thousand years, Catholics were the only people recognized as Christians.

In AD 1054, a formal split occurred between the Roman Catholic and Eastern Orthodox churches. This division remains in effect today. The 1054 split, also known as the "Great East-West Schism," marks an important date in the history of all Christian denominations because it designates the very first major division in Christianity and the beginning of "denominations."

The next major division occurred in the sixteenth century

with the Protestant Reformation. The Reformation was ignited in 1517 when Martin Luther posted his Ninety-five Theses, but the Protestant movement did not officially begin until 1529. It was during this year that the "Protestation" was published by German princes who wanted the freedom to choose the faith of their territory. They called for an individual interpretation of Scripture and religious freedom.

The Reformation marked the beginning of denomination-alism as we see it today. Those who remained faithful to Roman Catholicism believed that the central regulation of doctrine by church leaders was necessary to prevent confusion and division within the church and corruption of its beliefs. On the contrary, those who broke away from the church believed this central control was what led to the corruption of the true faith.

Protestants insisted that believers be allowed to read the Word of God for themselves. Up until this time, the Bible was only made available in Latin.

This look back at history is possibly the best way to make sense of the incredible volume and variety of Christian denominations today.[227]

Fractured Christianity

This report serves to confirm that Christianity is fractured into many pieces based on theology and orthopraxy. It can be said of most denominations that they are on the same page, but the real question is, in what book? If faith alone in Jesus is not enough to unite us, and the Bible is not universally accepted in its entirety, imagine the division among these denominations when it comes to Israel.

Consider the following article from the website, Washington Reports on Middle East Affairs:

The Alliance of Baptists, with 65,000 members, passed a resolution in 2017 opposing "efforts by Congress and state legislatures to punish entities that engage in Boycott, Divestment and Sanctions (BDS) or that provide sanctuary for immigrants." In 2016, the Baptists "affirmed the use of BDS strategies and comprehensive education and advocacy programs to end the 49-year Israeli military occupation of Palestinian land."

The Church of the United Brethren in Christ, with 23,000 members, took a stand in 2006, when the Brethren Benefit Trust divested "from ownership of Caterpillar Corporation and any other company that sells products that are used routinely as weapons of destruction or death in Israel and Palestine." Recently, the Brethren joined others in divesting from HP Inc. (Hewlett-Packard Company). Early in 2010, members of On Earth Peace (a Church of the Brethren agency) were arrested, jailed, and deported as they tried to enter Israel.

The Religious Society of Friends (Quakers) has 76,000 members. The American Friends Service Committee (the humanitarian services arm of the church) took a position in 2012 in support of BDS and the right of people to use economic activism tactics as tools for change in Israel and Palestine, after having passed a divestment screen (screening an investment portfolio reflects an organization's ethical stances) in 2009. The American Friends Service Committee (AFSC), the 1947 Nobel Peace Prize laureate, was the main provider of aid for Palestinian refugees forced from their lands and homes in 1948. The Friends Fiduciary Corporation investment firm, serving over 300 Quaker institutions in the U.S., has dropped its holdings in HP Inc. and Veolia Environment. Those actions were the result of a preexisting investment screen, and are explicitly not part of BDS.

The Mennonite Church USA, which has more than 75,000 members, approved a resolution by a majority of 98 percent in

2017 calling on "individuals and congregations to avoid the purchase of products associated with acts of violence or policies of military occupation, including items produced in [Israeli] settlements." The church explained, "The Palestinian people have suffered injustices, violence, and humiliation, including...life under Israeli military occupation and in refugee camps throughout the Middle East.

The Presbyterian Church (USA), which represents 1.5 million Americans, voted overwhelmingly in support of the international BDS campaign in 2018. Members voted on a slate of resolutions put forth by the Israel Palestine Mission Network (IPMN). The church also opposed congressional and state anti-BDS legislation, instead calling on Americans to "defend and advocate for the constitutional protection under the First Amendment for all United States citizens."

The Roman Catholic Church has 70.4 million members in the U.S., making it the largest denomination in the nation. The Catholic Conference of Major Superiors of Men voted in March 2016 to "join the boycott of settlement products and companies profiting from settlements." The U.S. Conference of Catholic Bishops has not made a similar statement. Pax Christi, a Catholic peace and justice organization, is a leader on this issue.

The Unitarian Universalist Association (UUA) has 155,000 members. Its Socially Responsible Investing Committee adopted a human rights investment screen in 2016 focusing on conflict zones. Human rights violations by Israel in the occupied Palestinian territories came under scrutiny. As a result, the UUA divested from HP Inc., Motorola Solutions, and Caterpillar Inc. A resolution specifically mentioning Palestine and calling for a broader, secure, and long-lasting commitment to screening out investments in corporations complicit in human rights violations in Palestine/Israel was not adopted by the delegates to the 2016 UUA General Assembly.

The United Church of Christ (UCC), with 850,000 members, voted in 2015 to divest from companies profiting from Israel's military occupation of the West Bank and Gaza Strip. The UCC Christ Palestine-Israel Network (UCC PIN) stated that the resolution was "the culmination of a process that began in 2005 to end the Church's complicity in Israel's nearly half-century-old occupation and other abuses of Palestinian human rights." The 2005 resolution stated, "economic leverage can be used to support the development of Palestine and Israel as two independent, secure, economically viable states."

The United Methodist Church (UMC), with an estimated 7 million members, divested from five Israeli banks on the grounds that they contribute to Israel's occupation of Palestinian land. Bank Hapoalim, Bank Leumi, First International Bank of Israel, Israel Discount Bank and Bank Mizrahi-Tefahot are among 39 companies blacklisted in 2018 by the UMC pension fund for failing to meet the guidelines of a human rights investment policy. An Israeli construction company, Shikun & Binui, was also excluded for involvement in settlement building. The pension board's assets in 2014 were valued at $20.9 billion.

The World Communion of Reformed Churches (WCRC), has 232 member churches on six continents. In 2017, WCRC called on its members to "examine their mission, education, and investment relationships with Israel and Palestine in light of the witness of Palestinian Christians and to respond as they understand the Reformed communion's commitments to human rights and the protections of international law." The WCRC is the largest association of Reformed churches in the world, with 11 member denominations in the U.S., including two (UCC and Presbyterians) appearing on this list.[228]

If this isn't enough to demonstrate how the church is no longer being guided by the Bible regarding Israel and the seed line of Messiah, then the shift in its theological stance confirms this.

Removing the Old Testament from the Christian Narrative

There exists today a sweeping movement within denominational Christianity to remove the Old Testament from the Christian narrative. The emphasis on Jesus only, relegating the Father to a supporting role and deemphasizing the Holy Spirit, has led to a biblically illiterate and "feel-good experience" body of "believers." The rise of the megachurch and the lack of depth of its messaging has contributed to a decline in the belief that church is relevant.

Denominational Christianity is engaged in a civil war over LGBTQ+ and have taken their eyes off the message of Messiah. When Christianity becomes irrelevant and the message of the cross is watered down, the church has lost its salt. In regards to its impact on the seed line of Messiah, it has been neutered and now sits on the sidelines of Christian history—having become ineffective in reaching the lost sheep of the House of Israel. Its internal battles have taken it off the frontlines and directed its focus on its own identity and survival.

Paul warned in 2 Corinthians 11:3–4:

> But I fear, lest by any means, as the serpent beguiled Eve through his subtilty, so your minds should be corrupted from the simplicity that is in Christ.
>
> For if he that cometh preacheth another Jesus, whom we have not preached, or if ye receive another spirit, which ye have not received, or another gospel, which ye have not accepted, ye might well bear with him.

This lack of discernment is leading many astray from the message of the gospel. In 2 Timothy 4:1–4, Paul again admonishes:

I charge thee therefore before God, and the Lord Jesus Christ, who shall judge the quick and the dead at his appearing and his kingdom;

Preach the word; be instant in season, out of season; reprove, rebuke, exhort with all longsuffering and doctrine.

For the time will come when they will not endure sound doctrine; but after their own lusts shall they heap to themselves teachers, having itching ears;

And they shall turn away their ears from the truth, and shall be urned unto fables.

In Romans 10:1–21, Paul again makes his appeal:

Brethren, my heart's desire and prayer to God for Israel is, that they might be saved.

For I bear them record that they have a zeal of God, but not according to knowledge.

For they being ignorant of God's righteousness, and going about to establish their own righteousness, have not submitted themselves unto the righteousness of God.

For Christ is the end of the law for righteousness to every one that believeth.

For Moses describeth the righteousness which is of the law, That the man which doeth those things shall live by them.

But the righteousness which is of faith speaketh on this wise, Say not in thine heart, Who shall ascend, into heaven? (that is, to bring Christ down from above:)

Or, Who shall descend into the deep? (that is, to bring up Christ again from the dead.)

But what saith it? The word is nigh thee, even in thy mouth, and in thy heart: that is, the word of faith, which we preach;

That if thou shalt confess with thy mouth the Lord Jesus, and shalt believe in thine heart that God hath raised him from the dead, thou shalt be saved.

For with the heart man believeth unto righteousness; and with the mouth confession is made unto salvation.

For the scripture saith, Whosoever believeth on him shall not be ashamed.

For there is no difference between the Jew and the Greek: for the same Lord over all is rich unto all that call upon him.

For whosoever shall call upon the name of the Lord shall be saved.

How then shall they call on him in whom they have not believed? And how shall they believe in him of whom they have not heard? And how shall they hear without a preacher?

And how shall they preach, except they be sent? As it is written, How beautiful are the feet of them that preach the gospel of peace, and bring glad tidings of good things!

But they have not all obeyed the gospel. For Isaias saith, Lord, who hath believed our report?

So then faith cometh by hearing, and hearing by the word of God.

But I say, Have they not heard? Yes verily, their sound went into all the earth, and their words unto the ends of the world.

But I say, Did not Israel know? First Moses saith, I will provoke you to jealousy by them that are no people, and by a foolish nation I will anger you.

But Esaias is very bold, and saith, I was found of them that sought me not; I was made manifest unto them that asked no after me.

But to Israel he saith, All day long I have stretched forth my hands unto a disobedient and gainsaying people.

Mainstream denominational Christianity has had a nullified impact on the Jews and is unwittingly clearing the path for Satan's agenda. Since most of denominational Christianity is focused on a watered-down gospel, or Israel's politics, and not the Great Commission, they have taken a stance against Israel. The denominational church has not only been ineffective in reaching the Jews with the gospel, but many have turned against Israel and, instead of the Great Commission, they are advancing the "Great Omission"—and God's people are perishing for lack of knowledge.

> *It is time for us to reach the Jews and the Muslims with the gospel.*

Politicizing Israel

Evangelicals, especially in light of the 2016 and 2020 election and the years leading up to these elections, became a focal point of the Israel narrative among Christians. The recognition of Israel's sovereignty and the moving of the United States embassy to Jerusalem further divided the body of Messiah into what appeared to be two very distinct camps. Both the nation and the church became more vocal regarding Israel, and the biblical stance on Israel was radically attacked by the political stance on Israel. The lines became blurred in the debate between God's Word and those who support a Two-State Solution.

Biblical View of Israel

The biblical stance is based on Scriptures such as:

- Amos 9: "And I will plant them upon their land, and they shall no more be pulled up out of their land which I have given them, saith the Lord thy God."
- Ezekiel 37:22: "And I will make them one nation in the land upon the mountains of Israel; and one king shall be king to them all: and they shall be no more two nations, neither shall they be divided into two kingdoms any more at all."

In addition, the Covenant Land given to Abram and his descendants in Genesis 15 predates the modern Palestinian narrative by over four thousand years.

Political View of Israel

The political stance coming from within the ranks of Protestant Christianity is based on a social justice narrative claiming that "the Palestinians" are indigenous people, and Israel is denying them their birthright. In consideration of this position, it is important to first address if there is even such a people group calling themselves "Palestinians." If there is, then in keeping with the teachings of the Bible, we as believers should be engaged in this dialogue.

Hard Fact 1: There never was a "Palestinian People"

By the early 20th century the land we now call Palestine-Israel was a mix of many peoples representing some 50 languages [1911 Encyclopedia Britannica]. These communities were "ethnologically a chaos of all the possible human combinations," and so did not share a common Arab identity. For instance, they included Balkans, Greeks, Syrians, Egyptians, Turks, Armenians, Italians, Persians, Kurds, Germans, Afghans, Bosnians, Sudanese, Algerians and others. So it is not surprising that, historically, there is no language known as Palestinian, or any Palestinian culture distinct from that of all the Arabs in the area.

There is no authoritative text on Palestinian history [Eyen Edward Said, graduate of Harvard & Princeton, former member of the Palestine National Council]

By 1917 there were 690,000 Arabs (Christian and Muslim) and 59,000 Jews in Palestine, but still no identifiable "Palestinian People." Even the 1922 British Mandate for Palestine didn't recognize the existence of a "Palestinian people" since they were not an ethnic group. Instead the Mandate referred to the local Arab population as "existing non-Jewish communities." It is only when Israel started to blossom mid 20th century that we see a "Palestinian People" emerge. Nur Masalha, a Palestinian academic, admits that is was the establishment of the State of Israel in 1948 which brought about "the crystallisation of a distinct and resistance Palestinian identity."

Hard Fact 2: There never was a "Palestinian Land"

Is 'Palestine' a historic land? Is it legitimate to use the term "Palestine" for the area we now call Israel? Where did the term come from?

To answer this, we first observe that the Hebrews entered the Land of Israel, specifically Canaan, under Joshua c1450 BC (Jos 6). This area was gradually extended by Israel's kings (Saul, David and Solomon) but still excluded "Philistia" (the land of the Philistines), a narrow coastal strip including Gaza. The Philistines were an Aegean people more closely related to Greeks than to Arabs. Linguistically, the term "Palestine" originated from the Greek word pronounced *Palaistina*, which is derived from the Hebrew word pronounced pel-eh-sheth, meaning "land of the Philistines." Historically then, the term "Palestine" only applied to the narrow coastal strip of land occupied by the Philistines, and Philistia itself did not survive the invasion of Nebuchadnezzar II c600 BC.

However, that was not the end of the matter and this land definition of Palestine was later expanded by the Romans. In the 2nd century AD, the Romans renamed Judea as "Palaestina" in an attempt, some say, to minimize Jewish identification with the land of Israel. In fact, it is claimed that the Roman Emperor Hadrian began using the term "Palestine" for the whole Land of Israel, and unfortunately this term has prevailed over the centuries. For example, under the Ottoman Empire (1517–1917), the term "Palestine" was used as a general term to describe the land south of Syria, and it was applied to the territory placed under the 1922 British Mandate. But according to historian Professor Bernard Lewis, even at the start of the 20th century, "the land was not a country and had no frontiers, only administrative boundaries."

So since there was no historic "Land of Palestine" there can be no legitimate Arab claim to such a land spanning large parts of modern Israel. Even Arab leaders themselves have admitted to this in the past:

There is no such country as Palestine
[Arab leader A. B. Abdul Hadi, 1937]
There is no such thing as Palestine in history, absolutely not
[Arab Prof Philip Hitti (Princeton University), 1946]
Palestine does not exist at all
[Ahmed Shkari (PLO founder), 1956]

Hard Fact 3: There is no "State of Palestine"

International recognition of the State of Palestine has been the objective of the Palestine Liberation Organization (PLO) since the Palestinian Declaration of Independence proclaimed the establishment of the State of Palestine on 15 November 1988. The declaration was promptly acknowledged by a range of countries, and as of August 2018, 137 of the 193 United Nations member states and two non-member states had recognized it. Britain would recognise the state of Palestine under a Labour government—a major shift in long-standing British foreign policy in the Middle East.

The fact is, as of August 2018 there was no such thing as a "Palestinian State." Palestine was not a state:

It's not a state now. It does not meet the customary international law test of statehood. It doesn't control defined boundaries. It doesn't fulfill normal functions of government. There are a whole host of reasons why it's not a state. [John Bolton, US National Security Adviser, October 2018]

Bolton said it is a "so-called state." He said to become a state requires diplomatic negotiations with Israel and others.

Today's "Palestinians"

In the face of this strong historical record, some still make the case for the existence of an amorphous Palestinian territory with an identifiable population existing before the emergence of political Zionism around 1890. On the other hand, as discussed, history shows that there was no distinctive Palestinian people at the start of the 20th century. It was only really after WWI that we find an emergence of Palestinian nationalism and an identifiable "Palestinian People." Some see this as a response to the threat posed by Zionism, when waves of Jewish immigrants arrived in Palestine between 1919 and 1939. It is interesting to note that, by 1948, a substantial portion of the "Palestinian People" resident in Palestine Mandate territory originated, not from that territory, but rather from the surrounding Arab lands of Lebanon, Syria, Jordan and Egypt! It is claimed they came for the jobs provided by newly established Zionist industry and agriculture.[229]

Reaching Jews with the Gospel

Evangelical Christian support for Israel has created many levels of misunderstanding even among those actively engaged in humanitarian work in Israel. Many Christian nonprofit organizations have been established to solicit financial support to aid Israel's many Holocaust survivors and those in need of food and shelter. All aid to Israel is greatly appreciated; however, there are those who are unwilling to support efforts to reach the Jewish people with the gospel. There are many who include "Christian" in their name to lead us to believe they are actively engaged in advancing the Kingdom and reaching the "lost sheep of the House of Israel," when, in fact, they are opposed to any form of outreach for the advancement of the gospel in Israel. Hundreds of millions of dollars are raised each year by these organizations, yet, in most cases, no money is spent on preaching about the Messiah.

Whether it is through the active and vocal stance against Israel by denominational Christianity or the more insidious and subtle diversion of humanitarian aid away from reaching the Jewish people with the truth of the gospel, Satan's assault on the seed line of Messiah is in full force. Every Jewish person who dies without knowing Messiah is one less left to call for His return. To put this in perspective, in 1939, there were approximately 16.8 million Jews in the world. The Holocaust took the lives of 6 million, reducing our numbers in 1945 equal to our population in 1900. At the writing of this book, the Jewish population of the world stands at 15.2 million. At least in the Holocaust, our enemy wore a uniform and was easily identified. Today, a profession of faith in the Jewish Messiah is no guarantee that the church's and the believer's position on Israel does not support Satan's agenda to eliminate us through opposition, misinformation, or simple inaction.

12

Islam

A common claim of Islam is that its founder, Mohammed, descended from Ishmael. However, Ishmael clearly is not the "Father of Islam," as so many credit him to be.

Because Ishmael received no spiritual call from God, his only historical descendants were the twelve tribes that descended from his sons. In subsequent generations, even his sons' descendants forgot about him, including his name, even though the time between Ishmael and these tribes was only about 1,200 years (between the seventh and ninth centuries BC). Since this is the case for the true descendants of Ishmael, how can a man who lived in Yemen, far from where Ishmael lived, conclude that he descended from Ishmael, who lived two thousand years before him? If the Ishmaelites themselves weren't aware of their ancestry from Ishmael, who would have told the twenty-first ancestor of Mohammed that he was descended from Ishmael?

There is no proof that Mohammed's ancestors, number thirteen or number twenty, ever claimed to be descendants from Ishmael. No written document before Mohammed makes such a claim. Even if such a document were to have existed, still, this ancestor would have no right to claim descendancy from a man who lived two thousand years before him, without written documents in each generation to prove his case.[230]

This rebuttal to Islam's claim that Mohammed descended from Ishmael sheds a different light on the evolution of Islam's birth.

God's Two Prophecies over Ishmael

God spoke two specific words of prophecy over Ishmael. The first was when Sarai convinced Abram to take her servant Hagar, since Sarai was barren:

> Now Sarai Abram's wife bar him no children: and she had an handmaid, an Egyptian, whose name was Hagar.
>
> And Sarai said unto Abram, Behold now, the LORD hath restrained me from bearing: I pray thee, go in unto my maid; it may be that I may obtain children by her. And Abram hearkened to the voice of Sarai.
>
> And Sarai Abram's wife took Hagar her maid the Egyptian, after Abram had dwelt ten years in the land of Canaan, and gave her to her husband Abram to be his wife.
>
> And he went in unto Hagar, and she conceived. (Genesis 16:1–4a)

The trouble came, however, when she realized she was pregnant and began to take pride in it.

> And when she saw that she had conceived, her mistress was despised in her eyes.

And Sarai said unto Abram, My wrong be upon thee: I have given my maid into thy bosom; and when she saw that she had conceived, I was despised in her eyes: the LORD judge between me and thee.

But Abram said unto Sarai, Behold, thy maid is in thy hand; do to her as it pleaseth thee. And when Sarai dealt hardly with her, she fled from her face. (Genesis 16:4b–6)

Hagar left to begin heading back to her home country of Egypt. Along the way, she had an encounter with "an angel of the Lord." Throughout the Hebrew Bible, this term always refers to the preincarnate Yeshua/Jesus, as He is the only visible manifestation of God Himself. After admonishing Hagar to return to Sarai, He spoke this prophetic word over her:

And the angel of the LORD said unto her, I will multiply thy seed exceedingly, that it shall not be numbered for multitude.

And the angel of the LORD said unto her, Behold, thou art with child, and shalt bear a son, and shalt call his name Ishmael; because the LORD hath heard thy affliction.

And he will be a wild man; his hand will be against every man, and every man's hand against him; and he shall dwell in the presence of all his brethren. (16:11–12)

The second prophecy God spoke over Ishmael was in response to the intercession of Abraham on his behalf. Since Abraham was a loving father and knew that Isaac was the son of the promise, he asked God to consider his son, Ishmael. We read God's response in Genesis 17:20:

And as for Ishmael, I have heard thee: Behold, I have blessed him, and will make him fruitful, and will multiply him exceedingly; twelve princes shall he beget, and I will make him a great nation.

The Ishmaelites played an important role when Joseph was sold to them by his brothers, paving the way for Joseph to take a seat at Pharaoh's right hand and bring about the redemption of the nearly extinct remnant of Abraham's lineage through Isaac and Jacob (only seventy were left).

Tension between Islam and Jews?

The preconceived notion of a longstanding tension between Islam and the Jews is not supported in the historical record. Although it is dramatically different today, the origins of Islam throughout the eighth and

Fulfillment of Prophecies Regarding Ishmael

History is the best testimony to the fulfillment of both the prophecies regarding Ishmael. In regards to him being a "wild donkey" of a man (ESV), we see God again using something of the natural to reveal a supernatural truth.

A wild donkey in the natural is an untamable, difficult-to-get-along-with animal that freely roams and cannot be contained. It is considered aggressive, and since it cannot be tamed, it provides no benefit to man.

In the natural, wild donkeys do not maintain harems, but will mate with and disrupt order in domesticated herds for the sole purpose of expanding their bloodline. Wild donkeys are known for their environmentally destructive behaviors and aggressive actions towards other males.

ninth centuries made accommodations for both Christians and Jews to be recognized as a part of a certain distinct group.

The term used to define the status of tolerated religions was *dhimma*, which meant "protection." The people belonging to tolerated religions were called *ahl al-dhimma*—"protected people," or in shortened form, *dhimmīs*. *Dhimmīs* were obligated to pay an annual tax and to abide by the sumptuary laws. Their "protection" meant that they were legal citizens of the state and were sheltered by the same basic laws that protected Muslim citizens, though at a subordinate level. For example, they could bring grievances to a Muslim court of law, but their witnesses weren't as powerful as that of Muslims, so they were required to bring twice

---

As we examine the longstanding division between Sunni and Shiite Muslims, we can trace this inclination toward dispute among family members to the prophecy spoken over Ishmael.

Ismael deliberately defied his father's wishes and took wives from Egypt, and his descendants foretold in the prophecy to Abraham settled in the nations surrounding Israel. The twelve sons born to his Egyptian wife, Keturah, intermarried with others in the region in Egypt and Assyria, and their tribal identity was less a part of their tradition. The Ishmaelites were given the territory from Havilah to Shur, which today extends from near Kuwait north through Iraq, through Jordan and Egypt and most of Saudi Arabia, where Mecca and Medina are located.

God blessed Ishmael's descendants to multiply and prosper. Although not all Arabs are Muslim and not all Muslims are Arab, there is a familial connection back to Ishmael that is implied, but cannot be documented.

---

the number of witnesses to court. They could pray undisturbed in their houses of worship, but—unlike Muslims—were forbidden from public displays of religion. *Dhimmīs* were allowed to build new houses of worship or to repair those already established, except with permission of the ruler.

Ups and Downs in Jewish-Muslim Relations: Ninth—Nineteenth Centuries

The period between the ninth and fourteenth centuries was marked not only by Jewish intellectual advances under Islamic influence, but by violence as well:

This period includes times and places (in Baghdad and Fostat/Cairo and much of Spain, for example) that are sometimes referred to as "the Golden Age" of Muslim-Jewish or Muslim-Jewish-Christian symbiosis and *convivencia*. The truth is never so simple. Violence and the threat of violence was a central aspect of communal relationship between hierarchies in the medieval world, and Jews as subalterns clearly suffered not only social discrimination but sometimes also violence and even occasional massacre. [It has been] established quite clearly, however, that while a utopian Golden Age was a myth, the situation for Jews in much of the medieval Muslim world was significantly better than in most of the medieval Christian world and was one of the better situations for pre-modern Jewry....

In the thirteenth century, some places in the Muslim world were already beginning a long decline that negatively impacted the position of its minorities, including Jews. The downward trend occurred at different speeds in different places, and was even reversed for various periods in some areas, such as those under Mongol Ilkhanid, Ottoman Turkish, Safavid Persian, and Mughal Indian rule. But the general direction was one of decline, and when this occurred, it caused difficulties and frictions between the majority Muslim population and the Jews and other minorities. Under the stresses brought about by weakening economic and political institutions, society became increasingly stratified; religious orthodoxy with a rigid perspective toward religious minorities became increasingly dominant; and social, political, and religious frictions emerged between various factions and communities....

Nevertheless, the Ottoman Empire was a particularly bright spot for Jews, especially during its height in the fifteenth through much of the seventeenth centuries when it welcomed Jews who had been expelled from the Spanish peninsula under Christian rule in the late fifteenth and early sixteenth centuries, or who subsequently fled from the horrors of the Inquisition that followed. Those Spanish (Sefardi) Jews who moved to Ottoman lands were able to reestablish themselves among their own indigenous communities in the empire and among their new Muslim and Christian neighbors.

As a rule, when the economic and political situation in the Muslim world was stable, so was the position of its Jews. Relations between Jews and Muslims improved through business and commerce, and that positively affected social associations as well. During periods of destabilization, however, the general relationship between Muslims and Jews deteriorated, though always with exceptions. Generally speaking, the more precipitous the decline, the worse for positive and productive Muslim-Jewish interaction. The long decline of the Muslim world reached its nadir in the nineteenth century, when virtually all the Muslim world came under the control of one or another European colonial power.

Rise of Zionism

The rise of Zionism and Zionist Jewish immigration to Israel in the early twentieth century added to the tensions between native Jews and Muslims in the surrounding lands as well. By the 1930s, another element added to the stresses: the rise of German National Socialism (Nazism). Germany was not a colonial power in the Middle East and North Africa, so it was free from the taint of colonialism. Moreover, Germany was the traditional enemy of France, which was particularly aggressive in its colonial policies. So the Arab Muslim lands tended to be ripe for absorbing and assimilating Nazi anti-Semitic propaganda, which exacerbated the tensions between Jews and Muslims. By the end of the 1930s, the rise of Nazi Germany and fascist Italy offered alternative models to French and British liberalism, increasing the receptivity among Muslims to their anti-Semitic perspectives.

As a result, the overwhelming bulk of Jewry that had been firmly established for millennia in the Muslim world fled under duress with the realization of national independence. Many suffered from violent pogroms and state nationalizing of their property, and many fled with nothing more than what they could stuff into a suitcase. Some went to the European states to which they had previously naturalized. Others escaped to wherever they could find refuge. The mass exodus/expulsion occurred at the same time the State of Israel was in formation, so many— especially those with no other alternatives—ended up in the new Jewish state. Some Muslim and Western accounts have emerged that attribute the mass exodus of the Jewish populations of the Middle East and North Africa strictly to Zionism, but as noted above, the situation was far more complex. Zionism certainly was a factor, but so was the destabilization of colonialism, religious prejudice, government corruption, and other causes.

The conflict over control of the land that Jews and their supporters call "Israel" and that Palestinians and their supporters call "Palestine" is at its core a conflict of nationalisms, national identities, and national rights. More precisely, it is a product of nineteenth-century ideologies of secular nationalism and secular national identity. Nonetheless, among both Jewish Israelis and Muslim Palestinians, definitional identities have proven to be elastic, and the boundaries between nation, tribe, and religion remain ambiguous. This is not surprising, given the complexity of identity in general, and it cannot be denied that the factors that make up Israeli and Palestinian identity (or Jewish and Arab identity) include religious indicators. Zionists have emphasized religious aspects of Jewish identity to appeal to a larger, non-Zionist religious community for support, and in the process have gradually identified the conflict in religious as well as national terms. Palestinians, in turn, have increasingly emphasized the Islamic connections to Jerusalem and Palestine in order to appeal to a larger religious community for support as well. As a result, the conflict has come to be identified increasingly in religious terms, which has negatively impacted Muslim-Jewish relations globally.

Muslim-Jewish relations in the State of Israel have always been tense because of the ongoing and unsettled conflict. Its intractability and ever-present violence have resulted in a general sense of distrust, and this has become embedded within the cultures of both the Jewish and the Muslim inhabitants of the state. That lack of trust has entered the worldview and discourse of many Jews and Muslims far removed from the conflict as well. Muslim and Jewish organizations and media outlets tend to portray the conflict in simplistic and binary terms, and they project negative views and stereotypes of the other, exacerbating the problem within their respective cultural and religious assumptions and worldviews.

Despite the problems brought about by the decline of Muslim economic and political might, the rise of the European powers and their colonial domination, the emergence of nationalist movements, and the particular problems resulting from the Israel-Palestine conflict, individual Jews and Muslims have always managed to maintain deep friendships. These friendships have not been limited to the elites who shared "enlightened" views that transcended stereotypes and religious hierarchies. In fact, many traditional, religious Muslims and Jews maintained friendships in Muslim lands despite the massive disruptions to their traditional worlds. We read about them in the stories and novels authored by members of both communities. Those friendships have been powerful and enduring, but they could not withstand the forces that brought an end to the once-vibrant Jewish life in most of the Muslim world.[231]

Jihad

In order to understand the modern-day stance of jihad, the holy war against Islam's enemies, we must first identify an enemy. An enemy, or infidel, is defined as anyone who does not submit to Islam. This clearly demonstrates the ideological vision to convert or annihilate all who will not subjugate themselves to Islam. From recent history, the stated high-value targets are Israel and the United States, with special emphasis on the Jews. The current advances made in Europe, Asia, and Africa have created a dispersed group of jihadists, who are funded by Iran and operate in Lebanon, Syria, Iraq, and Afghanistan, with sleeper cells throughout the world.

There are many sources of opinions on the threat of Shariah Law. In the West, we are not yet facing what the Middle East, Asia, Europe, and Africa have been dealing with as Islam expands its foothold on the more than fifty-five countries whose populations are in excess of 80 percent Muslim. In choosing what to include that would provide the most universally understandable approach to this subject, I was able to access the United States Joint Chiefs of Staff course materials. If this is what our Department of Defense is using to brief our military leaders and train our military, then we should be as informed as they are in preparation for this imminent threat. The following document is presented in its entirety, without edit.

Understanding Shari'ah's Role in the War

I. The Intent of this Section

a. The intent of this section of the publication is to define the enemy in the terms the enemy uses, and explain what these terms mean from the enemy's perspective. This will give the warfighter a clear understanding of the enemy's intentions, perspective, and the doctrinal support for these views, in order to give U.S. forces the best possible opportunity to defeat the enemy.

II. Our Doctrine

a. U.S. Military Doctrine, specifically the Intelligence Preparation of the Battlefield Manual (IPB) states the war planners must begin with who the enemy says he is and why he is fighting us. That becomes the basis for determining the enemy threat doctrine.

III. The Enemy's Stated Threat Doctrine

a. The overwhelming majority of individuals with whom the United States military is engaged states they are fighting "Jihad" in the "Cause of Allah" in order to establish an Islamic State (Caliphate) under Islamic Law—known as Shari'ah. In order to accurately understand what this means, our professional duty is to know how jihad is understood by the enemy when mapped against "Jihad" as defined in Islamic Doctrine, and to understand what Islamic Law is and what its role is in Islam. Without this knowledge, we cannot accurately identify, target and defeat this enemy.

IV. Framework for Shari'ah (Islamic Law)

a. Islam defines itself as a complete way of life—social, cultural, religious, military, and political—governed by Islamic Law (Shari'ah). Islamic Law is real law which governs all affairs of Muslims. The Shari'ah, as it is called, is primarily derived from the Qur'an and the Sunnah (the collection of the Hadith and the Sira).

b. For Muslims, the Qur'an is considered the "uncreated word of Allah." This means that Muslims believe that everything in the Qur'an was directly revealed to the Prophet Muhammad by Allah (the god in Islam) and cannot be altered or amended. The 114 Suras (Chapters) in the Qur'an are arranged by size from largest to smallest (not chronologically), with the exception of the first Sura. Sura 2 is the largest and Sura 114 is the smallest.

c. In Islam, the Prophet Muhammad is the most perfect example of a human being. All that he did and said is to be modeled by Muslims. The Hadith is the collection of all of the practices, sayings, and traditions of the Prophet Muhammad.

d. The Sira are the authorized sacred biographies of Muhammad.

e. Hadith: There are hundreds of thousands of Hadith, which have been evaluated by Islamic Legal Scholars (Jurists) as to their validity based on their chain of transmission from the Prophet to the reporting author. The Hadith are categorized as mawdu (false), munkar (ignored), da' if (weak), hasan (good), sahih (sound), and mutawatir (strongest, most rigorously authenticated).

f. There are six primary Hadith scholars and they are, in rank order, Bukhari, Muslim, Abu Dawud, ai-Sugra, Tirmidhi, and Ibn Maj ah. Bukhari and Muslim are considered the most reliable. In Islamic Law, Mutawatir Hadith from Bukhari rises to the level of being second only to the Qur'an.

V. Dar al Harb / Dar al Islam

a. In Islamic Law, the entire world is divided into the Dar al Harb, "the house or abode of war," and the Dar al Islam, "the house or abode of peace." All lands which are not under Muslim control and ruled by Shari'ah, are considered Dar al Harb—enemy lands. "Hat·bi" means enemy personnel, or inhabitants of the Dar al Harb. All non-Muslims, not submitted to Islamic Law in Muslim lands are considered enemy persons, persons from the territory of war." The term "non-combatants" does not exist in Islamic Law. All lands occupied by Muslim forces at any time in history are considered "Muslim Lands."

VI. Ijma (Scholarly Consensus)

a. Ijma is one of two critical legal concepts in Islamic Law, especially Sunni Islamic law, which is key to understanding the law. Ijma, or "scholarly consensus" means that when the Mujtahids (senior Islamic Legal Jurists) of a particular time period, gather together, rule on points of Islamic Law, and unanimously agree on these points of law, the ruling becomes a permanent part of Islamic Law for all time and can never be changed. The core issues within Islam have been ruled upon by scholarly consensus in Islamic Law—specifically the issues of Jihad, relations between Muslims and non-Muslims, and the requirement for the establishment of the Caliphate.

b. "When the four necessary integrals of consensus exist, the ruling agreed upon is. An authoritative part of Sacred Law that is obligatory to obey and not lawful to disobey. (Umdat al Salik, The Classic Manual of Islamic Sacred Law, al-Misri, b7.2)

c. A way to recognize when this "absolute" standard is being applied is when writings state "this is a matter over which all the scholars agree," "there is no disagreement among the scholars," or similar language.

VII. Abrogation

a. Abrogation is a second legal concept in Islamic Law critical to understanding the underpinnings of the threat doctrine. Simply put, abrogation means that anything revealed to Muhammad chronologically later. in the Qur'an, abrogates or overrules anything which came earlier. Abrogation comes from three verses in the Qur'an meaning, from the perspective of Islam, it came from god and, therefore, can never be changed. The last chronological Sura in the Qur'an to discuss relations with non-Muslims is Sura 5.

i. "It is a Qur'an which We have divided into parts from time to time, in order that though mightest recite it to men at intervals: We have revealed it by stages." (Qur'an 17:106)

ii. "When We substitute one revelation for another—and Allah knows best what He reveals in stages—They say, "Thou art but a forger": But most of them understand not." (Qur'an 16:101)

iii. "None of Our revelations do we abrogate or cause to be forgotten, but we substitute something better or similar; knowest thou not that Allah hath power over all things?" (Qur'an 2:106)

VIII. Relations with non-Muslims [Sura 5: Last to discuss relations with non-Muslims]

a. It is a permanent command in Islam for Muslims to hate and despise Jews and Christians and not take them as friends. This comes from both the Qur'an as well as from the sacred hadith scholars Bukhari and Muslim.

b. "Oh ye who believe! Take not the Jews and the Christians for your friends and protectors; they are but friends and protectors to each other. And he amongst you that turns to them for friendship is of them. Verily Allah guideth not the unjust." (Qur'an 5:51)

c. The Prophet said, "The hour [of judgment] will not come until the Muslims fight the Jews and kill them. It will not come until the Jew hides behind rocks and trees. it will not come until. the rocks or the trees say, 'O Muslim! O servant of God! There is a Jew behind me. Come and kill him. Except for the gharqad, which is a tree of the Jews.'" [Sacred Hadith, Bukhari, 103/6, number 2926]

d. Allah's Apostle said, "By Him in Whose Hands my soul is, surely (Jesus,) the son of Mary will soon descend amongst you and will judge mankind justly (as a Just Ruler); he will break the Cross and kill the pigs and there will be no Jizya (i.e. taxation taken from non Muslims). "[Sacred Hadith, Bukhari, vol 4, book 55, number 657] Note: this Hadith states that the Muslim prophet Jesus will return to earth with Muhammad and will cast all Christians to hell and, kill all Jews in order that Muslims may go to "Paradise."

IX Jihad [Sura 9: The last to discuss Jihad]

a. Jihad is a permanent obligation on the Muslim community until the entire world made the Dar al Islam.

b. Jihad is sixth Right of Pure Worship between god and man—the first five being the "pillars" of Islam.

c. The Quranic Basis for Jihad

i. Islamic Law provides three options for "People of the Book" (those who had a holy book prior to Muhammad): (1) They may convert to Islam; (2) they may be killed; or (3) they may pay the jizya (non-Muslim tax) and be subjugated to Islamic Law having little rights as non-Muslims under the law. Pagans and others who had no holy book prior to Muhammad must either convert to Islam or be killed.

ii. "Fight and slay the. unbelievers wherever ye find them, and lie in wait for them in every stratagem. of war. But if they repent, and establish regular prayers and practice regular charity, then open the way for them; for Allah is Oft-forgiving, Most Merciful." (Qur'an 9:5, the Sura of the Sword).

iii. "Fight those who believe not in Allah nor the Last Day, nor hold that forbidden which hath been forbidden by Allah and His Apostle, nor acknowledge the religion of truth, even if they are of the people of the Book, until they pay the jizya with willing submission, and feel themselves subdued." (Qur'an 9:29)

d. Jihad has only ever been defined in Islamic Law as 'warfare against non-Muslims:

i. "to war against non-Muslims...signifying warfare to establish Islam" and is "obligatory for every Muslim" [Umdat al Salik, Classic Manual of Islamic Law (Shafi), Ahmad ibn Naqib ai-Misri, d. 1368.]

ii. "war is obligatory on men who are free, have attained puberty, who find the means for going to war, are of sound health, and are neither ill nor suffer from a chronic disease…the jurists agreed, with respect to the people who are to be fought, that they are all of the polytheists, because of the words of the Exalted, "And fight them until persecution is no more, and religion is all for Allah."

[The Distinguished Jurist's Primer (Maliki), Ibn Rushd, d. 1198]

iii. "'Fight the unbeliever wherever you find them and lie and wait for them in every stratagem of war.' "I have been commended to fight the people until they testify that there is no deity worthy of worship except Allah and that Muhammad is the Messenger of Allah. This honorable Ayah (verse) 9:5 (Qur'an) was called the Ayah of the Sword, about which Ad-Kahhak bin Muzahim said, "It abrogated every agreement of peace between the Prophet and any idolator, every treaty, and every term.'" [Tafsir of ibn Kathir, d. 1373] tv. "Jihad is a communal obligation…Jihad is determined till the Day of Judgment…. 'Then shall ye fight, or they shall submit (Qur'an 48:16)' When the Muslims commence battle, and they have surrounded a city or a fort, they are to invite the inhabitants to accept Islam…. If they respond positively, they are to refrain from fighting them, due to the attainment of the purpose. If they refuse, they are to invite them to the payment of jizyah, and this is what the Prophet ordered the commanders of the armies to do for it is one of the consequences upon the conclusion of battle….if they reject the invitation, they are to seek the help of Allah and engage them in combat." [Al-Hidayah, A Classic Manual of Hanafi Law, Primary Hanafi Text since 767 AD]

v. "Fight in the name of God and in the 'path of God.' Combat only those who disbelieve in God…. Whenever you meet your polytheist enemies, invite them to adopt Islam. If they do so, accept it and let them alone…if they refuse then call upon them to pay the jizya. If they do, accept it and leave them alone...." [The Islamic Law of Nations (first book of Islamic Law), Shaybani's Siyar, 700's AD]

vi. "The jurists have distinguished four different ways in which the believer may fulfill his jihad obligation: by his heart; his tongue; his hands; and by the sword...the. believers are under the obligation of sacrificing their 'wealth and lives' in the prosecution of war." [War and Peace in the Law of Islam, Majid Khadduri, 1955]

vii. "The word jihad is most often associated with the act of physically confronting evil and wrong-doing...if anyone dies in a Jihad they automatically go to Paradise. A Shaheed or Martyr, is described this way by Allah, 'Don't think that those who were killed in Allah's Cause are dead. No they are alive, finding their bounty in the presence of their Lord...the Law of the Land is the Shari'ah of Allah...the duty of the Muslim citizen is to be loyal to the Islamic State."

["What Islam is All About" (most popular Islamic junior high school text in the U.S.—printed in English), 1997]

viii. "The Holy Qur'an spelt out the object of the divine war against Paganism soon after it commanded the Muslims to take recourse to fighting. 'And fight them on until there is no more tumult or oppression'...The Holy Qur'an wishes to see the Muslim armies always in an uppermost, dominating and commanding position over those of their adversaries.... Terror struck into the hearts of the enemies is not only a means, it is the end in itself. Once a condition of terror into the opponent's heart is obtained, hardly anything is left to be achieved. It is the point where the means and the end meet and merge.... Psychological dislocation is temporary; spiritual dislocation is permanent.... To instill terror into the hearts of the enemy, it is essential, in the ultimate analysis, to dislocate his Faith. An invincible Faith is immune to terror.... This rule is fully applicable to nuclear as well as conventional wars." [The Quranic Concept of War, Brigadier General SK Malik, Pakistani Army; Forward by Chief of Staff Pakistani Army Zia ul Haq (who became President of Pakistan), and Preface by Advocate General of Pakistan Brohy who. calls this a "Restatement" of the. Islamic Law of War. This was written in English in 1979 and is DOCTRINE in Pakistan]

e. Jihad as warfare must be fought when the Muslim community has the ability to do so. Even when this is not possible, a standing requirement exists to wage Jihad via the pen or with words. At a minimum, however, all Muslims are under permanent obligation to hate and despise the non-Muslim rule (Jihad of the Heart).

X. Truces

a. In Islamic Law, Muslim fighting forces may only call for a truce when they are in a position of weakness and require time to resupply and rebuild forces. It is a grave concern because it entails nonperformance of jihad.

b. "Truces are permissible, not obligatory. The only one who may effect a truce is the Muslim ruler of a region (or his representative).... There must be some interest served in making a truce other than mere preservation of the status quo. Allah Most High says, 'So do not be fainthearted and call for peace, when it is you who are the uppermost.'

(Qur'an 47:35) Interests that justify making a truce are such things as Muslim weakness because of lack of numbers or materiel, or hope of an enemy becoming Muslim." [Umdat al Salik, Book 0: Jihad, o9.16J]

XI. Lying

a. Islamic Law specifically allows, and in some cases obliges, Muslims to lie to non-Muslims if doing so furthers the cause of Islam.

b. "The Prophet said, 'He who settles disagreements between people to bring about good or says something commendable is not a liar.'" [Sacred Hadith, Bukhari & Muslim]

c. "I did not hear him (the Prophet Muhammad) permit untruth in anything people say except for three things: war, settling disagreements, and a man talking with his wife or she with him." [Sacred Hadith, Muslim]

d. "Speaking is a means to achieve objectives...it is permissible to lie if attaining the goal is permissible...and obligatory to lie if the goal is obligatory." [Imam Abu Hamid Ghazali, Renowned Islamic Jurist, quoted in Umdat al Salik, Sacred Islamic Law, Book R: Holding One's Tongue, r8.2]

XII. Slander

a. Slander in Islamic Law means "to mention anything concerning a person that he would dislike." [Umdat al Salik, r2.2]

b. "As for talebearing, it consists of quoting someone's words to another in a way that worsens relations between them." [Umdat al Salik, r2 .3]

c. "The above define slander and talebearing. As for the ruling on them, it is that they are unlawful, by the consensus of Muslims." [Umdat al Salik, r2.4]

d. Summary—in Islamic Law, anyone who criticizes a Muslim, Islam, or the Prophet is guilty of "Slander." The punishment for slander in Islamic Law is death.

XIII. Apostasy

a. Apostasy is when a Muslim leaves Islam. This is a capital crime and is punishable by death. There is a requirement for the Muslim to be advised of his error before he is killed.

b. "Leaving Islam is the ugliest form of unbelief and the worst." [Umdat al Salik, o8.0]

c. "When a person who has reached puberty and is sane voluntarily apostatizes from Islam, he deserves to be killed. In such a case, it is obligatory for the caliph (or his representative) to ask him to repent and return to Islam. If he does, it is accepted from him, but if he refuses, he is immediately killed.... There is no indemnity for killing an apostate since it is killing someone who deserves to die." [Umdat al Salik, o8.1-o8.4] [232]

This is the current Islamic Agenda in play in 2021 with Iran backing Syria, Lebanon, Gaza, and funding proxy groups throughout the world to advance the caliphate, the one-world movement ruled by Islamic leadership whose main objectives are to annihilate Israel and the United States.

Although some of the Islamist nations are a part of the Ezekiel 38–39 confederacy, they will ultimately be defeated in that campaign. Until then, they are motivated by the same agenda of eliminating the seed of the woman through the same agenda promoted by Haman, who was also based in Persia and plotted the annihilation of the Jews.

13

The Holocaust, the Church, and the Allies

In all of modern history, the greatest attack on the seed line of Messiah was orchestrated by the Nazi[233] regime headed by Adolf Hitler.[234] Many have portrayed him as a madman, but it is clear that he was more committed to his sin than the church was committed to the Lord. Hitler's stated personal goal was to own the largest collection of artifacts of an extinct people.

My Family's Experiences

Many in my age group are referred to as "Baby Boomers";[235] however, there are many who see themselves as the first post-Holocaust[236] generation. That description is most often used by those, like me, who have a family member or members who survived the Holocaust. Here's a look at some of the things my family experienced.

Since my mother's parents emigrated to America in 1904 and half of my father's family fled Hungary in 1934, we were impacted by the loss of extended family in Kiev and Odessa, Ukraine, Austria, and Hungary.

Only one of my grandfather's relatives was the sole survivor of her Austrian family and was reunited with us after being found in a camp for displaced persons. Her name was Gisella.

Gisella and her entire family were taken by the Nazis, but because she was a very adept seamstress and the SS officers liked the way she repaired their uniforms, her life was spared. Each day she was escorted to a sewing machine, but not before her bare feet were beaten until they were bloodied so that she would not attempt to leave her station. The only time she was allowed to leave was to bear witness to one of her relatives being marched to their death. The database at Yad Vashem,[237] the Holocaust Museum, recorded twenty of her family members being put to death. The last displaced persons camp,[238] located in Wels, Germany, closed in 1959. I was only seven years old when Gisella came to live with my grandparents. Even with her very thick Austrian accent, I would spend hours with her listening to her stories. The most notable feature of this 4'10" petite woman was her oddly shaped and oversized shoes.

In October 2012, I took a group to minister at a conference in Odessa, Ukraine, and a part of that trip was a visit to Babi Yar in Kiev, Ukraine, to see the site where many of my grandmother's family members perished. Beginning on September 29, 1941, more than thirty thousand Jews were lined up on the edge of this large ravine, stripped naked, and shot. On that one day, seventy-eight members of my grandmother's family met their death.

After the conference, we traveled to Poland to visit the city of Krakow[239] and tour Auschwitz[240] and Birkenau,[241] where fifty-seven of my grandfather's relatives were marched to their death. As we drove down the streets of Krakow, we could see the rail line used to transport cattle cars filled with Jewish people from all over the region. We passed by homes and churches that were close enough for those inside to hear the cries and see the smoke bellowing from the chimneys of the crematoriums that ran twenty-four hours a day. It would have been impossible not to smell the burning flesh.

As we turned to drive to Auschwitz, we navigated up a city street with houses on either side. The camp immediately came into view. How could those who lived in close proximity to the rail line and could hear the cries of those being led to slaughter claim they didn't know?

Yad Vashem, the Holocaust Memorial Museum, estimates that 1.3 million people were sent to the death camp in occupied Poland. Of this total, nearly 1.1 million were Jews, 960,000 of whom died in the camp. The other group, numbering approximately two hundred thousand people, was predominantly made up of non-Jewish Poles,[242] the mentally challenged, Roma[243] people, homosexuals, and Soviet[244] prisoners of war. Of the total of 1.3 million, only seven thousand were liberated in 1945.

Where Was the Church?

Germany, like the rest of Europe, was primarily Christian when the Nazis rose to power. In 1933, the country had approximately forty-five million Protestant Christians, twenty-two million Catholic Christians, five hundred thousand Jews, and twenty-five Jehovah's Witnesses. Religion was a huge part of people's everyday life and culture.

Those of us who are a part of the first post-Holocaust generation grew up hearing bits and pieces from those willing to discuss their experiences. For many, it was just too difficult—and, in spite of it being a rich part of our history, few could understand how such an atrocity could take place in plain sight. Dr. Michael Rydelnik, professor of Jewish Studies and Bible at Moody Bible Institute, is the son of Holocaust survivors, and makes this statement: "There are two types of Holocaust survivors, those who never speak of the Holocaust and those who only speak about the Holocaust."

In an attempt to understand the sequence of events and the world's response, I felt it best to share exactly what is reflected in the article entitled "The Sounds of Silence: World Responses to the Holocaust" from the Holocaust Survivor Oral History Archive. Who better to tell this story than those who were there?

I. What the Allies Knew and How They Responded:

A. The Newspapers:

1. 1938: There was extensive press coverage by American, British and French newspapers of the attacks on Jews and the anti-Jewish riots during the Kristallnacht.

a. The newspaper accounts prompted President Roosevelt to recall the American Ambassador from Germany for a brief time.

b. Roosevelt also issued a public statement condemning German behavior.

2. 1941: In December, the New York Herald Tribune noted that reports of mistreatment of Jews were no longer news; what was news was the "sheer mass" of those who had already been killed.

3. 1942: American reporters were allowed to stay in Germany until May 1942. They regularly reported the public humiliation and mistreatment of Jews in the streets of Germany.

a. In June 1942, the Polish government in exile reported that the Germans were systematically killing all the Jews of Poland.

1) The New York Times gave the story 17 lines on the bottom of page five.

2) The Daily Telegraph, a London newspaper reported the gassing of 700,000 Jews in a small article in the middle of the paper.

3) A later report of the death of a million Jews got 13 lines on page three of the Los Angeles Times.

b. Almost every newspaper in the United States treated the stories the same way—burying them in short articles in the middle of the papers next to the weather reports or on the comic pages.

1) This included stories with details of deportations to Auschwitz. Massacres of entire communities and eyewitness accounts of mass murder.

2) On April 20,1943, the Detroit Evening Times printed an article whose headline read: "2,000,000 Jews Murdered." The article was two inches long and appeared next to a group of large ads.

RESPONSE:

Denials: Allied government officials, including President Roosevelt, denied the reports of the Holocaust or labeled the newspaper accounts as "unconfirmed."

B. Other Sources of Information:

1. World Jewish Congress: In June 1942, a German industrialist told representatives of this Jewish agency in Switzerland precise details about the "Final Solution." The report was immediately sent to the Allied governments.

RESPONSE:

1. The news was suppressed, that is, blocked, and no action was taken because of the urging of U.S. Secretary of State Cordell Hull and later Acting Secretary of State Sumner Welles. On December 17, 1942, the American and British governments announced that the Nazis were murdering the Jews of Europe. In the U.S., officials still voiced doubts in private and sometimes in public. By the time this statement was issued, over three million European Jews were already dead.

2. U.S. Air Force: In the fall of 1943, American reconnaissance, or scouting planes, flew over Birkenau and photographed the gas chambers. The photos showed lines of people moving into a gas chamber.

RESPONSE: When the reconnaissance photos were sent to the U.S. Department of War, the Assistant Secretary of the War Department, John McCloy, insisted they be kept secret and no action taken.

3. Polish Underground: Reports for members of the Polish underground resistance movement against the Germans began arriving in Allied countries starting in 1941. These reports, along with photographs or mass graves and mass murders, were circulated among government offices.

RESPONSE:

a. All reports from the Polish underground and the World Jewish Congress were kept secret by Allied governments.

b. All requests for aid from Allied armed forces were refused because the reports were either denied or called "unconfirmed."

1) When Polish and Jewish leaders asked the U.S for planes to bomb the gas chambers or the railroads at Auschwitz, they were told it was a British responsibility. All requests were turned down by the Assistant Secretary of War, John McCloy.

2) Prime Minister Winston Churchill demanded that Auschwitz be bombed. But his orders were undermined by the Foreign Office and Air Ministry. The British told Jewish and Polish leaders that such bombings were "outside the realm of tactical efficiency"; in other words, they refused on military grounds.

3) Both governments claimed that these were non-military issues, not directly related to the war efforts, and that the only way to destroy Auschwitz was to destroy the Germans in the war. Auschwitz, it seemed, was a "civilian target."

WHEN THE ALLIES REFUSED TO BOMB AUSCHWITZ IN 1944, THE NAZIS WERE KILLING 15,000

JEWS EACH DAY. ONE BOMB, DESTROYING ONE GAS CHAMBER OR ONE RAILROAD LINE, MIGHT HAVE SAVED THOUSANDS OF LIVES.

4. Jan Karski: This Polish messenger between the underground and the Polish government in exile was taken into the Warsaw Ghetto on two separate occasions in 1943.

a. The two Jews who smuggled him in and out pleaded with him to tell his story to the outside world.

b. Karski did what they asked—even speaking personally to President Roosevelt.

RESPONSE:

After listening to his moving and impassioned plea for help, President Roosevelt told Jan Karski that the U.S. and the Allies were helping the Jews by winning the war. They, therefore, had to focus all their efforts on fighting the Germans, not rescuing the Jews.

ROOSEVELT INSISTED THE WAR AND THE HOLOCAUST WERE THE SAME. TO HIM, FIGHTING THE GERMANS WAS AUTOMATICALLY HELPING THE JEWS. THIS OPINION ALLOWED THE HOLOCAUST TO CONTINUE AND RESULTED IN THE DEATHS OF HUNDREDS OF THOUSANDS OF INNOCENT PEOPLE.

5. Romanian Government: In 1943, the Romanian government revealed the extent of the massacres of the Jews of Romania to American Officials. The Romanians offered to aid in the rescue if 72,000 Jews from the region of Transnistria. They asked only for the cost of the passage of each person out of Romania (about $130 per person).

RESPONSE:

The American authorities refused to consider or publicize the offer. Over 125,000 Jews died in Transnistria between 1943 and the end of 1944.

6. Bermuda Conference: With public pressure increasing, especially in England, the American State Department met with the British Foreign Office at the Bermuda Conference on Refugees on April 19, 1943. Coincidentally, it was the day the Warsaw Ghetto Rebellion began. The members of the conference were to discuss what should be done about the refugees of the Nazi invasions-especially the Jews.

RESPONSE:

Nothing was accomplished. The American and British representatives decided the following: There would be no negotiations with the Nazis. Nor would there be any contact with Jewish and other refugees. No food would be sent to the ghettos or camps. No ships would be made available for those who were able to escape on their own. The America and British people were told that important, secret decisions were reached to help rescue the refugees. Both governments lied to their people.

7. Adolf Eichmann: In 1944, Adolf Eichmann, in charge of Jewish deportations, contacted the British and offered to exchange one million Jews for 10,000 Allied trucks.

RESPONSE:

The Allies refused. When he was asked why he has refused to negotiate with Eichmann, Lord Moyne, British Deputy Minister of State, later responded: "What would I do with one million Jews? Where would I put them?"

8. War Refugee Board: Three members of the U.S. Treasury Department had learned of the murder of the Jews through all

the reports received by the government offices. They prepared a "Report for the Secretary of the Treasury on this Country's Acquiescence in the Murder of the Jews." As Secretary of the Treasury of the United States, Henry Morgenthau thus learned the fate of the Jews. He changed the title of the report and presented it to President Roosevelt as "A Report to the President."

RESPONSE:

As a result, in January 1944, the President had the War Refugee Board formed "to take all measures consistent with the successful prosecution of the war" to "rescue the victims of enemy oppression." The Board was given a free hand to negotiate with foreign governments, including enemies, for the rescue and/or relief of those "victims." Although the WRB rescued some Jews, by the time they began their efforts most of Hungary's Jews had been killed.

9. Escaped Prisoners: Two escaped prisoners from Auschwitz managed to reach high officials in the British and American governments through representatives of the War Relief Board in Spring 1944. They gave exact statistics and descriptions of what was happening to the Jews of Europe. In June 1944, two months after German forces had occupied Hungary, their report reached President Roosevelt. Deportations of Hungarian Jews to the gas chambers at Auschwitz had already begun.

RESPONSE:

At first, the report of the two escapees from Auschwitz was ignored, kept secret or denied. It finally became public when it was sent to the leaders of every government. The pope received the report. As a result:

a. President Roosevelt issued a public warning to the German and the Hungarian governments about punishment for what he called the "systematic persecution of helpless minority groups" and the "insane desire to wipe out the Jewish race." He warned that "the criminals" would pay.

b. British Foreign Secretary Anthony Eden also made a public statement to the British Parliament condemning the Nazis.

c. The pope instructed Vatican diplomats to hide Hungarian Jews and warned members of the Hungarian government not to cooperate with the Germans.

d. On July 2, 1944, American planes bombed Budapest, the capital of Hungary.

e. In September 1944, British planes bombed the factories and railway yards at Auschwitz.

C. Some Reasons for the Allied Responses:

1. War Propaganda: Newspapers like the Daily Telegraph had reported stories of German atrocities in World War I. These had been proven false. Reports of mass killings in World War II were considered a return of war atrocity propaganda.

2. Disbelief: Reports of mass killings, extermination camps, gas chambers, mass graves and crematoria were simply unbelievable. People found it impossible to accept that such inhuman behavior could occur on such a grand scale.

3. German Denials: The Germans denied the reports, and the Allies chose to believe the official denials.

4. Anti-Semitism: Statements like that of Lord Moyne indicate that there was anti-Semitism among the Allied Leaders.

5. "Useless People": Some of the Allied officials seemed to have expressed the belief that the Jews were a "useless" people— they had no state, no political or military power.

THE LAST REASON IS PERHAPS THE MOST DISTURBING BECAUSE IT SUGGESTS THAT THE MORALITY OF SOME ALLIED BUREAUCRATS WAS NOT UNLIKE THE MORALITY OF GERMAN BUREAUCRATS.

II. What the Christian Churches Knew and How They Responded:

A. The Vatican: There is much conflicting evidence over the Vatican's, that is, the pope's response to the murder of the Jews. During World War II, the Vatican made no pronouncement against the "Final Solution." Yet, there is much evidence that the pope directed the rescue of Jews when he could.

1. The Pope: The Catholic popes during World War II and the Holocaust were Pius XI (1922–1939) and Pius XII (1939–1958).

2. The Concordat: In 1933, Pope Pius XI negotiated a Concordat or agreement with Hitler. The Vatican recognized the Nazi government thus giving it Catholic approval. The Vatican also disbanded all Catholic political parties. The pope believed it was his duty to protect the 30 million German Catholics by maintaining a good relationship with Hitler. Hitler agreed to leave the Catholic Churches alone. Catholics, as Catholics, would remain out of politics; the Nazis, as Nazis, would remain out of religious issues.

a. Papal Silence: By signing the Concordat, Pope Pius XI hoped to silence the Catholic opponents of Hitler because he believed they were endangering the other German Catholics.

b. Vatican Opposition to the Third Reich: In general, Catholic opposition to the Nazis was based on fear of Nazi interference in Catholic matters: closing Catholic schools, disbanding Catholic youth groups, attacking Catholic doctrine. The Vatican did not openly oppose anti-Semitism.

3. "Final Solution": By the summer of 1942, the pope and other leading Catholics knew about the "Final Solution." They knew that Jews who were deported to Poland were not only being used for labor but were being annihilated there in a policy known as the "Final Solution."

4. The Fate of Italian Jews: In October 1943, after Italy was occupied by the Germans, the SS began the first round-ups of Jews in Rome. The Germans scheduled over 8,000 Jews for deportation. By the end of October, 1,007 Jews had been sent to Auschwitz.

a. German officials were worried that the Vatican would publicly protest the treatment of the Italian Jews.

1) When similar events had occurred in France, Catholic bishops there had staged open protests.

2) The French bishops and some Italian clergymen began to put pressure on the Pope to protest against the unchristian treatment of Italian Jews.

b. Catholic priests and people on the staff of the Vatican hindered the round up by hiding Jews and protecting them.

c. Of the 8,000 Jews marked for deportation, 7,000 were rescued from the SS—seven out of every eight Jews in Rome. Catholic clergymen had been

very important in the rescue.

d. Papal Silence: The pope had said nothing about the fate of the Italian Jews.

1) Many Catholic clergymen from around the world called on the pope to speak out.

2) Protestant leaders began to criticize the pope's silence as Jews were being rounded up "right beneath his window."

3) The pope, however, remained silent. After the first round-up of Jews in October 1943, the German Ambassador to the Vatican noted with relief that the pope had "done everything in order not to burden relations with the German government and German agencies in Rome."

5. Rescue: In 1944, after the secret publication of the report of the two escaped Auschwitz prisoners, the pope approved the protection of Jews by Vatican diplomats in Hungary. With this single action, thousands of lives were saved.

VATICAN SOURCES ESTIMATE POPE PIUS XII WAS RESPONSIBLE FOR SECRETLY DIRECTING OR APPROVING CATHOLIC ASSISTANCE TO HUNDREDS OF THOUSANDS OF JEWS. HAD THE POPE MORE OPENLY AND OFFICIALLY CONDEMNED NAZI ACTIONS, MORE JEWS MIGHT HAVE BEEN SAVED.

6. Some Reasons for the Vatican Responses:

a. Fear of Reprisals: The Vatican feared Nazi reprisals against German Catholics and for that reason tried to preserve good diplomatic relations with Germany.

b. Fear for the Jews: Some scholars argue that Pope Pius XII believed that a formal protest from him would have caused more harm to the Jews and endangered Catholics as well. Vatican sources say he knew that Hitler would not have changed his anti-Jewish policies.

c. Catholic Lands: There was concern in the Vatican that the Nazi government would seize Catholic lands—including Vatican City—when the Germans occupied Italy in 1943.

d. Anti-Communism: The Catholic Church was strongly anti-Communist and anti- Socialist. The Vatican saw Hitler as a safeguard against Communism.

B. Individual Protests: Many individual Catholic, including clergy, actively spoke out against the persecution and murder of the Jews.

1. German Catholic Opponents of Nazism: Many German Catholic leaders had opposed Nazism in the 1920s and 1930s. They were among the first concentration camp prisoners in 1933.

a. One priest, Bernhard Lichtenberg, after the Kristallnacht, told his congregation: "Outside this church the synagogue is burning, and that also is a house of God."

b. Bishop Faulhaber of Munich condemned Nazi racist teachings.

c. The British Catholic Archbishop of Westminster and the Anglican Archbishop of Canterbury issued strong letters of protest to their own government and to the German governments.

d. Cardinal Archbishop of Lvov, Count Andreas Szeptycki, ordered his clergy to save Jews. The Ursuline sisters and some village priests did the same.

e. Individual Catholic priests and higher clergymen all over Europe hid Jews, helped them escape and often hindered the German efforts. Four thousand priests were murdered by the Nazis, many for hiding Jews or opposing the "Final Solution."

C. Some

No major Protestant church took an official stand against the persecution of the Jews. There were, however, just as among Catholic, thousands of individuals who opposed the "Final Solution" and helped Jews when and where they could.

1. Individuals: Individual Protestant ministers and congregations protested against Nazi anti-Jewish policies in Germany and later in the occupied countries.

a. Andre Trocme: Andre Trocme, a Protestant (Huguenot) minister, led the village of Le Chambon in Southern France in their efforts to rescue Jews from the "Final Solution."

b. Archbishop Damskinos: In Greece, the Greek Orthodox Archbishop Damskinos of Athens helped to rescue Jews by declaring them Christians and/or by hiding them in Greek Orthodox churches.

Protestant Responses to the Holocaust: Just as with the Catholic Church, 2. The Confessing Church: In 1934, Pastor Martin Niemoeller, fearing the Nazi takeover of the Protestant churches, founded the Confessing Church in Germany.

a. Niemoeller and Barth: Leading members of this church, like Niemoeller and Karl Barth, spoke out publicly against the Nazis but not against persecution of the Jews.

b. The Barmen Confession: Leading theologians, Niemoeller and Barth, did not mention the persecution of the Jews in the "Barmen Confession," their formal declaration of principles. Barth later admitted that his church's neglect of this issue was a serious omission.

c. Dietrich Bonhoeffer: Dietrich Bonhoeffer stated that a good Christian must protest against evil state policies, even those outside the realm of religion. He was murdered in a Nazi prison.

d. Protestant Opponents of Nazism: Thousands of ministers and pastors were imprisoned in concentration camps. About 500 died.

3. Church Policy: As Church policy, no Protestant church declared that Nazism or the murder of the Jews were unchristian or immoral.

D. Some Reasons for the Protestant Responses:

1. Danger: Protestant churches felt endangered by the Nazis.

2. Religious Principles: Some Protestants actively opposed anti-Jewish policies on religious grounds. One pastor quoted Jesus' words on the good Samaritan who had helped a Jew attacked by robbers: "Go and do as he (the Samaritan) did."

III. Summary

Shmuel Zygelboim wrote that the primary responsibility for the murder of the Jews was with the murderers themselves. But, what drove him to despair and suicide was the realization that the Allies, too, shared the responsibility by refusing to help when and where they could.

THE PRIMARY RESPONSIBILITY FOR THE MURDER OF THE JEWS LIES WITH THE PERPETRATORS, THE GERMAN DESTRUCTION MACHINE. BUT THE SECONDARY RESPONSIBILITY COMES FROM INDIFFERENCE AND REFUSAL TO ACT. THE

ALLIES DID NOT DETERMINE "WHO SHALL LIVE AND WHO SHALL DIE," BUT THEY WERE INDIRECTLY INVOLVED IN SUCH DECISIONS. CHURCH OFFICIALS OF DIFFERENT CHRISTIAN DENOMINATIONS DID NOT CONTROL THOSE LIFE AND DEATH DECISIONS. YET, SOME OF THEM FAILED AS MORAL LEADERS OF THE CHRISTIAN WORLD.[245]

Catholic Church Complicity in the Holocaust

From its very creation, the Catholic Church has made every effort remove itself from its Jewish foundation into the creation of a religious nation-state that wields power over 1.2 billion members. Their history, as outlined in chapters 8–10, reaches the pinnacle of anti-Semitism upon examination of their role in the Holocaust. One-third of the Jewish population was murdered and the seed line of Messiah sustained its most devastating blow in all of history. What began as silence morphed into support and pastoral service to the Nazi regime. To the Jewish world, Catholicism is Christianity regardless of the Reformation. No other branch of Christianity has a single leader who is as visible and holds as much power as the pope.

The public denial of the Catholic Church's complicity in the Holocaust[246] remained the party line up until the early unveiling of Pope Pius XII.[247] Under normal circumstances, papers covering Pius' papacy would have been under lock and key until 2028, or seventy years after the end of his tenure. But last year, at a gathering marking the eightieth anniversary of Pius' election, Pope Francis[248] announced the archives' impending opening, telling those gathered that the Church "is not afraid of history; rather, she loves it." Speaking with Reuters' Philip Pullella[249] in February, Father Norbert Hofmann,[250] the Vatican's top official in charge of religious relations with Jews, added, "I don't think [researchers] will find a smoking gun."[251]

"In 'confession of guilt,' German Catholic Church admits 'complicity' with Nazis." The caption reads, "After decades of ambivalence, document prepared by clergy says hundreds of priests gave spiritual guidance to Hitler's soldiers on front, 'lent war an additional sense of purpose.'"

In a new report after decades of ambivalence, Germany's council of Catholic bishops has finally admitted to the church's complicity in the actions of the Nazi regime during World War II, The Times reported Friday.

The 23-page document by the council reportedly states, "Inasmuch as the bishops did not oppose the war with a clear 'no,' and most of them bolstered the [German nation's] will to endure, they made themselves complicit in the war."

This included providing hundreds of priests who joined Nazi soldiers on the front lines of the war to offer spiritual guidance between 1939 and 1945 and the conversion of thousands of church properties into military hospitals where tens of thousands of nuns worked as nurses, says the document, produced 75 years after the collapse of Hitler's Third Reich.

It added: "The bishops may not have shared the Nazis' justification for the war on the grounds of racial ideology, but their words and their images gave succor both to soldiers and the regime prosecuting the war, as they lent the war an additional sense of purpose."

One Catholic Church official cited by The Times called the report a "confession of guilt" by the church.

The document said most German bishops, motivated by nationalism and anti-communist sentiment and a desire to preserve the church by avoiding confrontation with the Nazis, told their followers to support the regime during the war.

"Even if we can perceive that the bishops' perspective on events shifted over the course of the war, they did not pay enough attention to the suffering of others," The Times quoted Heiner Wilmer, bishop of Hildesheim and head of the conference's foreign affairs committee, as saying.

The Times report came days after the Washington Post reported that researchers studying the newly opened Vatican archives of Pius XII have found evidence that the World War II-era pope knew about the mass killing of Jews from his own sources but kept the matter from the US government.

The archives were opened on March 2, but closed soon after due to the coronavirus crisis. Many of the 200 scholars who had applied for access delayed their trips. However, a German team lead by award-winning religious historian Hubert Wolf from the University of Münster made a start and has already found some damning discoveries.

Some Jewish groups and historians have said Pius, who was pope from 1939 to 1958, stayed silent during the Holocaust and didn't do enough to save lives. His defenders at the Vatican and beyond say he used quiet diplomacy and encouraged convents and other religious institutes to hide Jews.

In September 1942, a US diplomat gave the Vatican a secret report prepared by the Jewish Agency that documented the mass murder of some 100,000 Jews from the Warsaw Ghetto. It also said some 50,000 Jews were killed in Lviv in German-occupied Ukraine. The US asked if the Vatican could confirm the report from its own sources among Catholics, but were told they could not.

However, in the week the archive was open, Wolf and his team discovered a note confirming that Pius had read the American report and also two instances where the Vatican had independently corroborated reports of the killings.

Pope Benedict XVI moved Pius one step closer to possible sainthood in December 2009, when he confirmed that Pius lived a life of "heroic" Christian virtue. All that is needed now is for the Vatican to determine a "miracle" occurred. Pope Francis said in 2014 that the miracle hadn't been identified, suggesting that the process would remain on hold, at least for now.[252]

Out of The Ashes

Who hath heard such a thing? Who hath seen such things? Shall the earth be made to bring forth in one day? Or shall a nation be born at once? For as soon as Zion travailed, she brought forth her children. (Isaiah 66:8)

Out of the ashes of the Holocaust, the State of Israel was formed, giving the Jewish people their own homeland. For the Jewish world, this was a dream come true and the fulfillment of God's covenant promise, but to the rest of the world, the centralized gathering of an ever-growing Jewish population would allow the seed line of Messiah to become a target that would come under frequent attack. The regathering of the outcasts of Israel would become the blessing of God that came with a steep price. Prophetically, the birth of Israel fulfilled the fig tree prophecy from Matthew:

...it is the hope and promise of God that all of Israel will be saved.

Immediately after the tribulation of those days shall the sun be darkened, and the moon shall not give her light, and the stars shall fall from heaven, and the powers of the heavens shall be shaken:

And then shall appear the sign of the Son of man in heaven: and then shall all the tribes of the earth mourn, and they shall see the Son of man coming in the clouds of heaven with power and great glory.

And he shall send his angels with a great sound of a trumpet, and they shall gather together his elect from the four winds, from one end of heaven to the other.

Now learn a parable of the fig tree; When his branch is yet tender, and putteth forth leaves, ye know that summer is nigh:

So likewise ye, when ye shall see all these things, know that it is near, even at the doors.

Verily I say unto you, this generation shall not pass, till all these things be fulfilled.

Heaven and earth shall pass away, but my words shall not pass away. (Matthew 24:29–35)

This would start the clock for the great day of the Coming of the Lord, the Tribulation spoken of in Daniel.

In the most dramatic attempt to rid the world of the Jews in the modern era, Satan's plan to use the power of the Third Reich combined with the complicity of the silent church was defeated. God had reserved for Himself a remnant of survivors that would use this atrocity to bring about the birth of the Jewish State, the Promised Land. Although God began the ingathering of the Jews in Israel in unbelief, it is the hope and promise of God that all of Israel will be saved.

And so all Israel shall be saved: as it is written, There shall come out of Sion the Deliverer, and shall turn away ungodliness from Jacob:

For this is my covenant unto them, when I shall take away their sins. (Romans 11:26–27)

Maranatha (Aramaic, "Come Lord")
Bo Yeshua Bo (Hebrew, "Come Jesus Come")

14

Rise in Anti-Semitism

"Anti-Semitism is often considered the world's longest form of hatred; it has existed for over two millennia."[253] With this statement, Walter Reich, former director of the US Holocaust Memorial Museum, was referring to the systemic anti-Semitism dating back to the crucifixion of Yeshua/Jesus. What started as blame for the killing of Jesus has ignited a global conflagration of anti-Semitism that has exponentially grown since the birth of Israel in 1948. What began as a hatred toward the Jews has now become intermixed with an indelible connection to Israel and Middle East politics.

An examination of both is required to understand the divide in theological anti-Semitism and social justice-based anti-Semitism. The former is summarized in replacement theology and other error-filled doctrine, while the latter is more politically charged and tied to Israel's position on Palestinian matters.

Theological Anti-Semitism: Replacement Theology (Supersessionism)

Around the year AD 200, a new theological conviction began to sweep Gentile Christianity, one that had to rationalize and justify what was already happening. In later centuries, this system was called "supersessionism" or "replacement theology." According to replacement theology, in His anger with the Jews for killing the Messiah, God revoked His covenant with Israel. Since they were no longer the covenant people, the Jews lost their birthright and, as a people, were deprived of divine grace. No longer the chosen people, they had to remain in a state of collective sin under condemnation from God. In their place was a new "chosen people," the Church, seen as the "New Israel"—replacing "Israel of the flesh."

Church Fathers Turn against Israel

The **Letter to Barnabas,**[254] written around AD 100, though not officially part of the Bible, was understood to be inspired by God and considered an important document of the apostolic times. The letter speaks about the loss of the Jewish birthright and, because they had killed the Messiah, the Jews were excluded from the people of God and the Church.

Irenaeus (AD 135–202) strongly emphasized that Christians should avoid any kind of relationship with Jews in order to prevent confusion in their faith. He wanted the Church to be cleansed from all Jewish elements.

For **Ambrose**[255] (AD 337–397), it wasn't enough to affirm that the Jews were no longer a part of the Church; the Church must also exert the judgment of God upon them.

Augustine (AD 354–430) wrote that Christians were not allowed to kill Jews. However, God had to keep the Jews alive to use them as a negative example of divine judgment on a nation that abandons Him. Thus, Christians felt authorized to persecute the Jews without killing them.

John Chrysostom[256] (AD 344 or 355–407) hated Jews and preached eight famous sermons full of venom against them. He warned his listeners to have nothing to do with the Jews—neither in their daily contact nor by visiting their synagogues or participating in religious occasions. For him, it was necessary that Christians avoid any kind of contact with Jews in order to avoid getting "infected with the Jewish disease."

All of these theologians had great revelations concerning the Kingdom of God. But concerning the role of the Jews in God's plan for salvation, they were blind. The devil fomented this, knowing that as long as Christians fail to understand the "mystery of Israel," he would remain dominant in the world.

Replacement Theology Becomes Anti-Semitic Politics

The replacement theology of the church fathers established principles that guided Christian practice and politics for centuries. Church and state legislation against the Jews followed. From the third century onward, a systematic "cleansing" of the Church from all its Jewish heritage began. From synod to convention, anti-Semitic legislation became stricter to make sure that nothing of Jewish life remained in the Church.

Emperor Constantine, who stopped all persecution against Christians and began to use the Christian Church as a unifying factor for the Roman Empire, forced all Gentile bishops at the First Council of Nicea (AD 325) to "cleanse" the Church from all things Jewish. He ordered (AD 321) Sunday instead of Shabbat (Saturday) as the holy day of the week and changed the dates for Easter so that its relationship with Passover would be lost.

In AD 365, the Synod of Laodicea ordered all Christians who still kept Shabbat in their private homes to be publicly excommunicated from the Church and, in some cases, even sentenced to death.

There were more than six hundred thousand Jews in Spain and Portugal before 1492 when they were expelled from their countries or forced to convert to Christianity. The Jews who were forced to convert and be baptized were called *Marranos* (pig). Most lived a double life.

Acting as Catholics outwardly, they remained Jews in the privacy of their homes. Terrorized by the Holy Inquisition, thousands fled to the colonies of the Americas in hope of freedom. But the Inquisition followed them to South America, and the persecution continued there. Based on the Nicene decision, the Inquisition forced the new converts to deny any link with Judaism.

Anti-Jewish ideology is also found in almost all streams of Protestantism, beginning with Martin Luther (1483–1546) and his anti-Semitic rhetoric during the later years of his ministry. Frustrated about the small number of converted Jews after years of biblical preaching and reformation, he finally ordered the persecution of Jews and justified these atrocities in his sermons and writings influencing future Protestant generations. The poison of replacement theology is still working in many Protestant denominations.

> *The poison of replacement theology is still working in many Protestant denominations.*

The End of the Jewish Part of the Church and the Consequences

It was no longer possible to believe in Christ and remain a Jew. A Jew who believed in Yeshua had to deny all his Jewishness. Replacement theology, therefore, brought two very tragic consequences:

- The persecution of the Jews in general.
- The extinction of the Messianic Jewish presence in the Church.

This extinction was catastrophic not only for the Jewish part of the Church, but also for the Gentile part. As a result of this loss, the Gentile

Church became disoriented and incomplete. The separation between Jews and Gentiles was the Church's first division.

Numerous other divisions followed. This separation worked like a virus and contaminated the Church. It was perpetuated in every following division according to the model of replacement theology. Even though it may not be apparent at first sight, this replacement strategy is a fundamental characteristic operating within every Christian division. There are more than thirty thousand different denominations—and in some way, each one believes it is "the true Church."

The loss of the Jewish component not only caused divisions, but also produced many other negative consequences. If it is true that we are now part of the "commonwealth of Israel" (Ephesians.2:12), and if it is true that our identity as Jewish and non-Jewish believers lies in the fact that we have been grafted into the olive tree (Romans 11), replacement theology has robbed us of our foundations.

Can Christians Understand the Bible without the Jews?

The lack of a Hebraic mindset has resulted in much misunderstanding and misinterpretation of the Hebrew Scriptures of both the Old and the New Testaments. Although the New Testament Scriptures were written in Greek, the original text was construed according to the Hebrew worldview of its original authors. In the following centuries, this fact provoked endless and unresolved debates among theologians.

As a consequence, many divisions within the Church occurred because each stream had a different mindset when it came to interpreting the Scriptures. Like Karl Barth (1886–1968), other theologians of the twentieth century stated that the Jewish issue is at the heart of many of the ecumenical problems we face. Unless this first division is addressed and healed, all the efforts to foster unity in the divided Body of Christ will continue to be frustrated.

Wolves in Sheep's Clothing

The most disturbing part of all of this are those who masquerade as friends of Israel, yet believe they have replaced Israel. They raise funds in support of humanitarian aid and establish high-level political connections, but prohibit the preaching of the gospel in Israel. Some who raise millions of dollars in support of Israel are actually enemies of the gospel. Through the widespread use of media showing pictures of Holocaust survivors and Russian immigrants struggling in Israel, they appeal to the hearts of well-meaning Christians and then channel a portion of the funds to organizations that persecute the advancement of the gospel in Israel.

> *The New Testament was written in Greek by Hebrew thinkers and Jewish followers of Jesus. The Bible is not a work of Greek literature or philosophy.*

Others raise humanitarian aid and, undoubtedly, they make a positive contribution to the physical well-being of those in need, but they are playing right into the hands of Satan's plan to eliminate the seed line of Messiah by filling their stomachs and clothing their bodies, but depriving them of the truth of the gospel. They claim to love Israel, but are loving Israel to death.

Dual-Covenant Theology

Although there have been many denials made publicly that certain well-recognized ministers do not believe that the Jewish people have their own covenant and that Jesus did not come to be the Messiah to the Jews, their fundraising, humanitarian-aid arms are told to steer clear of anything to do with the gospel. In essence, they have become a public charity for Israel—feeding their bellies, but starving their souls. Yet, in many settings, they have stated that the Jews are saved by their own covenant with Abraham.

Both replacement theology, which is adopted by most mainstream denominations, and dual covenant theology are representative of Christian theological anti-Semitism.

Church-Supported Anti-Semitism: The Boycott, Divest, and Sanction Movement (BDS)

Boycott, Divestment, Sanctions (BDS) is a Palestinian-led movement for freedom, justice and equality. BDS upholds the simple principle that Palestinians are entitled to the same rights as the rest of humanity.

Israel is occupying and colonizing Palestinian land, discriminating against Palestinian citizens of Israel and denying Palestinian refugees the right to return to their homes. Inspired by the South African anti-apartheid movement, the BDS call urges action to pressure Israel to comply with international law.

For nearly seventy years, Israel has denied Palestinians their fundamental rights and has refused to comply with international law.

Israel maintains a regime of settler colonialism, apartheid and occupation over the Palestinian people. This is only possible because of international support. Governments fail to hold Israel to account, while corporations and institutions across the world help Israel to oppress Palestinians.

Because those in power refuse to act to stop this injustice, Palestinian civil society has called for a global citizens' response of solidarity with the Palestinian struggle for freedom, justice and equality.

BDS is now a vibrant global movement made up of unions, academic associations, churches and grassroots movements across the world. Since its launch in 2005, BDS is having a major impact and is effectively challenging international support for Israeli apartheid and settler-colonialism.[257]

The inherent problem with the BDS movement lies in the fact that there are no such people in history known as "Palestinians."[258] There is no such thing as a Palestinian history, and no Palestinian language exists. There has never been any independent, sovereign Palestinian state in all of recorded history—let alone an Arab independent state of Palestine.

We would search in vain if we were to look for Palestinian Arab coinage or Palestinian Arab archaeological artifacts specifically related to any Palestinian Arab king or ancient leader. But what we would find are coins, pottery, and ancient scrolls, all providing conclusive, empirical, and millennial evidence of Jewish civilization dotting the land known correctly as "Israel," not "Palestine."

"There is no such thing as Palestine in history, absolutely not."
—Professor Philip Hitti, Arab historian, 1946

The present-day, so-called Palestinians are an Arab people sharing an overwhelmingly Muslim Arab culture, ethnicity, and language identical to their fellow Arabs in the Middle East and North Africa, with few, if any, distinctions.

Many non-governmental organizations (NGOs) that claim to promote human rights and humanitarian agendas in the context of the Arab-Israeli conflict often use anti-semitic themes and imagery to demonize the Jewish people and state of Israel.

This "new anti-semitism" is evidenced in NGO political campaigns based on the 2001 Durban Conference, including the boycott, divestment, and sanctions movement (BDS) movement and legal attacks ("lawfare") against Israeli officials and companies that do business with Israel.

Contrary to NGO claims that they are engaging in "legitimate criticism" of Israel, the NGO rhetoric, publications, and activities often violate accepted standards, including the EU and U.S. definitions of anti-Semitism.

> "It is common knowledge that Palestine is nothing but Southern Syria."[259]

However, despite the extensive evidence of NGO antisemitism, governments continue to fund these groups, often claiming that the funding is intended for distinct "projects" unrelated to the grantee's wider agenda and expressions of antisemitism. However, funders are enablers, and share full responsibility for the activities of their grantees.

The ongoing government funding for NGOs that engage in antisemitic activities and use antisemitic rhetoric highlights the persistent double standard: Hatred of Jews is tolerated in a way that would be unthinkable for other racial, ethnic, or religious groups; moreover, Jewish and Israeli targets are often denied the right to define what constitutes discrimination against them.[260]

Today, many churches find themselves on the wrong side of both history and the Bible. Since there is no such thing as a Palestinian either in history or in the Bible, the following denominations have engaged in support of the BDS movement, which is patently anti-Semitic and advances Satan's plan of turning believers in the Jewish Messiah into advocates for a nonexistent people group who have systematically attacked Israel and launched over twenty thousand rockets onto Israeli soil. As of February 2019, a total of ten major US denominations have gone a step beyond statements of affirmation; they are now materially participating, to some degree, in the BDS movement, which aims to hold Israel accountable to international law. These are the Alliance of Baptists, Church of the United Brethren in Christ, Religious Society of Friends (Quakers), Mennonite Church USA, Presbyterian Church (USA), Roman Catholic Church, Unitarian Universalist Association, United Church of Christ, and United Methodist Church, as well as the World Communion of Reformed Churches (a confederation that overlaps some of the above). These numbers represent over 1.5 billion Christians whose denominations support the agenda of BDS. These are also the same denominations that subscribe to replacement theology.

Systemic Rise in Anti-Semitism

The Anti-Defamation League's (ADL[261]) most recent "Audit of Anti-Semitic[262] Incidents in the United States" recorded more than 2,100 acts of assault, vandalism, and harassment, an increase of 12 percent over the previous year.

> This is the highest level of anti-Semitic incidents since ADL's tracking began in 1979. The year included five fatalities directly linked to anti-Semitic violence and another ninety-one individuals targeted in physical assaults. Assault, harassment, and vandalism against Jews remain at near-historic levels in the US. The deadly attacks in synagogues in Pittsburgh, Pennsylvania, and Poway, California, have made American Jews feel more vulnerable than they've felt in decades.

In its attempt to stem the rise in anti-Semitism in America, the US Senate passed by a voice vote on June 14, 2021, a resolution (S.Res.252 www.congress.gov):

Unequivocally condemning the recent rise in antisemitic violence and harassment targeting Jewish Americans, and standing in solidarity with those affected by antisemitism, and for other purposes.

Whereas antisemitism remains a serious and growing danger for Jews in the United States and around the world;

Whereas, in May 2021, antisemitic incidents and rhetoric have surged in the United States and around the world as hostilities between Hamas and Israel escalated;

Whereas, since the beginning of 2021, there has been an increase in acts of antisemitism, including—

(1) individuals in London calling for Jewish "daughters to be raped";

(2) a German synagogue being pelted with rocks;

(3) an attack on Jewish diners in Los Angeles, California;

(4) fireworks hurled at a crowd in New York City, New York;

(5) synagogues in Tucson, Arizona, and Skokie, Illinois, being vandalized;

(6) Pakistan's Foreign Minister Shah Mahmood Qureshi's claim in an interview that Israel "controls the media" and has "deep pockets," perpetuating an antisemitic conspiracy theory; and

(7) Turkey's President Recep Tayyip Erdogan's invocation of the blood libel myth, which has historically been used to justify violence against Jews;

Whereas such antisemitic incidents are part of a broader increase in the number and intensity of antisemitic incidents in the United States and around the world, as evidenced by—

(1) studies by the Kantor Center for the Study of Contemporary European Jewry, finding that violent antisemitic attacks worldwide rose 18 percent in 2019 and shifted online in 2020

during the COVID–19 pandemic, which resulted in antisemitic conspiracy theories related to the pandemic proliferating; and

(2) hate crime statistics collected by the Federal Bureau of Investigation, demonstrating—

(A) a 14-percent increase in antisemitic hate crimes in the United States in 2019; and

(B) that Jewish Americans were the target of 60.2 percent of all religiously motivated hate crimes in 2019, despite accounting for 2 percent of the population of the United States;

Whereas Holocaust denial and distortion, including intentional efforts to excuse or minimize the impact of the Holocaust, dishonors those who were persecuted and murdered and reinforces the need for advancing accurate Holocaust education globally;

Whereas, over the course of the past decade, Holocaust distortion has grown in intensity;

Whereas protecting the history of the Holocaust and recognizing and confronting Holocaust denial and distortion is critical to preventing antisemitism;

Whereas Jewish houses of worship are increasingly targets of violent attacks in the United States, as evidenced by the deadly assaults on synagogues in Pittsburgh, Pennsylvania, in 2018 and Poway, California, in 2019;

Whereas, in October 2020, the Department of Homeland Security warned that "racially and ethnically motivated violent extremists—specifically white supremacist extremists—will remain the most persistent and lethal threat in the [United States] Homeland";

Whereas the Nonprofit Security Grant Program of the Department of Homeland Security provides critical funding to support physical security enhancements to Jewish organizations and institutions, including synagogues, that are at high risk of a terrorist attack or targeted violence;

Whereas the United States has played a crucial leadership role in combating antisemitism internationally, including by working to promote Holocaust education, improve the safety and security of at-risk Jewish communities, combat online radicalization, ensure foreign public officials and faith leaders condemn antisemitic discourse, and strengthen foreign judicial systems in their prosecution of antisemitic incidents;

Whereas section 59 of the State Department Basic Authorities Act of 1956 (22 U.S.C. 2731) establishes the Office to Monitor and Combat Anti-Semitism of the Department of State, which is headed by an individual who has the rank of ambassador and reports directly to the Secretary of State, to develop and implement policies and projects to combat global antisemitism by working closely with foreign governments, intergovernmental organizations, and civil society; and

Whereas the Never Again Education Act (36 U.S.C. 2301 note; Public Law 116–141), which was signed into law on May 29, 2020, expands United States Holocaust Memorial Museum education programming, requires the museum to develop and nationally disseminate accurate, relevant, and accessible resources to improve awareness and understanding of the Holocaust, and authorizes various Holocaust education program activities to engage prospective and current teachers and educational leaders: Now, therefore, be it

Resolved, That the Senate—

(1) unequivocally condemns the recent rise in antisemitic violence and harassment targeting Jewish Americans, and stands in solidarity with those affected by antisemitism;

(2) recommits to combating antisemitism in all forms;

(3) calls on elected officials, faith leaders, and civil society leaders to denounce and combat all manifestations of antisemitism;

(4) urges the President to—

(A) continue the leadership role of the United States in combating antisemitism internationally, including by nominating a qualified Ambassador to Monitor and Combat Antisemitism and engaging intergovernmental organizations to ensure that the anti-discrimination efforts of the organizations include combating antisemitism;

(B) advance accurate Holocaust education and counter Holocaust denial and distortion, including by fully implementing the Never Again Education Act (36 U.S.C. 2301 note; Public Law 116–141);

(C) ensure the physical security of Jewish institutions and organizations, including by requesting sufficient resources for the Nonprofit Security Grant Program of the Department of Homeland Security to keep at-risk houses of worship, schools, and community centers safe from terrorist attacks and other forms of antisemitic violence; and

(D) produce an analysis that accounts for the level and scope of the threat that antisemitism poses to the people of the United States; and

(5) urges Federal, State, local, and Tribal law enforcement agencies to fully participate in the data collection process of the Federal Bureau of Investigation in order to improve antisemitic hate crime data collection.

The Squad

America has enjoyed the blessing of Genesis 12:3, but with unbridled vocal anti-Semitic statements being posted daily by a group of four Democratic congresswomen referred to in mainstream media as "the Squad."

On May 21, 2021, the BBC reported in an article entitled "Israel-Gaza: The Democrats' 'Tectonic' Shift on the Conflict":

> To track the shift within the Democratic Party on Israel and the Palestinians, one can start by looking at that most representative US political institution, Congress. In the national legislature, US foreign policy sympathies have tended to tilt historically toward Israel's perspective in Middle East conflicts—in part because of the preferences of both Jewish voters (a key Democratic constituency) and evangelicals (important for Republicans).
>
> As the US Congress has become an increasingly diverse body, however, that has had some serious consequences for US policy toward Israel. In 2021, a record 23% of members of the House and Senate were people of black, Hispanic, Asian/Pacific Islander or Native American heritage, according to a Pew Foundation study.
>
> Two decades earlier, that number was 11%. In 1945, it was 1%.
>
> A diversity of backgrounds has led to a wider diversity of viewpoints and a diffusion of power. The influential group of young liberal congresswomen, known informally as "The Squad," includes Palestinian-American Rashida Tlaib[263] of Michigan and Somalian refugee Ilhan Omar[264] of Minnesota, and Alexandria Ocasio-Cortez[265] for instance.[266]

Although the Senate has just recently taken a stance on anti-Semitism and is labeling it as "hate speech," the media still has not taken up the cause and continues to focus on all other minority groups. The fact that one or more sitting members of Congress repeatedly engages in blatant anti-Semitic rhetoric and social media posts without any consequence is a blot on America's support for Israel. In the 2019 vote to condemn anti-Semitism, a surprising twenty-nine Republicans said no to the bill, demonstrating that America's unequivocal support of Israel is eroding. Without condemnation at the highest levels of government, America can and will suffer the same consequences that every nation or empire that has ever stood against Israel has suffered. History shows that no empire that has ever stood against Israel stands today.

Global Anti-Semitism on the Rise

A Rabbi attacked in the street. A synagogue daubed with a swastika. Hate shouted from a loudspeaker in a Jewish neighborhood.

These are only a few of the alarming incidents of antisemitic hatred witnessed in Europe last weekend, including in the UK, Germany, and Austria. As Jewish groups have been warning, antisemitism is on the rise again in Europe.

These anti-Semites use human rights abuses by the Israeli state against Palestinians as cover for hatred of Jews everywhere.

Pro-Palestinian activists, the Palestinian Mission to the United Kingdom, and Muslim religious leaders in Europe are among those condemning efforts to instrumentalize the suffering of Palestinians to justify hate against Jews.

There is work to be done in the realm of education, both in history and citizenship education, to ensure Europeans understand the horrors of the Holocaust, the profound impact of ideologies based on hatred, and to differentiate between legitimate criticism of governments and expressions of hate against people based on religion, including against Muslims.

In recent years, Jews in many European countries have reported an increase in hate incidents and say they feel increasingly unsafe. Synagogues have been attacked. Jewish cemeteries desecrated. Jewish children bullied in school for their faith.

Those who want a world where everyone is treated with dignity and humanity should stand up against anti-Semitic hate in Europe.[267]

The more frequent and intense the attacks become, the more fearful the Jewish community around the world becomes. Nothing would please Satan more than to build an even greater army and incite more violence against the seed line of Messiah.

United Nations Bias

Legal scholar Robert A. Caplen wrote that institutional bias against Israel within the UN has deprived the country of its ability to lawfully exercise those rights accorded to member states under the UN Charter.

In order to understand the view of the United Nations from the Israeli perspective, I have included, without edit, the comprehensive question-and-answer document created by former Israeli ambassador, Danny Ayalon, founder of the Truth About Israel website who has contributed to the site for the past twenty-five years to inform the public from the inside of government and politics. In an article entitled, "The Comprehensive Guide to the Truth about the United Nations," he writes:

History shows that no empire that has ever stood against Israel stands today.

> The United Nations (UN) was created following World War II, in order to prevent war and terror and to promote human rights and justice for individuals and nations. Article 51 of Chapter VII of the United Nations Charter states that: "Nothing in the present Charter shall impair the inherent right of individual or

collective self-defense if an armed attack occurs against a Member of the United Nations." Therefore, Israel has every right to defend herself and her citizens, even if it means preventing and preempting a terrorist rocket or mortar attack from Gaza on innocent Israeli citizens, or conducting military operations in order to locate and release Israeli civilians abducted by Palestinian terrorists.

Is the United Nations objective in its dealing with the Israel-Palestinian conflict?

Absolutely not. The United Nations General Assembly has consistently voted against Israel, denying Israel its fundamental right to self-defense according to the United Nations' own charter. The General Assembly consistently condemns Israel, calls to investigate and boycott Israel, and in a biased and hypocritical move, unconditionally backs the uncompromising Palestinian positions. With this very partial conduct, the UN is damaging the prospects for peace, emboldens the uncompromising Palestinian positions, and erodes Israeli trust in the organization. With such conduct, no Israeli would agree to make concessions for peace, because not only will they not be appreciated, but the UN will never come to Israel's defense if attacked.

Why is the UN biased against Israel?

The UN is biased against Israel because of the political composition of the General Assembly. Out of 193 countries in the General Assembly, the Arab states control an absolute majority, made up of Islamic states, the Arab League and the Non-Aligned Movement which make up a voting bloc of 124 countries. In the 2012 General Assembly, there were 26 Resolutions passed against specific countries. 22 out of those 26, an astonishing 85%, were against Israel. Israel is criticized for doing what every other country would do because Israel is not treated as all other countries, due to Palestinian delegitimization and the automatic majority in the UN. For instance, Israel is criticized for building the Security Fence, while similar fences exist on the US-Mexico border, the EU border, between India and Pakistan, Yemen and Saudi Arabia, Morocco and Algeria, and there is even a UN-sanctioned security fence on Cyprus. Similarly, even though the Israeli blockade on Gaza is an entirely legal one, as determined by the UN commissioned Palmer Report, Israel is still condemned for it. The United Nations Human Rights Council (HRC) in Geneva singles out Israel, where 50% of all resolutions are against one country, Israel, and is the only country which is on the HRC's permanent agenda. Many of the HRC are the world perpetrators of human rights violations.

But didn't the UN vote in 1947 to create a Jewish state in Israel?

Yes, it did, but this was when the UN had a total of 50 member states, most of them open and democratic. Today, the UN is comprised of 193 countries, most of them non-democratic and yield to the Arab and Muslim pressure.

But at least they are doing some good with regards to human rights, no?

True, they are doing some good, but in places that are already working on their own to fix the situation. They are unwilling to attack the tough situations. The Palestinians, backed with the support of human rights organizations as well as the United Nations Commission on Human Rights and the Human Rights Council, accuse Israel of human rights violations, when violations which are hundreds and even thousands of times worse are occurring in the Palestinian West Bank every day, and we have not even begun to discuss Hamas' actions in Gaza.

Human rights organizations were originally intended to investigate closed dictatorial regimes, and to investigate actual human rights issues. Today they don't deal with closed societies. They don't deal with Cuba, Venezuela, North Korea, etc. They are betraying their ideal. Instead, they investigate the USA, UK and Israel for war crimes, open societies with free press, where you are allowed to criticize the government, and where there are independent judicial systems which maintain the law and which guard human rights. A glaring example is how the UN treats refugees around the world and Palestinian refugees differently. Again, this is the result of the automatic majority enjoyed by the Arab and undemocratic countries in the United Nations.

How are Palestinian refugees treated any differently from any other refugees around the world?

Palestinian refugees have their own private agency, the United Nations Relief and Works Agency for Palestine Refugees in the Near East (UNRWA), unlike refugees from the rest of the world, who are treated for by the United Nations High Commissioner for Refugees (UNHCR). UN resources for Palestinian refugees are three times higher than any other refugees in the world. The UN's objective with regards to refugees around the world is to resettle them, while UNRWA's objective is to perpetuate their status. While all refugees are considered thus for only the first generation, Palestinian refugees maintain this status and pass it down from generation to generation, aggravating the problem instead of resolving it.

Can the UN be a broker in the peace between Israel and the Palestinians?

Absolutely not. Because of their inherent bias and hostility towards Israel, as well as the Arab majority that backs the Palestinians and supports even their most aggressive behavior and capricious demands. This is why any peace agreement between Israel and the Palestinians cannot be based upon UN resolutions, which are reflections of Palestinian demands. Unfortunately, the UN does not represent international law, but in most cases is used against Israel as a kangaroo court.[268]

In Israel today, the most notable presence of the United Nations' peace-keeping forces are in the Golan Heights with an encampment visible from Mount Bental overlooking Syria with a clear view of Damascus. As the UN vehicles pass by, many Israelis will ask "Do you know what 'UN' stands for?" The reply is "UNnecessary!" The United Nation's presence along the border as an observer has done nothing to advance a deescalation of the Syrian conflict. Many who understand what the Bible says about Damascus await the day when the prophecy of Isaiah 17 comes to pass.

While we wait, Russian, Iranian, Lebanese Hezbollah, and Syrian forces have exerted great force and financial investment to back the Assad regime. In addition, armed militia men from Iraq, Afghanistan, and Yemen have lent their support to a stand against the Kurds, who are backed by Turkey. Israel, meanwhile, has been so concerned by what it calls Iran's "military entrenchment" in Syria and shipments of Iranian weapons to Hezbollah and other Shia militias that it has conducted air strikes with increasing frequency in an attempt to thwart them.

Where is the UN in bringing an end to this ten-year-old war that has taken the lives of over 387,000, which includes civilians, in addition to the missing 205,300 missing civilians that are presumed dead?

Damascus is sixty kilometers from the border of Israel, and its enemies are using the civil war in Syria to set up military installations that will unite many of the confederates of the Ezekiel 38–39 Gog/Magog war. When combining the arsenals in Syria, Lebanon, and Gaza, there are estimated to be more than forty thousand rockets within striking range of Israel. When we add Iran's new long-range missile program, the numbers increase dramatically.

Anti-Israel Jews

As surprising as it may be, there are many members of the Jewish community who are not in support of Israel. They don't challenge Israel's right to exist, but they focus mainly on the fabricated narrative regarding Palestinians and the one-state or two-state solution. Although it is often said that Israel is America's only democratic ally in the Middle East, this in no way implies that the majority of the American Jewish population supports Israel's sovereignty over the often-referred-to "occupied territories."

Jewish Congressman Andy Levin (D-MI) is featured in the following article entitled "Rep. Levin on Bennet: 'Gentleman That Represents 6 Seats'":

A group of progressive, pro-Israel Democrats introduced a comprehensive piece of legislation on Thursday aimed at keeping alive the dimming prospects for a two-state solution to Israel's conflict with the Palestinians.

The Two-State Solution Act introduced by Rep. Andy Levin with over a dozen co-sponsors aims "to preserve conditions for, and improve the likelihood of, a two-state solution that secures Israel's future as a democratic state and a national home for the Jewish people, a viable, democratic Palestinian state."

However, it faces an uphill battle to become law. The bill is strongly opposed by more moderate Democrats, who say it demands nothing of the Palestinians.

If passed, the bill orders the US government to take a series of steps aimed at limiting Israeli entrenchment in the West Bank.

The bill bars US defense aid from use in acts by Israel to expand its control beyond the Green Line, through moves such as settlement building, demolitions of Palestinian homes, or evictions of Palestinian residents. It also mandates strict oversight of how Israel spends defense assistance more broadly.

The legislation says the West Bank, including East Jerusalem, and the Gaza Strip are all occupied territories and should be referred to as such in all official US policies, documents and communications.

Israel captured those areas in the 1967 Six Day War and later annexed East Jerusalem. Israel withdrew from the Gaza Strip in 2005, handing over control to the Palestinian Authority, which was ousted in 2007 from the coastal enclave in a bloody coup by the Hamas terror group that still rules the Strip.

Israel regards all of Jerusalem as its capital. Former US president Donald Trump recognized Jerusalem as Israel's capital and shifted the US embassy there from Tel Aviv.

The centrist Democratic Majority for Israel group quickly announced its opposition to the new bill, which it called "counterproductive, one-sided, and bad policy." It added: "The bill wrongly blames Israel alone for the failure to achieve a two-state solution. The reality is that Israel has offered Palestinians—and Palestinian leaders have refused—a state of their own on several occasions."

Said group CEO Mark Mellman in a statement: "This one-sided Two-State Solution Act seems less about actually achieving a two-state solution and more about rewriting history—both ancient and modern—and stirring up anti-Israel hostility."

The bill also seeks to reverse a 2020 Trump administration directive requiring goods made in Israeli settlements to be marked as "Made in Israel." Under the bill, imports to the US produced outside of Israel proper should be marked as made in the West Bank or Gaza.

In addition, the legislation seeks to advance the Lowey Fund passed by Congress last year, setting aside $250 million in funding for Israeli-Palestinian dialogue programs and Palestinian business development. The Two-State Solution Act urges the State Department to authorize grants to support human rights, democracy and the rule of law in Gaza and the West Bank as provided by the Lowey Fund.

The legislation urges US President Joe Biden to follow through on campaign pledges to reopen the US Consulate in Jerusalem, which served as the de facto mission to the Palestinians, along with the PLO Diplomatic Mission in Washington. Both were shuttered by the Trump administration.

The bill also calls for the scrapping of the 1987 Anti-Terrorism Act, which deems the PLO and its affiliates a terror organization.

To get around the hurdle, the legislation says the US should encourage the PA to reform its so-called "pay-to-slay" practice of providing regular stipends to security prisoners and families of dead terrorists through its welfare program.

Levin unveiled the legislation at a Thursday's press conference on the steps of Capitol Hill where he was joined by several of his bill's cosponsors—Reps. Jan Schakowsky of Illinois, Sara Jacobs and Alan Lowenthal of California, and Peter Welch of Vermont.

All five of them said they supported a separate bill approved by the House later in the day to expand funding for Israel's Iron Dome missile defense system. The moderate Democrats who introduced the Iron Dome legislation are unlikely to return the favor though, and the Two-State Solution Act will most likely have a difficult time passing in Congress, due to its heavy criticism of Israeli actions in the West Bank.

Despite the moderate opposition, the progressive, pro-Israel lawmakers at Thursday's press conference were optimistic about their bill's chances.

"We need a new center of gravity for actually doing something to bring long-term peace for Israel and human rights for Palestinians," said Levin.

"We're speaking for the American public. The American public wants a two-state solution," added Lowenthal.

"I have a master's degree in international conflict resolution. I've been working on these issues for a very long time," said Jacobs, a first-term Congresswoman. "It's not a question of will we make peace right now… That doesn't mean we should do nothing, or lose hope."

Levin said in an interview with the Jewish Telegraphic Agency that the vast majority of the American Jewish community backs his approach, which is to advocate for aid for Israel, but with rigid oversight to make sure the money does not inhibit the two-state outcome.

Levin referred to a Jewish Electoral Institute poll in July, taken after the Gaza conflict, in which 58% of Jewish voters said it would be appropriate to restrict aid to Israel so it could not spend US money on settlements.

During the press conference, he downplayed "excuses" commonly used by opponents to dismiss working toward a two-state solution, citing Hamas rule in Gaza, the PA's lack of legitimacy or Prime Minister Naftali Bennett's opposition to a Palestinian state. He dismissively referred to him as a "gentleman that represents six seats in the Knesset."

"We can come up with a lot of excuses, but what's missing is the US playing a muscular role by saying we support you and bring you together through thick and thin to reach a two-state solution," he explained.

Levin rolled out his bill at the press conference with J Street, the liberal Jewish Middle East policy group that in recent years has endorsed some restrictions on US assistance to Israel. Also joining him and speaking was Americans for Peace Now CEO Hadar Susskind, whose group espouses similar views.[269]

Rarely a day goes by that the name George Soros is not mentioned in one or more media outlets. Yes, Soros is Jewish, and it is clear from the following article, "Billionaire's Cash Helps 'Flip' Evangelicals Away from Israel," exactly where he stands:

He's Jewish, but George Soros is no friend to Israel. The radical billionaire told the *New York Times* in 2006 he is "very critical of Israel."

That's an understatement. The Israeli government has blasted the deep-pocketed philanthropist and atheist for "funding organizations that defame the Jewish state." And former U.S. Ambassador to Israel David Friedman says Soros has done "more to vilify the state of Israel…than almost any individual on the face of the earth."

One of the world's wealthiest men, Soros has used his philanthropy to steer the American Jewish community away from its traditional support for Israel. He helped launch J Street, a left-wing, Palestinian-friendly Jewish lobby now positioned as an alternative to the American Israel Political Action Committee (AIPAC), the long-recognized pro-Israel powerhouse.

And Soros is also using his wealth to distance evangelicals—long the leading pro-Israel constituency in the U.S.—from the Jewish state. For a decade, Soros has been giving six-figure grants to the Telos Group, which takes evangelical influencers on expense-paid tours to Israel and brings "Israeli and Palestinian leaders and activists" to speak in the U.S.

Soros has been an "angel investor" for Telos. He gave it half of its start-up funding in its first three years, a total of $713,500. And Soros pumped another $1.6 million into Telos from 2012 to 2019.

The listed purpose for Soros' largesse is "to educate U.S. leaders in faith communities…about the reality on the ground in Palestine/Israel." In plain terms, that means cooling evangelical fervor for Israel.

"Telos Group purports to promote a 'pro-Israel, pro-Palestinian and pro-peace' agenda, but the problem is that this slogan has become a cover for broadcasting a lot of misinformation that invariably cuts against Israel," Dexter Van Zile, Christian media analyst for the Committee for Accuracy in Middle East Reporting in America (CAMERA) told JNS.org. "It's part of a propaganda or cognitive war against Israel."

Co-founded in 2009 by Todd Deatherage, an evangelical Christian, and Gregory Khalil, an American attorney of Palestinian descent, Telos has taken more than 110 groups to Israel, giving evangelical leaders a decidedly pro-Palestinian perspective. Telos tours have featured speakers like Mitri Raheb and Elias Chacour, severe critics of the Jewish state who dive into the deep end of the anti-Semitic pool.

Raheb, the former pastor of a Lutheran Church in Bethlehem, has advanced the contemptible theory that Jews have no historic association with the land of Israel. And Chacour, the former Melkite Catholic Bishop of Galilee, "has frequently drawn comparisons between the state of Israel and Nazi Germany," writes Tricia Miller, a senior analyst for CAMERA.

"Experts" like these make a pronounced impact on high-profile evangelicals. Lynne Hybels, co-founder of the influential megachurch Willow Creek Community Church, has taken over 100 Willow Creek staffers and leaders on Telos tours to "Israel/Palestine," the Telos Group's loaded term for the Jewish state and the disputed Palestinian territories. Hybels has disparaged Israel for its "occupation of the West Bank and the continuing blockade of Gaza," which she calls "a violation of human rights"—accusations that echo Palestinian talking points.

Likewise, *Relevant* magazine founder Cameron Strang offered his readers a heavily slanted picture of "Israel/Palestine" in his "Blessed Are the Peacemakers" 2014 cover story, published after his Telos-guided visit to the Holy Land. Strang's account gave readers—without comment or correction—this bit of blatant misinformation from PLO leader Hanan Ashrawi: "Palestinians are the descendants of the early Christians. We are probably the straightest line to original Christianity."

This would be news, no doubt, to the apostles—all Jewish—who struggled at first with the idea of gentile followers of Jesus. It also shoehorns the Palestinians into the first century despite their invention as a people in the late 1960s.

Google's "Ngram Viewer," which maps the appearance of unique terms in books from 1800 to the present, documents the Palestinians' late arrival. A search for "Palestinian state" or "Palestinian people" turns up almost no hits before the late 1960s, when the number shoots upward.

But it's not just evangelical elites who sour on Israel after Soros-funded Telos tours. The rank-and-file do, too. A 2017 excursion left Katie Kallam, the daughter of an evangelical pastor, disenchanted with the Jewish state. "I didn't realize how much of our defense budget goes to Israel," Kellam told Jewish Currents. "It was jarring to learn how complicit I am as an American."

Of course, Israel is the lone democracy in the Middle East, a pro-Western state and strong U.S. ally. It's also surrounded by enemies who want it destroyed. But reasons like that for aiding Israel may not be heard on Telos tours.

Perhaps that's why Telos Group co-founder Todd Deatherage told Jewish Currents it's "easy to almost flip people" from sympathy for Israel to sympathy for Palestinians.

Telos, which leverages evangelical celebrities to reach into the evangelical community, may be eroding support for Israel among younger evangelicals. A recent survey registered a 42% drop since 2018 in support for Israel among evangelicals aged 18–29. Some say the drop is not that steep, but it's still cause for alarm.

George Soros might consider it a return on investment. Dubbed "one of Israel's most dangerous and powerful enemies in the Western world," Soros is at least getting his money's worth.[270]

If the Holocaust and Hitler's agenda to annihilate the Jews is not horrific enough, imagine how diabolical a force was at work as Jews served the Third Reich and turned and spied on their own relatives. Even today, as we read these articles, we see Satan's handiwork. None of this is in alignment with God's Word and only serves to advance Satan's agenda.

America No Longer Safe

Fear of antisemitism spurred 40 percent of American Jews to change their behavior over the past year, according to a new survey about antisemitism in America.

The survey, released [June 2021], is the latest in an annual series commissioned by the American Jewish Committee to understand how Jewish Americans and the general public experience and perceive antisemitism.

A survey of American Jews found that over the last year, 17% said they "avoided certain places, events, or situations," 22% avoided making themselves visually identifiable as a Jew and 25% refrained from posting Jewish-related content online.

A companion survey of the general public, meanwhile, found that the proportion of Americans who say they understand what antisemitism is rose sharply in the last year, from 53% in 2020 to 65% this year.

Last year's survey was taken shortly before the presidential election in which Joe Biden defeated incumbent Donald Trump, whom many Jews perceived as stoking antisemitism. At the time, just 4% of American Jews said they felt more secure than they had in the past; this year that proportion was significantly higher, at 10%.

"Almost 40% of Jews have changed their behavior. This is horrible and heartbreaking data," Holly Huffnagle, the AJC's US director for combating antisemitism, told the Jewish Telegraphic Agency about this year's findings.

"But I think we can't hide the fact that more Jews feel secure today," she added, noting that when the surveyors asked for an explanation, "The change in the administration was by far the biggest response to that."

This year's surveys were taken in September and early October and included 1,214 Americans overall and 1,433 Jews. The margin of error for each survey was 3.9%. In a shift, the majority of the surveys were completed online, rather than by phone, although Huffnagle said researchers had concluded that the change had not influenced results in any particular way.

Some of the results, including the finding about the proportion of American Jews who changed their behavior out of fear, cannot be directly compared to the AJC's past antisemitism surveys because this year's version asked about experiences only in the last year. Previous surveys asked about experiences and perceptions in the past two or five years.

"We decided to lose the trend data in favor of accurate information," Huffnagle said.

Other findings are comparable over time, and suggest that much has remained unchanged in American Jewish sentiment. The vast majority of American Jews continue to say that antisemitism is a problem in the United States; antisemitism on college campuses remains a concern for many American Jews; and American Jews continue to say they are more concerned about antisemitism emanating from the extreme right than the extreme left.

Half of American Jews say the "extreme political right" poses a "very serious" antisemitic threat, and 91% said they believed the far right poses at least some threat, similar to last year's finding. In a shift, however, the proportion of American Jews who said they thought "the extreme political left" represents at least a slight antisemitic threat increased sharply, from 61% last year to 71% this year.

Huffnagle said she attributed the increase in the general public's awareness of antisemitism to multiple high-profile incidents related to right-wing activity, including penetration of the QAnon conspiracy theory, which has antisemitic overtones, and the January 6 insurrection at the US Capitol, where one participant was photographed wearing a "Camp Auschwitz" sweatshirt.

She also said a broader discourse around combating discrimination and hate, spurred in part by a response to attacks on Asian Americans, may have played a role.

"I think there might have been this national wakeup call," Huffnagle said, adding, "at least about how to answer survey questions."

Three-quarters of Jews said they had heard "a lot" or "some" about Jews being attacked in the United States and abroad during Israel's conflict with Hamas in Gaza in May. Three-quarters of those respondents—representing a majority of Jews—said those reports had made them feel less safe as Jews in the United States.

Huffnagle said there was little evidence that the incidents of antisemitism reported at the time had contributed to the shift in sentiment within the general public.

Still, she said, the general public remains notably supportive of Israel—perhaps more so than American Jews. She pointed to the fact that the proportion of general-public respondents who said they viewed the statement "Israel has no right to exist" as antisemitic was higher this year: 85% of respondents said the statement is antisemitic, compared to 77% last year.[271]

God's Word

We need look no further than the first book of the Bible to find how God feels about the People of the Book and the Land of the Book. May of 1948 was the first time in human history that Israel had sovereignty over even one-twelfth of what God had promised in His Word in regards to the biblically mandated borders of Israel.

> In the same day the LORD made a covenant with Abram, saying, Unto thy seed have I given this land, from the river of Egypt unto the great river, the river Euphrates:
> The Kenites, and the Kenizzites, and the Kadmonites,
> And the Hittites, and the Perizzites, and the Rephaims, And the Amorites, and the Canaanites, and the Girgashites, and the Jebusites. (Genesis 15:18–21)

This is the land covenant made with Abram (Abraham) and his seed line to Isaac and Jacob; it encompasses all of its current borders after 1967 in addition to all of Lebanon, Syria, Jordan, and most of Iraq, Northern Saudi Arabia, and Northern Egypt including the Sinai Peninsula.

In Joel 3:1–2, God says:

> For, behold, in those days, and in that time, when I shall bring again the captivity of Judah and Jerusalem,
>
> I will also gather all nations, and will bring them down into the valley of Jehoshaphat, and will plead with them there for my people and for my heritage Israel, whom they have scattered among the nations, and parted my land.

Ezekiel 37:22:

> And I will make them one nation in the land upon the mountains of Israel; and one king shall be king to them all: and they shall be no more two nations, neither shall they be divided into two kingdoms any more at all.

America, like every nation or empire throughout the course of history, is subject to God's blessings according to Genesis 12:3:

> And I will bless them that bless thee, and curse him that curseth thee: and in thee shall all families of the earth be blessed.

In fact, as stated earlier, no empire that has ever stood against Israel is intact today; there is now no longer an Egyptian, Assyrian, Babylonian, Persian, Greek, Roman, Byzantine, Ottoman, or British Empire. All share one thing in common: their rule over Israel.

If God says that He will not allow His land to be divided, then those who stand against His Word are subject to His judgment. According to William (Bill) Koenig,[272] author of *Eye to Eye*,[273] every major natural disaster over the past one hundred years that has cost Americans over $1 billion can be tied to decisions we, as a nation, have made regarding Israel that go against God's Word. The increase in the numbers of wildfires, floods, tornadoes, hurricanes, earthquakes, and more is not because of global warming; it is the consequences of our stand against Israel and God in any attempt we make to divide what God has said will never be divided again. This anti-Israel agenda and our lukewarm position concerning Israel's enemies put us all in jeopardy. One can only imagine how the stage is being set to accomplish Satan's goal to eliminate the seed line of Messiah in a staged attack against Israel.

15

The Coming Battle

Since its creation as a nation-state, Israel has been engaged in a series of wars. In order to examine the coming biblical war, we must first take a look at history. Prophetic camps are divided as to whether or not the Psalm 83 war has been fulfilled or is the one before the war that positions Israel to meet the prerequisites stated in Ezekiel 38.

Israel has been involved in a number of wars and large-scale military operations, including:

1948 Arab–Israeli War (November 1947–July 1949)—Started as 6 months of civil war between Jewish and Arab militias at the end of the British Mandate of Palestine and turned into a regular war after the declaration of independence of Israel and the intervention of several Arab armies. In its conclusion, a set of agreements were signed between Israel, Egypt, Jordan, Lebanon, and Syria, called the 1949 Armistice Agreements, which established the armistice lines between Israel and its neighbors, also known as the Green Line.

Reprisal operations (1950s–1960s)—Military operations carried out by the Israel Defense Forces during the 1950s and

1960s. These actions were in response to constant fedayeen during which Arab guerillas infiltrated from Syria, Egypt, and Jordan into Israel to carry out attacks against Israeli civilians and soldiers. [Fedayeen (Arabic: فِـدائِيِّـن fidāʾīyīn [fɪdaːʔɪjiːn] "self-sacrificers") is an Arabic term used to refer to various Islamic military groups willing to sacrifice themselves for a larger campaign.] The policy of the reprisal operations was exceptional due to Israel's declared aim of getting a high "blood cost" among the enemy side which was believed to be necessary in order to deter them from committing future attacks.

Suez Crisis (October 1956)—A military attack on Egypt by Britain, France, and Israel, beginning on 29 October 1956, with the intention to occupy the Sinai Peninsula and to take over the Suez Canal. The attack followed Egypt's decision of 26 July 1956 to nationalize the Suez Canal after the withdrawal of an offer by Britain and the United States to fund the building of the Aswan Dam. Although the Israeli invasion of the Sinai was successful, the US and USSR forced it to retreat. Even so, Israel managed to re-open the Straits of Tiran and pacified its southern border.

Six-Day War (June 1967)—Fought between Israel and Arab neighbors Egypt, Jordan, and Syria. The nations of Iraq, Saudi Arabia, Kuwait, Algeria, and others also contributed troops and arms to the Arab forces. Following the war, the territory held by Israel expanded significantly ("The Purple Line") : The West Bank (including East Jerusalem) from Jordan, Golan Heights from Syria, Sinai, and Gaza from Egypt.

War of Attrition (1967–1970)—A limited war fought between the Israeli military and forces of the Egyptian Republic, the USSR, Jordan, Syria, and the Palestine Liberation Organization from 1967 to 1970. It was initiated by the Egyptians as a way of recapturing the Sinai from the Israelis, who had been in control of the territory since the mid-1967 Six-Day War. The hostilities ended with a ceasefire signed between the countries in 1970 with frontiers remaining in the same place as when the war began.

Yom Kippur War (October 1973)—Fought from October 6 to October 26, 1973 by a coalition of Arab states led by Egypt and Syria against Israel as a way of recapturing part of the territories which they lost to the Israelis back in the Six-Day War. The war began with a surprise joint attack by Egypt and Syria on the Jewish holiday of Yom Kippur. Egypt and Syria crossed the cease-fire lines in the Sinai and Golan Heights, respectively. Eventually Arab forces were defeated by Israel and there were no significant territorial changes.

Palestinian insurgency in South Lebanon (1971–1982)—PLO relocate to South Lebanon from Jordan and stage attacks on the Galilee and as a base for international operations. In 1978, Israel launches Operation Litani—the first Israeli large-scale invasion of Lebanon, which was carried out by the Israel Defense Forces in order to expel PLO forces from the territory. Continuing ground and rocket attacks, and Israeli retaliations, eventually escalate into the 1982 War.

1982 Lebanon War (1982)—Began in 6 June 1982, when the Israel Defense Forces invaded southern Lebanon to expel the PLO from the territory. The Government of Israel ordered the invasion as a response to the assassination attempt against Israel's ambassador to the United Kingdom, Shlomo Argov, by the Abu Nidal Organization and due to the constant terror attacks on northern Israel made by the Palestinian guerilla organizations which resided in Lebanon. The war resulted in the expulsion of the PLO from Lebanon and created an Israeli Security Zone in southern Lebanon.

South Lebanon conflict (1982–2000)—Nearly 20 years of warfare between the Israel Defense Forces and its Lebanese proxy militias with Lebanese Muslim guerrilla, led by Iranian-backed Hezbollah, within what was defined by Israelis as the "Security Zone" in South Lebanon.

First Intifada (1987–1993)—First large-scale Palestinian uprising against Israel in the West Bank and the Gaza Strip.

Second Intifada (2000–2005)—Second Palestinian uprising, a period of intensified violence, which began in late September 2000.

2006 Lebanon War (summer 2006)—Began as a military operation in response to the abduction of two Israeli reserve soldiers by the Hezbollah. The operation gradually strengthened, to become a wider confrontation. The principal participants were Hezbollah paramilitary forces and the Israeli military. The conflict started on 12 July 2006 and continued until a United Nations-brokered ceasefire went into effect on 14 August 2006, though it formally ended on 8 September 2006, when Israel lifted its naval blockade of Lebanon. The war resulted in the pacification of southern Lebanon and in the weakness of the Hezbollah (which suffered serious casualties but managed to survive the Israeli onslaught).

Gaza War (December 2008–January 2009)—Three-week armed conflict between Israel and Hamas during the winter of 2008–2009. In an escalation of the ongoing Israeli–Palestinian conflict, Israel responded to ongoing rocket fire from the Gaza Strip with military force in an action titled "Operation Cast Lead." Israel opened the attack with a surprise air strike on December 27, 2008. Israel's stated aim was to stop such rocket fire from and the import of arms into Gaza. Israeli forces attacked military and civilian targets, police stations, and government buildings in the opening assault. Israel declared an end to the conflict on January 18 and completed its withdrawal on January 21, 2009.

Operation Pillar of Defense (November 2012)—Military offensive on the Gaza Strip

Guardians on the Wall (May, 2021)—Israeli Military response to 4,000 rockets fired from Gaza over an 11-day period.

Psalm 83 War

Keep not thou silence, O God: hold not thy peace, and be not still, O God.

For, lo, thine enemies make a tumult: and they that hate thee have lifted up the head.

They have taken crafty counsel against thy people, and consulted against thy hidden ones.

They have said, "Come, and let us cut them off from being a nation; that the name of Israel may be no more in remembrance."

For they have consulted together with one consent: they are confederate against thee:

The tabernacles of Edom, and the Ishmaelites; of Moab, and the Hagarenes;

Gebal, and Ammon, and Amalek; the Philistines with the inhabitants of Tyre;

Assur also is joined with them: they have holpen the children of Lot. Selah.

Do unto them as unto the Midianites; as to Sisera, as to Jabin, at the brook of Kison:

Which perished at Endor: they became as dung for the earth.

Make their nobles like Oreb, and like Zeeb: yea, all their princes as Zebah, and as Zalmunna:

Who said, "Let us take to ourselves the houses of God in possession."

O my God, make them like a wheel; as the stubble before the wind.

As the fire burneth a wood, and as the flame setteth the mountains on fire;

So persecute them with thy tempest, and make them afraid with thy storm.

Fill their faces with shame; that they may seek thy name, O LORD.

Let them be confounded and troubled for ever; yea, let them be put to shame, and perish:

That men may know that thou, whose name alone is JEHOVAH, art the most high over all the earth. (Psalm 83)

Listed within this ten-people group confederacy are the biblical references; they must be translated into their twenty-first-century locations. While these groups are no longer identifiable by their ancient names, Bill Salus, author of *Israelistine and Psalm 83: The Missing Prophecy Revealed*, ascertains the modern-day equivalents/descendants of these coalition members as the following:

- Tents of Edom: Palestinians and Southern Jordanians
- Ishmaelites: Saudis (Ishmael is the father of the Arabs)
- Moab: Palestinians and Central Jordanians
- Hagrites: Egyptians (Hagar is the matriarch of Egypt)
- Gebal (Byblos): Hezbollah and Northern Lebanese
- Ammon: Palestinians and Northern Jordanians
- Amalek: Arabs of the Sinai area
- Philistia: Hamas of the Gaza Strip
- Tyre: Hezbollah and Southern Lebanese

In an expanded view of these confederates, not only are they identified by geography, but by their current position on the State of Israel:

Assyria: Syrians and Northern Iraqis: Of course, these Psalm 83 countries are actively conspiring today to either take over the land of Israel and make it their own or to prevent Israel from being a Jewish state. In other words, they want to make Israel a country that cannot protect and shelter the Jewish people from those who hate them. Let's look a little closer at these groups:

Palestinians—Tents of Edom (Esau); Moab and Ammon (sons of Lot): Mahmoud Abbas, the Palestinian Authority (PA) president, has made his intentions about Israel's existence very clear: "We won't recognize and accept the Jewishness of Israel. We have many excuses and reasons that prevent us from doing so," Abbas said. "We will march to Jerusalem in the millions, as free people and heroes," he asserted. (JPost) And that sentiment remains to this day.

Jordanians—Tents of Edom; Moab and Ammon: Although Jordan and Israel have enjoyed a peace treaty since 1994, Jordan's foreign minister Nasser Judeh told his parliament that Israel should not be recognized as a Jewish state nor should Jordan take in the Palestinian refugees (Tents of Edom). (ArutzSheva) Jordan's parliament voted to not recognize Israel as a Jewish state. That sentiment permeates society as well, where even 81 percent of Jordanians have anti-Semitic views and 70 percent have positive views of Hamas.

Hezbollah and Lebanon—Gebal (Byblos) and Tyre: While Hezbollah, the terrorist group based in Lebanon, has been helping Syrian President Assad wage war against the rebels. Hezbollah leader, Hassan Nasrallah, came out of hiding to remind the people of Lebanon that "Israel poses a danger on all people of this region…including Lebanon, and removing it is a Lebanese national interest." (That belief remains today.)

Hamas—Philistines: Although Gaza is officially a part of the Palestinian Authority ruled by President Abbas, the terrorist group Hamas (similar to the word for "violence" in Hebrew) rules Gaza and is ready to form a coalition with any Muslim group willing to resist Israel. Its charter states: "[Hamas] will only be of help to all associations and orga-nizations which act against the Zionist enemy and those who revolve in its orbit." Hamas Interior Minister Fathi Hamad said that the goal of Hamas is total destruction of Israel. "We are coming after the Zionists with all our leaders and soldiers," Hamad said. "You have only eight years on the land of Palestine before your demise." We now have about five years left.

Egyptians (or possibly Northern Jordanians)—Hagrites or Hagarenes: Some commentators believe that Egypt and Israel are experi-encing the highest level of peace and cooperation since they signed their peace treaty of 1979, especially in security against Hamas, where they have been destroying hundreds of terror tunnels that smuggle weapons to ISIS in the Sinai Peninsula from Gaza.

This makes sense if prophecy watchman Joel Richardson[274] is cor-rect. He believes that the Hagarenes are not Egyptians but northern Jordanians (based on 1 Chronicles 5:10, which specifies a region east of Gilead). In this scenario, the peace and cooperation that Israel is cur-rently enjoying with Egypt might continue through the coming war.

Saudis (or all Arabs)—Ishmaelites: Author Salus[275] believes Saudi Arabia represents the Ishmaelite people in Psalm 83. Like most Arabs throughout the Middle East and Africa, the Saudis claim to be the true chosen people (as descendants of Ishmael). Considering that Saudi Ara-bia is an ally of the US and a foe of Iran, it may seem that it is not involved in a coalition against Israel. Nevertheless, Saudi Arabia voted "no" to the 1947 UN resolution to create a Jewish state and supported the Arab invasions of 1948, 1967 and 1973 with troops as well as finances. They do not have diplomatic relations with Israel.

Arabs of the Sinai (or of the Negev area)—Amalek (grandson of Esau): Salus places the Amalekites in Sinai. He believes they were a part of Esau's family (the Edomites) who migrated into the Sinai area, which is part of Egypt.

Others, however, think that the Amalekites originated near Mecca, and by the tenth century BC, had migrated to the Negev area of modern Israel. It is possible, therefore, that some Arab-Israelis currently enjoying citizenship within Israel are of this group.

Indeed, some Arabs inside of Israel look for its destruction as a Jewish state, and even have representation in the Knesset (parliament): "Israel should be defined as a state of its own nationalities. There are two nationalities in Israel. One is [the] Jewish majority, one is [the] Arab-Palestinian minority," said the deputy speaker of the Knesset Ahmad Tibi[276] in January 2014. "Saying that Israel is the Jewish state is neglecting our existence, our very existence and our narrative, and I will not accept that," he added.

Syrians and Northern Iraqis (and possibly Turkey)—Assyria: Since the creation of both Israel and Syria in the mid-twentieth century, diplomatic ties have never been established between these two countries, which share a border.

Syria has attacked Israel in three major wars in 1948, 1967, and 1973. The situation in Syria is incredibly volatile. While its President Bashar Assad[277] shares his neighbors' common hatred for Israel, if he is defeated in his civil war, the many thousands of jihadist rebels, including Hezbollah and ISIS, could take control and eagerly rally support for a war against Israel. Any invasion could potentially include Russia someday, which now has a permanent navy and air base in this nation to Israel's north.

Have these confederates ever worked in complete concert to align against Israel? In a review of the wars listed up to and including the May 2021 Israeli operation Guardians on the Wall, these ten have never worked in concert in fulfillment of Psalm 83. Since these ten confederates are not named as players in the Ezekiel 38–39 Gog/Magog campaign of Armageddon, there is a reasonable expectation that the purpose behind a future Psalm 83 war will set the stage for the prerequisites of Ezekiel 38 to be in place. In addition, the Psalm 83 war does cause Jewish casualties that advance Satan's plan to eliminate the seed line of Messiah, whereas the Ezekiel 38–39 conflict advances the armies of the Antichrist, but the Jews are warned to flee before Jerusalem falls.

Prerequisites for the Ezekiel 38–39 Campaign of Armageddon

Ezekiel 38:1–39:29:

And the word of the LORD came unto me, saying,

Son of man, set thy face against Gog, the land of Magog, the chief prince of Meshech and Tubal, and prophesy against him,

And say, Thus saith the Lord GOD; Behold, I am against thee, O Gog, the chief prince of Meshech and Tubal:

And I will turn thee back, and put hooks into thy jaws, and I will bring thee forth, and all thine army, horses and horsemen, all of them clothed with all sorts of armour, even a great company with bucklers and shields, all of them handling swords:

Persia, Ethiopia, and Libya with them; all of them with shield and helmet:

Gomer, and all his bands; the house of Togarmah of the north quarters, and all his bands: and many people with thee.

Be thou prepared, and prepare for thyself, thou, and all thy company that are assembled unto thee, and be thou a guard unto them.

After many days thou shalt be visited: in the latter years **thou shalt come into the land that is brought back from the sword,** and is gathered out of many people, against the mountains of Israel, which have been always waste: but it is brought forth out of the nations, and they shall dwell safely all of them.

Thou shalt ascend and come like a storm, thou shalt be like

a cloud to cover the land, thou, and all thy bands, and many people with thee.

Thus saith the Lord GOD; It shall also come to pass, that at the same time shall things come into thy mind, and thou shalt think an evil thought:

And thou shalt say, **I will go up to the land of unwalled villages**; I will go to them that are at rest, that dwell safely, **all of them dwelling without walls, and having neither bars nor gates,**

To take a spoil, and to take a prey; to turn thine hand upon the desolate places that are now inhabited, and upon the people that are gathered out of the nations, which have gotten cattle and goods, that dwell in the midst of the land.

Sheba, and Dedan, and the merchants of Tarshish, with all the young lions thereof, shall say unto thee, Art thou come to take a spoil? hast thou gathered thy company to take a prey? **to carry away silver and gold**, to take away cattle and goods, to take a great spoil?

Therefore, son of man, prophesy and say unto Gog, Thus saith the Lord GOD; **In that day when my people of Israel dwelleth safely**, shalt thou not know it?

And thou shalt come from thy place out of the north parts, thou, and many people with thee, all of them riding upon horses, a great company, and a mighty army:

And thou shalt come up against my people of Israel, as a cloud to cover the land; it shall be in the latter days, and I will bring thee **against my land**, that the heathen may know me, when I shall be sanctified in thee, O Gog, before their eyes.

Thus saith the Lord GOD; "Art thou he of whom I have spoken in old time by my servants the prophets of Israel, which prophesied in those days many years that I would bring thee against them?

And it shall come to pass at the same time when Gog shall come against the land of Israel, saith the Lord GOD, that my fury shall come up in my face.

For in my jealousy and in the fire of my wrath have I spoken, Surely in that day there shall be a great shaking in the land of Israel;

So that the fishes of the sea, and the fowls of the heaven, and the beasts of the field, and all creeping things that creep upon the earth, and all the men that are upon the face of the earth, shall shake at my presence, and the mountains shall be thrown down, and the steep places shall fall, and every wall shall fall to the ground.

And I will call for a sword against him throughout all my mountains," saith the Lord GOD: every man's sword shall be against his brother.

And I will plead against him with pestilence and with blood; and I will rain upon him, and upon his bands, and upon the many people that are with him, an overflowing rain, and great hailstones, fire, and brimstone.

Thus will I magnify myself, and sanctify myself; and I will be known in the eyes of many nations, and they shall know that I am the LORD.

Therefore, thou son of man, prophesy against Gog, and say, Thus saith the Lord God; Behold, I am against thee, O Gog, the chief prince of Meshech and Tubal:

And I will turn thee back, and leave but the sixth part of thee, and will cause thee to come up from the north parts, and will bring thee upon the mountains of Israel:

And I will smite thy bow out of thy left hand, and will cause thine arrows to fall out of thy right hand.

Thou shalt fall upon the mountains of Israel, thou, and all thy bands, and the people that is with thee: I will give thee unto the ravenous birds of every sort, and to the beasts of the field to be devoured.

Thou shalt fall upon the open field: for I have spoken it, saith the Lord GOD.

And I will send a fire on Magog, and among them that dwell carelessly in the isles: and they shall know that I am the LORD.

So will I make my holy name known in the midst of my people Israel; and I will not let them pollute my holy name any more: and the heathen shall know that I am the LORD, the Holy One in Israel.

Behold, it is come, and it is done, saith the Lord GOD; this is the day whereof I have spoken.

And they that dwell in the cities of Israel shall go forth, and shall set on fire and burn the weapons, both the shields and the bucklers, the bows and the arrows, and the handstaves, and the spears, and they shall burn them with fire seven years:

So that they shall take no wood out of the field, neither cut down any out of the forests; for they shall burn the weapons with fire: and they shall spoil those that spoiled them, and rob those that robbed them," saith the Lord GOD.

And it shall come to pass in that day, that I will give unto Gog a place there of graves in Israel, the valley of the passengers on the east of the sea: and it shall stop the noses of the passengers: and there shall they bury Gog and all his multitude: and they shall call it The valley of Hamongog.

And seven months shall the house of Israel be burying of them, that they may cleanse the land.

Yea, all the people of the land shall bury them; and it shall be to them a renown the day that I shall be glorified, saith the Lord GOD.

And they shall sever out men of continual employment, passing through the land to bury with the passengers those that remain upon the face of the earth, to cleanse it: after the end of seven months shall they search.

And the passengers that pass through the land, when any seeth a man's bone, then shall he set up a sign by it, till the buriers have buried it in the valley of Hamongog.

And also the name of the city shall be Hamonah. Thus shall they cleanse the land.

And, thou son of man, thus saith the Lord GOD; Speak unto every feathered fowl, and to every beast of the field, Assemble yourselves, and come; gather yourselves on every side to my sacrifice that I do sacrifice for you, even a great sacrifice upon the mountains of Israel, that ye may eat flesh, and drink blood.

Ye shall eat the flesh of the mighty, and drink the blood of the princes of the earth, of rams, of lambs, and of goats, of bullocks, all of them fatlings of Bashan.

And ye shall eat fat till ye be full, and drink blood till ye be drunken, of my sacrifice which I have sacrificed for you.

Thus ye shall be filled at my table with horses and chariots, with mighty men, and with all men of war, saith the Lord God.

And I will set my glory among the heathen, and all the heathen shall see my judgment that I have executed, and my hand that I have laid upon them.

So the house of Israel shall know that I am the LORD their God from that day and forward.

And the heathen shall know that the house of Israel went into captivity for their iniquity: because they trespassed against me, therefore hid I my face from them, and gave them into the hand of their enemies: so fell they all by the sword.

According to their uncleanness and according to their transgressions have I done unto them, and hid my face from them.

Therefore thus saith the Lord GOD; Now will I bring again the captivity of Jacob, and have mercy upon the whole house of Israel, and will be jealous for my holy name;

After that they have borne their shame, and all their trespasses whereby they have trespassed against me, when they dwelt safely in their land, and none made them afraid.

When I have brought them again from the people, and gathered them out of their enemies' lands, and am sanctified in them in the sight of many nations;

Then shall they know that I am the LORD their God, which caused them to be led into captivity among the heathen: but I have gathered them unto their own land, and have left none of them anymore there.

Neither will I hide my face any more from them: for I have poured out my spirit upon the house of Israel, saith the Lord GOD. (Emphasis added)

As we read in the above passages, the prerequisites for the future campaign of Armageddon are as follows:

1. "Thou shalt come into the land that is brought back from the sword" (Ezekiel 38:8).

In Genesis 15, God made an unconditional covenant with Abraham—a land covenant outlining the borders of sovereign Israel. At no point in biblical history has Israel ever had sovereignty over these borders. Man has confined Israel to one-twelfth of the promised land of Genesis 15, which includes all of modern-day Israel plus Lebanon, Syria, most of Iraq, Jordan, Northern Saudi Arabia, and Northern Egypt, including the Sinai Peninsula. In order for Israel to be sovereign in the land that meets God's definition of the borders of Israel, an event must take place that expands its tent pegs to fulfill its God-appointed borders. A victory over the Psalm 83 confederates accomplishes this.

2. "I will go up to the land of unwalled villages" (Ezekiel 38:11a).

Modern-day Israel is a nation divided by walled villages separating Jewish settlements from Palestinian settlements. In order for there to be a "land of unwalled villages," Israel must be sovereign over all the land under the authority of the Israeli government.

3. "All of them dwelling without walls, and having neither bars nor gates" (Ezekiel 38:11b).

Walls, bars, and gates are boundary dividers throughout Israel today. In order to pass in to the West Bank (Judea and Samaria), one must enter and exit through security checkpoints. For this to be a land "without walls, bars, and gates," Israel must be sovereign in the land according to the Genesis 15 boundaries.

4. "To carry away silver and gold" (Ezekiel 38:13).

At no point in Israel's history has either silver or gold been a natural geological resource. Although there were a number of periods when gold and silver adorned the First and Second Temples, Israel does not mine these commodities. Yet, two major discoveries have recently been made in Israel that, in modern terms, would place the nation in a position to have enough "gold and silver" to plunder. The Leviathan gas discovery off the coast of Haifa now has silver pipes distributing natural gas both within Israel and across the Mediterranean. The silver is now understood to be the silver pipelines containing the vast wealth of one of the largest natural gas deposits in the world.

With the discovery of one of the world's largest oil reserves under the Golan Heights, which is now sovereign Israel, we see a new form of gold—black gold, in the form of this incredibly valuable resource.

5. "In that day when my people of Israel dwelleth safely" (Ezekiel 38:14).

For Israel to dwell safely, it has to be protected by more than just treaties that can be easily broken. Israel must be sovereign in the land God promised. It appears that the Psalm 83 war will grant Israel full occupancy of the bordering nations that once posed a threat to the nation's peace and safety. Through this expansion into the biblically mandated boundaries of Israel, safety is assured through new military installations directly bordering Iran to the east, Turkey to the north, and deeper into Egypt and Saudi Arabia.

No timeline is given between the expansion of Israel's borders and the invasion of the confederates of Ezekiel 38 and 39; however, Israel is in a much better position to prepare and follow God's instructions to flee to safety to avoid the loss of life.

As in any military threat to a nation, a plan is in place to protect the leadership of that nation to ensure a continuity of government. In the case of Israel, through the expansion of its borders, the safety and security of Petra is now under Israel's sovereignty. Isaiah 63 gives us great insight into where the leadership of Israel may be sequestered to avoid the armies of the Antichrist:

Who is this that cometh from Edom, with dyed garments from Bozrah? this that is glorious in his apparel, travelling in the greatness of his strength? I that speak in righteousness, mighty to save.

Wherefore art thou red in thine apparel, and thy garments like him that treadeth in the winefat?

I have trodden the winepress alone; and of the people there was none with me: for I will tread them in mine anger, and trample them in my fury; and their blood shall be sprinkled upon my garments, and I will stain all my raiment.

For the day of vengeance is in mine heart, and the year of my redeemed is come.

And I looked, and there was none to help; and I wondered that there was none to uphold: therefore mine own arm brought salvation unto me; and my fury, it upheld me.

And I will tread down the people in mine anger, and make them drunk in my fury, and I will bring down their strength to the earth.

I will mention the loving kindnesses of the LORD, and the praises of the LORD, according to all that the LORD hath bestowed on us, and the great goodness toward the house of Israel, which he hath bestowed on them according to his mercies, and according to the multitude of his loving kindnesses.

For he said, Surely they are my people, children that will not lie: so he was their Saviour.

In all their affliction he was afflicted, and the angel of his presence saved them: in his love and in his pity he redeemed them; and he bare them, and carried them all the days of old.

Bozrah in Hebrew means "sheepfold" or "enclosure." In Micah, we find a prophecy from the Lord declaring Bozrah as the sheep pen of the remnant of Israel:

I will surely assemble, O Jacob, all of thee; I will surely gather the remnant of Israel. I will put them together as the sheep of Bozrah, as the flock in the midst of their fold. (Micah 2:12a)

As the armies of the Antichrist march across Israel, the leadership is sequestered in the safe place with limited access. Petra meets all the requirements, as its entrance is narrow like the sheep's path, and an advancing army would only be able to enter two by two. However, the invading armies can surround the leadership of Israel and cut off all paths of escape.

Is this the scene of Isaiah 63? Do the leaders of Israel find themselves on the verge of destruction and in desperation cry out the very words Jesus predicted must be said to call for His return in Matthew 23:37–39? That being the case, Jesus returns to singlehandedly defeat the armies of the Antichrist and save Israel. This then leads to the two-hundred-mile victory march from Petra to the Mount of Olives and the fulfillment of Zechariah 14.

16

The Events Leading to the Millennial Reign

This encapsulated list of events as described in Scripture, in some cases, defies the traditional thinking that the Second Coming is being referred to in Zechariah 14 with the description of the Messiah planting His feet on the Mount of Olives. Upon examination of the Scriptures and Jesus' declaration in Matthew 23:37–39 that requires "Jerusalem" to call for His return, traditional thinking is that the Jews are in Jerusalem at the time of His return. According to Scripture, the Jews that He is addressing are not in Jerusalem when the call for His return goes out. There is no question that Zechariah 14 is the final destination point that ushers in the millennial reign, but it is at the end of a series of events that must take place in order for all that must happen.

1. The assembling of the allies of Antichrist. When the sixth bowl is poured out, the Euphrates River is dried up and the kings of the earth are gathered to the valley of Jezreel.

Revelation 16:12–16:

And the sixth angel poured out his vial upon the great river Euphrates; and the water thereof was dried up, that the way of the kings of the east might be prepared.

And I saw three unclean spirits like frogs come out of the mouth of the dragon, and out of the mouth of the beast, and out of the mouth of the false prophet.

For they are the spirits of devils, working miracles, which go forth unto the kings of the earth and of the whole world, to gather them to the battle of that great day of God Almighty.

Behold, I come as a thief. Blessed is he that watcheth, and keepeth his garments, lest he walk naked, and they see his shame.

And he gathered them together into a place called fin the Hebrew tongue Armageddon.

Joel 3:9–11:

Proclaim ye this among the Gentiles; Prepare war, wake up the mighty men, let all the men of war draw near; let them come up:

Beat your plowshares into swords, and your pruninghooks into spears: let the weak say, I am strong.

Assemble yourselves, and come, all ye heathen, and gather yourselves together round about: thither cause thy mighty ones to come down, O Lord.

2. The destruction of Babylon. Babylon is rebuilt on the banks of the Euphrates to become the world economic capital.
Zechariah 5:5–11:

Then the angel that talked with me went forth, and said unto me, Lift up now thine eyes, and see what is this that goeth forth.

And I said, What is it? And he said, This is an ephah that

goeth forth. He said moreover, This is their resemblance through all the earth.

And, behold, there was lifted up a talent of lead: and this is a woman that sitteth in the midst of the ephah.

And he said, This is wickedness. And he cast it into the midst of the ephah; and he cast the weight of lead upon the mouth thereof.

Then lifted I up mine eyes, and looked, and, behold, there came out two women, and the wind was in their wings; for they had wings like the wings of a stork: and they lifted up the ephah between the earth and the heaven.

Then said I to the angel that talked with me, Whither do these bear the ephah?

And he said unto me, To build it an house in the land of Shinar: and it shall be established, and set there upon her own base.

While the Antichrist is away at Megiddo, Babylon undergoes catastrophic destruction.

Jeremiah 50:1–20

The word that the LORD spake against Babylon and against the land of the Chaldeans by Jeremiah the prophet.

Declare ye among the nations, and publish, and set up a standard; publish, and conceal not: say, Babylon is taken, Bel is confounded, Merodach is broken in pieces; her idols are confounded, her images are broken in pieces.

For out of the north there cometh up a nation against her, which shall make her land desolate, and none shall dwell therein: they shall remove, they shall depart, both man and beast.

In those days, and in that time, saith the LORD, the children of Israel shall come, they and the children of Judah together, going and weeping: they shall go, and seek the LORD their God.

They shall ask the way to Zion with their faces thitherward, saying, Come, and let us join ourselves to the LORD in a perpetual covenant that shall not be forgotten.

My people hath been lost sheep: their shepherds have caused them to go astray, they have turned them away on the mountains: they have gone from mountain to hill, they have forgotten their resting place.

All that found them have devoured them: and their adversaries said, We offend not, because they have sinned against the LORD, the habitation of justice, even the LORD, the hope of their fathers.

Remove out of the midst of Babylon, and go forth out of the land of the Chaldeans, and be as the he goats before the flocks.

For, lo, I will raise and cause to come up against Babylon an assembly of great nations from the north country: and they shall set themselves in array against her; from thence she shall be taken: their arrows shall be as of a mighty expert man; none shall return in vain.

And Chaldea shall be a spoil: all that spoil her shall be satisfied, saith the LORD.

Because ye were glad, because ye rejoiced, O ye destroyers of mine heritage, because ye are grown fat as the heifer at grass, and bellow as bulls;

Your mother shall be sore confounded; she that bare you shall be ashamed: behold, the hindermost of the nations shall be a wilderness, a dry land, and a desert.

Because of the wrath of the LORD it shall not be inhabited, but it shall be wholly desolate: every one that goeth by Babylon shall be astonished, and hiss at all her plagues.

Put yourselves in array against Babylon round about: all ye

that bend the bow, shoot at her, spare no arrows: for she hath sinned against the LORD.

Shout against her round about: she hath given her hand: her foundations are fallen, her walls are thrown down: for it is the vengeance of the LORD: take vengeance upon her; as she hath done, do unto her.

Cut off the sower from Babylon, and him that handleth the sickle in the time of harvest: for fear of the oppressing sword they shall turn every one to his people, and they shall flee every one to his own land.

Israel is a scattered sheep; the lions have driven him away: first the king of Assyria hath devoured him; and last this Nebuchadnezzar king of Babylon hath broken his bones.

Therefore thus saith the LORD of hosts, the God of Israel; Behold, I will punish the king of Babylon and his land, as I have punished the king of Assyria.

And I will bring Israel again to his habitation, and he shall feed on Carmel and Bashan, and his soul shall be satisfied upon mount Ephraim and Gilead.

In those days, and in that time, saith the LORD, the iniquity of Israel shall be sought for, and there shall be none; and the sins of Judah, and they shall not be found: for I will pardon them whom I reserve.

3. The fall of Jerusalem. The Antichrist receives news that his capital city has been destroyed and moves south against Jerusalem.
Zechariah 12:1–3:

The burden of the word of the LORD for Israel, saith the LORD, which stretcheth forth the heavens, and layeth the foundation of the earth, and formeth the spirit of man within him.

Behold, I will make Jerusalem a cup of trembling unto all

the people round about, when they shall be in the siege both against Judah and against Jerusalem.

And in that day will I make Jerusalem a burdensome stone for all people: all that burden themselves with it shall be cut in pieces, though all the people of the earth be gathered together against it.

Zechariah 14:1–9:

Behold, the day of the LORD cometh, and thy spoil shall be divided in the midst of thee.

For I will gather all nations against Jerusalem to battle; and the city shall be taken, and the houses rifled, and the women ravished; and half of the city shall go forth into captivity, and the residue of the people shall not be cut off from the city.

Then shall the LORD go forth, and fight against those nations, as when he fought in the day of battle.

And his feet shall stand in that day upon the mount of Olives, which is before Jerusalem on the east, and the mount of Olives shall cleave in the midst thereof toward the east and toward the west, and there shall be a very great valley; and half of the mountain shall remove toward the north, and half of it toward the south.

And ye shall flee to the valley of the mountains; for the valley of the mountains shall reach unto Azal: yea, ye shall flee, like as ye fled from before the earthquake in the days of Uzziah king of Judah: and the LORD my God shall come, and all the saints with thee.

And it shall come to pass in that day, that the light shall not be clear, nor dark:

But it shall be one day which shall be known to the LORD, not day, nor night: but it shall come to pass, that at evening time it shall be light.

And it shall be in that day, that living waters shall go out from Jerusalem; half of them toward the former sea, and half of them toward the hinder sea: in summer and in winter shall it be.

And the LORD shall be king over all the earth: in that day shall there be one LORD, and his name one.

The Jews will put up a mighty defense, but Jerusalem will eventually fall.

4. The armies of the Antichrist at Bozrah. The Jewish remnant flees to the mountains.

Matthew 24:15–16:

When ye therefore shall see the abomination of desolation, spoken of by Daniel the prophet, stand in the holy place, (whoso readeth, let him understand:)

Then let them which be in Judaea flee into the mountains.

Micah 2:12:

I will surely assemble, O Jacob, all of thee; I will surely gather the remnant of Israel; I will put them together as the sheep of Bozrah, as the flock in the midst of their fold: they shall make great noise by reason of the multitude of men.

5. The national regeneration of Israel. The Jews confess their national sin: the rejection and crucifixion of Messiah Jesus.

Leviticus 26:40–42:

If they shall confess their iniquity, and the iniquity of their fathers, with their trespass which they trespassed against me, and that also they have walked contrary unto me.

And that I also have walked contrary unto them, and have brought them into the land of their enemies; if then their uncircumcised hearts be humbled, and they then accept of the punishment of their iniquity:

Then will I remember my covenant with Jacob, and also my covenant with Isaac, and also my covenant with Abraham will I remember; and I will remember the land.

Jeremiah. 3:11–18:

And the LORD said unto me, The backsliding Israel hath justified herself more than treacherous Judah.

Go and proclaim these words toward the north, and say, Return, thou backsliding Israel, saith the LORD; and I will not cause mine anger to fall upon you: for I am merciful, saith the LORD, and I will not keep anger for ever.

Only acknowledge thine iniquity, that thou hast transgressed against the LORD thy God, and hast scattered thy ways to the strangers under every green tree, and ye have not obeyed my voice, saith the LORD.

Turn, O backsliding children, saith the LORD; for I am married unto you: and I will take you one of a city, and two of a family, and I will bring you to Zion:

And I will give you pastors according to mine heart, which shall feed you with knowledge and understanding.

And it shall come to pass, when ye be multiplied and increased in the land, in those days, saith the LORD, they shall say no more, The ark of the covenant of the LORD: neither shall it come to mind: neither shall they remember it; neither shall they visit it; neither shall that be done any more.

At that time they shall call Jerusalem the throne of the Lord; and all the nations shall be gathered unto it, to the name of the Lord, to Jerusalem: neither shall they walk any more after the imagination of their evil heart.

In those days the house of Judah shall walk with the house of Israel, and they shall come together out of the land of the north to the land that I have given for an inheritance unto your fathers.

Hosea 5:14:

For I will be unto Ephraim as a lion, and as a young lion to the house of Judah: I, even I, will tear and go away; I will take away, and none shall rescue him.

They then plead for His return; Psalm 79:1–13:

O God, the heathen are come into thine inheritance; thy holy temple have they defiled; they have laid Jerusalem on heaps.

The dead bodies of thy servants have they given to be meat unto the fowls of the heaven, the flesh of thy saints unto the beasts of the earth.

Their blood have they shed like water round about Jerusalem; and there was none to bury them.

We are become a reproach to our neighbours, a scorn and derision to them that are round about us.

How long, LORD? wilt thou be angry for ever? shall thy jealousy burn like fire?

Pour out thy wrath upon the heathen that have not known thee, and upon the kingdoms that have not called upon thy name.

For they have devoured Jacob, and laid waste his dwelling place.

O remember not against us former iniquities: let thy tender mercies speedily prevent us: for we are brought very low.

Help us, O God of our salvation, for the glory of thy name: and deliver us, and purge away our sins, for thy name's sake.

Wherefore should the heathen say, Where is their God? let him be known among the heathen in our sight by the revenging of the blood of thy servants which is shed.

Let the sighing of the prisoner come before thee; according to the greatness of thy power preserve thou those that are appointed to die;

And render unto our neighbours sevenfold into their bosom their reproach, wherewith they have reproached thee, O Lord.

So we thy people and sheep of thy pasture will give thee thanks for ever: we will shew forth thy praise to all generations.

And finally, Matthew 23:39:

For I say unto you, Ye shall not see me henceforth, till ye shall say, Blessed is he that cometh in the name of the Lord.

6. The Second Coming of Messiah. Christ returns to Bozrah, where the remnant has been preserved.
Isaiah 34:1–7:

Come near, ye nations, to hear; and hearken, ye people: let the earth hear, and all that is therein; the world, and all things that come forth of it.

For the indignation of the LORD is upon all nations, and his fury upon all their armies: he hath utterly destroyed them, he hath delivered them to the slaughter.

Their slain also shall be cast out, and their stink shall come up out of their carcases, and the mountains shall be melted with their blood.

And all the host of heaven shall be dissolved, and the heavens shall be rolled together as a scroll: and all their host shall fall down, as the leaf falleth off from the vine, and as a falling fig from the fig tree.

For my sword shall be bathed in heaven: behold, it shall come down upon Idumea, and upon the people of my curse, to judgment.

The sword of the LORD is filled with blood, it is made fat with fatness, and with the blood of lambs and goats, with the fat of the kidneys of rams: for the LORD hath a sacrifice in Bozrah, and a great slaughter in the land of Idumea.

And the unicorns shall come down with them, and the bullocks with the bulls; and their land shall be soaked with blood, and their dust made fat with fatness.

Isaiah 63:1–6:

Who is this that cometh from Edom, with dyed garments from Bozrah? this that is glorious in his apparel, travelling in the greatness of his strength? I that speak in righteousness, mighty to save.

Wherefore art thou red in thine apparel, and thy garments like him that treadeth in the winefat?

I have trodden the winepress alone; and of the people there was none with me: for I will tread them in mine anger, and trample them in my fury; and their blood shall be sprinkled upon my garments, and I will stain all my raiment.

For the day of vengeance is in mine heart, and the year of my redeemed is come.

And I looked, and there was none to help; and I wondered that there was none to uphold: therefore mine own arm brought salvation unto me; and my fury, it upheld me.

And I will tread down the people in mine anger, and make them drunk in my fury, and I will bring down their strength to the earth.

Micah 2:12–13:

I will surely assemble, O Jacob, all of thee; I will surely gather the remnant of Israel; I will put them together as the sheep of Bozrah, as the flock in the midst of their fold: they shall make great noise by reason of the multitude of men.

The breaker is come up before them: they have broken up, and have passed through the gate, and are gone out by it: and their king shall pass before them, and the LORD on the head of them.

Habakkuk 3:1–19:

A prayer of Habakkuk the prophet upon Shigionoth.

O LORD, I have heard thy speech, and was afraid: O LORD, revive thy work in the midst of the years, in the midst of the years make known; in wrath remember mercy.

God came from Teman, and the Holy One from mount Paran. Selah. His glory covered the heavens, and the earth was full of his praise.

And his brightness was as the light; he had horns coming out of his hand: and there was the hiding of his power.

Before him went the pestilence, and burning coals went forth at his feet.

He stood, and measured the earth: he beheld, and drove asunder the nations; and the everlasting mountains were scattered, the perpetual hills did bow: his ways are everlasting.

I saw the tents of Cushan in affliction: and the curtains of the land of Midian did tremble.

Was the LORD displeased against the rivers? was thine anger against the rivers? was thy wrath against the sea, that thou didst ride upon thine horses and thy chariots of salvation?

Thy bow was made quite naked, according to the oaths of the tribes, even thy word. Selah. Thou didst cleave the earth with rivers.

The mountains saw thee, and they trembled: the overflowing of the water passed by: the deep uttered his voice, and lifted up his hands on high.

The sun and moon stood still in their habitation: at the light of thine arrows they went, and at the shining of thy glittering spear.

Thou didst march through the land in indignation, thou didst thresh the heathen in anger.

Thou wentest forth for the salvation of thy people, even for salvation with thine anointed; thou woundedst the head out of the house of the wicked, by discovering the foundation unto the neck. Selah.

Thou didst strike through with his staves the head of his villages: they came out as a whirlwind to scatter me: their rejoicing was as to devour the poor secretly.

Thou didst walk through the sea with thine horses, through the heap of great waters.

When I heard, my belly trembled; my lips quivered at the voice: rottenness entered into my bones, and I trembled in myself, that I might rest in the day of trouble: when he cometh up unto the people, he will invade them with his troops.

Although the fig tree shall not blossom, neither shall fruit be in the vines; the labour of the olive shall fail, and the fields shall yield no meat; the flock shall be cut off from the fold, and there shall be no herd in the stalls:

Yet I will rejoice in the LORD, I will joy in the God of my salvation.

The LORD God is my strength, and he will make my feet like hinds' feet, and he will make me to walk upon mine high places. To the chief singer on my stringed instruments.

Revelation 19:11–19:

And I saw heaven opened, and behold a white horse; and he that sat upon him was called Faithful and True, and in righteousness he doth judge and make war.

His eyes were as a flame of fire, and on his head were many crowns; and he had a name written, that no man knew, but he himself.

And he was clothed with a vesture dipped in blood: and his name is called The Word of God.

And the armies which were in heaven followed him upon white horses, clothed in fine linen, white and clean.

And out of his mouth goeth a sharp sword, that with it he should smite the nations: and he shall rule them with a rod of iron: and he treadeth the winepress of the fierceness and wrath of Almighty God.

And he hath on his vesture and on his thigh a name written, KING OF KINGS AND LORD OF LORDS.

And I saw an angel standing in the sun; and he cried with a loud voice, saying to all the fowls that fly in the midst of heaven, Come and gather yourselves together unto the supper of the great God;

That ye may eat the flesh of kings, and the flesh of captains, and the flesh of mighty men, and the flesh of horses, and of them that sit on them, and the flesh of all men, both free and bond, both small and great.

And I saw the beast, and the kings of the earth, and their armies, gathered together to make war against him that sat on the horse, and against his army.

7. The battle from Bozrah to the Valley of Jehoshaphat. Christ fights the forces of Antichrist from Bozrah continuing all the way back to the eastern walls of Jerusalem, which overlook a section of the Kidron Valley, also known as the Valley of Jehoshaphat. Antichrist is destroyed.

Joel 3:2:

I will also gather all nations, and will bring them down into the valley of Jehoshaphat, and will plead with them there for my people and for my heritage Israel, whom they have scattered among the nations, and parted my land.

Joel 3:13–14:

Put ye in the sickle, for the harvest is ripe: come, get you down; for the press is full, the fats overflow; for their wickedness is great.

Multitudes, multitudes in the valley of decision: for the day of the LORD is near in the valley of decision.

2 Thessalonians 2:8:

And then shall that Wicked be revealed, whom the Lord shall consume with the spirit of his mouth, and shall destroy with the brightness of his coming.

Zechariah 14:12–14:

And this shall be the plague wherewith the LORD will smite all the people that have fought against Jerusalem; Their flesh shall consume away while they stand upon their feet, and their eyes shall consume away in their holes, and their tongue shall consume away in their mouth.

And it shall come to pass in that day, that a great tumult from the LORD shall be among them; and they shall lay hold every one on the hand of his neighbour, and his hand shall rise up against the hand of his neighbour.

And Judah also shall fight at Jerusalem; and the wealth of all the heathen round about shall be gathered together, gold, and silver, and apparel, in great abundance.

Revelation 14:19–20:

And the angel thrust in his sickle into the earth, and gathered the vine of the earth, and cast it into the great winepress of the wrath of God.

And the winepress was trodden without the city, and blood came out of the winepress, even unto the horse bridles, by the space of a thousand and six hundred furlongs.

Revelation 19:20:

And the beast was taken, and with him the false prophet that wrought miracles before him, with which he deceived them that had received the mark of the beast, and them that worshipped his image. These both were cast alive into a lake of fire burning with brimstone.

8. The victory ascent up the Mount of Olives. This is not the initial return of Christ, for He will save the tents of Judah first.

Zechariah 12:7:

The LORD also shall save the tents of Judah first, that the glory of the house of David and the glory of the inhabitants of Jerusalem do not magnify themselves against Judah.

Nor will his initial return be to the same place He ascended, the Mount of Olives, but merely in the same manner (Acts 1:11: "shall so come in like manner as ye have seen him go into heaven").

His ascent to the mount is accompanied by cataclysmic events associated with the seventh bowl judgment.

Matthew 24:29:

Immediately after the tribulation of those days shall the sun be darkened, and the moon shall not give her light, and the stars shall fall from heaven, and the powers of the heavens shall be shaken.

Zechariah 14:4–5:

And his feet shall stand in that day upon the mount of Olives, which is before Jerusalem on the east, and the mount of Olives shall cleave in the midst thereof toward the east and toward the west, and there shall be a very great valley; and half of the mountain shall remove toward the north, and half of it toward the south.

And ye shall flee to the valley of the mountains; for the valley of the mountains shall reach unto Azal: yea, ye shall flee, like as ye fled from before the earthquake in the days of Uzziah king of Judah: and the LORD my God shall come, and all the saints with thee.

Revelation 16:17–21:

And the seventh angel poured out his vial into the air; and there came a great voice out of the temple of heaven, from the throne, saying, It is done.

And there were voices, and thunders, and lightnings; and there was a great earthquake, such as was not since men were upon the earth, so mighty an earthquake, and so great.

And the great city was divided into three parts, and the cities of the nations fell: and great Babylon came in remembrance before God, to give unto her the cup of the wine of the fierceness of his wrath.

And every island fled away, and the mountains were not found.

And there fell upon men a great hail out of heaven, every stone about the weight of a talent: and men blasphemed God because of the plague of the hail; for the plague thereof was exceeding great.

And the seed of the serpent, the Antichrist, has been destroyed. This fatal blow to the agenda of Satan brings an end to plans to cut off the seed line of Messiah. But this is not the end of his story, and Satan's fate is now in the hands of Messiah. For almost six thousand years, Satan has hung onto the hope that he could usurp the dominion of the seed of the woman in the same manner he has usurped man's dominion of the earth. Every diabolical scheme and deception has now failed, and the next thousand years will be nothing like the first six thousand. The prophecy of Genesis 3:15 will now have been fulfilled in part, but God's work to rid all the workings of evil and sin from the face of the earth will have become an addendum to the prophecy. Until all things can be made new and we can return to the Garden of Eden for eternity, the work of God is not finished.

17

Genesis 3:15 Fulfilled

With the elimination of the seed of the serpent, the Antichrist, God will ultimately focus on ridding humanity from evil and dealing with Satan and those who followed him out of heaven, those who took the mark of the Beast, and the remainder of humanity that has not accepted His plan of atonement through the shed blood of Yeshua/Jesus.

In a world that is desperate for peace, the millennial reign of Messiah will be a welcomed time of peace for all of mankind. It will be a period in which Yeshua/Jesus will have sovereign rule on earth for one thousand years, in fulfillment of many Old and New Testament prophecies. During Jesus' reign, Satan will be bound and sealed in the bottomless pit so that he will have no influence on the earth to deceive mankind. Jesus' supremacy will span the entire world, over which He will be King of Kings and Lord of Lords. He will also sit on the throne of His Father, David, ruling over Israel.

The millennium will be the period of the full manifestation of the glory of the Lord Jesus Christ. There will be the manifestation of glory associated with the humanity of Christ. There will be the glory of a glorious dominion, in which Christ, by virtue of his obedience unto death, is given universal dominion to replace that dominion which Adam lost. There will be the glory of a glorious government, in which Christ, as David's son is given absolute power to govern. There will be the glory of a glorious inheritance, in which the land and the seed promised to Abraham are realized through Christ.[278]

The Beginning of the End

In John's vision on Patmos, God revealed a vivid picture summarizing a series of events that connect the prophecies of the Old Testament with the final period of judgment that ultimately leads to the cleansing of both Heaven and earth of all sin. In the following passages from Revelation, the story is made complete without much needed commentary. In keeping with God's commandment not to add or take away anything from His Word, I have chosen to let the Word of God speak for itself. In these passages, Genesis 3:15, "And I will put enmity between thee and the woman, and between thy seed and her seed; it shall bruise thy head, and thou shalt bruise his heel," is fulfilled. As believers in Messiah, we return to the beginning and take our place in the Garden of Eden for all eternity. As Yeshua/Jesus said in his last breath, "IT IS FINISHED."

Revelation 12 (1–17):

And there appeared a great wonder in heaven; a woman clothed with the sun, and the moon under her feet, and upon her head a crown of twelve stars:

And she being with child cried, travailing in birth, and pained to be delivered.

And there appeared another wonder in heaven; and behold a great red dragon, having seven heads and ten horns, and seven crowns upon his heads.

And his tail drew the third part of the stars of heaven, and did cast them to the earth: and the dragon stood before the woman which was ready to be delivered, for to devour her child as soon as it was born.

And she brought forth a man child, who was to rule all nations with a rod of iron: and her child was caught up unto God, and to his throne.

And the woman fled into the wilderness, where she hath a place prepared of God, that they should feed her there a thousand two hundred and threescore days.

And there was war in heaven: Michael and his angels fought against the dragon; and the dragon fought and his angels,

And prevailed not; neither was their place found any more in heaven. And the great dragon was cast out, that old serpent, called the Devil, and Satan, which deceiveth the whole world: he was cast out into the earth, and his angels were cast out with him.

And I heard a loud voice saying in heaven, Now is come salvation, and strength, and the kingdom of our God, and the power of his Christ: for the accuser of our brethren is cast down, which accused them before our God Day and night.

And they overcame him by the blood of the Lamb, and by the word of their testimony; and they loved not their lives unto the death.

Therefore rejoice, ye heavens, and ye that dwell in them. Woe to the inhabiters of the earth and of the sea! for the devil is come down unto you, having great wrath, because he knoweth that he hath but a short time.

And when the dragon saw that he was cast unto the earth, he persecuted the woman which brought forth the man child.

And to the woman were given two wings of a great eagle, that she might fly into the wilderness, into her place, where she is nourished for a time, and times, and half a time, from the face of the serpent.

And the serpent cast out of his mouth water as a flood after the woman, that he might cause her to be carried away of the flood.

And the earth helped the woman, and the earth opened her mouth, and swallowed up the flood which the dragon cast out of his mouth.

And the dragon was wroth with the woman, and went to make war with the remnant of her seed, which keep the commandments of God, and have the testimony of Jesus Christ.

Now sin will have been expelled from Heaven; no longer will Satan have any power by which to bring an accusation against man before the Divine Council. But this will not yet be the end.

Revelation 13:1–18:

And I stood upon the sand of the sea, and saw a beast rise up out of the sea, having seven heads and ten horns, and upon his horns ten crowns, and upon his heads the name of blasphemy.

And the beast which I saw was like unto a leopard, and his feet were as the feet of a bear, and his mouth as the mouth of a lion: and the dragon gave him his power, and his seat, and great authority.

And I saw one of his heads as it were wounded to death; and his deadly wound was healed: and all the world wondered after the beast.

And they worshipped the dragon which gave power unto the beast: and they worshipped the beast, saying, Who is like unto the beast? who is able to make war with him?

And there was given unto him a mouth speaking great things and blasphemies; and power was given unto him to continue forty and two months.

And he opened his mouth in blasphemy against God, to blaspheme his name, and his tabernacle, and them that dwell in heaven.

And it was given unto him to make war with the saints, and to overcome them: and power was given him over all kindreds, and tongues, and nations.

And all that dwell upon the earth shall worship him, whose names are not written in the book of life of the Lamb slain from the foundation of the world.

If any man have an ear, let him hear.

He that leadeth into captivity shall go into captivity: he that killeth with the sword must be killed with the sword. Here is the patience and the faith of the saints.

And I beheld another beast coming up out of the earth; and he had two horns like a lamb, and he spake as a dragon.

And he exerciseth all the power of the first beast before him, and causeth the earth and them which dwell therein to worship the first beast, whose deadly wound was healed.

And he doeth great wonders, so that he maketh fire come down from heaven on the earth in the sight of men,

And deceiveth them that dwell on the earth by the means of those miracles which he had power to do in the sight of the beast; saying to them that dwell on the earth, that they should make an image to the beast, which had the wound by a sword, and did live.

And he had power to give life unto the image of the beast, that the image of the beast should both speak, and cause that as many as would not worship the image of the beast should be killed.

And he causeth all, both small and great, rich and poor, free and bond, to receive a mark in their right hand, or in their foreheads:

And that no man might buy or sell, save he that had the mark, or the name of the beast, or the number of his name.

Here is wisdom. Let him that hath understanding count the number of the beast: for it is the number of a man; and his number is Six hundred threescore and six.

Revelation 15:1–8:

And I saw another sign in heaven, great and marvelous, seven angels having the seven last plagues; for in them is filled up the wrath of God.

And I saw as it were a sea of glass mingled with fire: and them that had gotten the victory over the beast, and over his image, and over his mark, and over the number of his name, stand on the sea of glass, having the harps of God.

And they sing the song of Moses the servant of God, and the song of the Lamb, saying, Great and marvelous are thy works, Lord God Almighty; just and true are thy ways, thou King of saints.

Who shall not fear thee, O Lord, and glorify thy name? for thou only art holy: for all nations shall come and worship before thee; for thy judgments are made manifest.

And after that I looked, and, behold, the temple of the tabernacle of the testimony in heaven was opened:

And the seven angels came out of the temple, having the seven plagues, clothed in pure and white linen, and having their breasts girded with golden girdles.

And one of the four beasts gave unto the seven angels seven golden vials full of the wrath of God, who liveth for ever and ever.

And the temple was filled with smoke from the glory of God, and from his power; and no man was able to enter into the temple, till the seven plagues of the seven angels were fulfilled.

Revelation 19:1–21:

And after these things I heard a great voice of much people in heaven, saying, Alleluia; Salvation, and glory, and honour, and power, unto the Lord our God:

For true and righteous are his judgments: for he hath judged the great whore, which did corrupt the earth with her fornication, and hath avenged the blood of his servants at her hand.

And again they said, Alleluia And her smoke rose up for ever and ever.

And the four and twenty elders and the four beasts fell down and worshipped God that sat on the throne, saying, Amen; Alleluia.

And a voice came out of the throne, saying, Praise our God, all ye his servants, and ye that fear him, both small and great.

And I heard as it were the voice of a great multitude, and as the voice of many waters, and as the voice of mighty thunderings, saying, Alleluia: for the Lord God omnipotent reigneth.

Let us be glad and rejoice, and give honour to him: for the marriage of the Lamb is come, and his wife hath made herself ready.

And to her was granted that she should be arrayed in fine linen, clean and white: for the fine linen is the righteousness of saints.

And he saith unto me, Write, Blessed are they which are called unto the marriage supper of the Lamb. And he saith unto me, These are the true sayings of God.

And I fell at his feet to worship him. And he said unto me, See thou do it not: I am thy fellow servant, and of thy brethren that have the testimony of Jesus: worship God: for the testimony of Jesus is the spirit of prophecy.

And I saw heaven opened, and behold a white horse; and

he that sat upon him was called Faithful and True, and in righteousness he doth judge and make war.

His eyes were as a flame of fire, and on his head were many crowns; and he had a name written, that no man knew, but he himself.

And he was clothed with a vesture dipped in blood: and his name is called The Word of God.

And the armies which were in heaven followed him upon white horses, clothed in fine linen, white and clean.

And out of his mouth goeth a sharp sword, that with it he should smite the nations: and he shall rule them with a rod of iron: and he treadeth the winepress of the fierceness and wrath of Almighty God.

And he hath on his vesture and on his thigh a name written, KING OF KINGS, AND LORD OF LORDS.

And I saw an angel standing in the sun; and he cried with a loud voice, saying to all the fowls that fly in the midst of heaven, Come and gather yourselves together unto the supper of the great God;

That ye may eat the flesh of kings, and the flesh of captains, and the flesh of mighty men, and the flesh of horses, and of them that sit on them, and the flesh of all men, both free and bond, both small and great.

And I saw the beast, and the kings of the earth, and their armies, gathered together to make war against him that sat on the horse, and against his army.

And the beast was taken, and with him the false prophet that wrought miracles before him, with which he deceived them that had received the mark of the beast, and them that worshipped his image. These both were cast alive into a lake of fire burning with brimstone.

And the remnant were slain with the sword of him that sat

upon the horse, which sword proceeded out of his mouth: and all the fowls were filled with their flesh.

Revelation 20:1–15:

And I saw an angel come down from heaven, having the key of the bottomless pit and a great chain in his hand.

And he laid hold on the dragon, that old serpent, which is the Devil, and Satan, and bound him a thousand years,

And cast him into the bottomless pit, and shut him up, and set a seal upon him, that he should deceive the nations no more, till the thousand years should be fulfilled: and after that he must be loosed a little season.

And I saw thrones, and they sat upon them, and judgment was given unto them: and I saw the souls of them that were beheaded for the witness of Jesus, and for the word of God, and which had not worshipped the beast, neither his image, neither had received his mark upon their foreheads, or in their hands; and they lived and reigned with Christ a thousand years.

But the rest of the dead lived not again until the thousand years were finished. This is the first resurrection.

Blessed and holy is he that hath part in the first resurrection: on such the second death hath no power, but they shall be priests of God and of Christ, and shall reign with him a thousand years.

And when the thousand years are expired, Satan shall be loosed out of his prison,

And shall go out to deceive the nations which are in the four quarters of the earth, Gog, and Magog, to gather them together to battle: the number of whom is as the sand of the sea.

And they went up on the breadth of the earth, and compassed the camp of the saints about, and the beloved city: and fire came down from God out of heaven, and devoured them.

And the devil that deceived them was cast into the lake of fire and brimstone, where the beast and the false prophet are, and shall be tormented day and night for ever and ever.

And I saw a great white throne, and him that sat on it, from whose face the earth and the heaven fled away; and there was found no place for them.

And I saw the dead, small and great, stand before God; and the books were opened: and another book was opened, which is the book of life: and the dead were judged out of those things which were written in the books, according to their works.

And the sea gave up the dead which were in it; and death and hell delivered up the dead which were in them: and they were judged every man according to their works.

And death and hell were cast into the lake of fire. This is the second death.

And whosoever was not found written in the book of life was cast into the lake of fire.

Revelation 21:1–27:

And I saw a new heaven and a new earth: for the first heaven and the first earth were passed away; and there was no more sea.

And I John saw the holy city, new Jerusalem, coming down from God out of heaven, prepared as a bride adorned for her husband.

And I heard a great voice out of heaven saying, Behold, the tabernacle of God is with men, and he will dwell with them, and they shall be his people, and God himself shall be with them, and be their God.

And God shall wipe away all tears from their eyes; and there shall be no more death, neither sorrow, nor crying, neither shall there be any more pain: for the former things are passed away.

And he that sat upon the throne said, Behold, I make all things new. And he said unto me, Write: for these words are true and faithful.

And he said unto me, It is done. I am Alpha and Omega, the beginning and the end. I will give unto him that is athirst of the fountain of the water of life freely.

He that overcometh shall inherit all things; and I will be his God, and he shall be my son.

But the fearful, and unbelieving, and the abominable, and murderers, and whoremongers, and sorcerers, and idolaters, and all liars, shall have their part in the lake which burneth with fire and brimstone: which is the second death.

And there came unto me one of the seven angels which had the seven vials full of the seven last plagues, and talked with me, saying, Come hither, I will shew thee the bride, the Lamb's wife.

And he carried me away in the spirit to a great and high mountain, and shewed me that great city, the holy Jerusalem, descending out of heaven from God,

Having the glory of God: and her light was like unto a stone most precious, even like a jasper stone, clear as crystal;

And had a wall great and high, and had twelve gates, and at the gates twelve angels, and names written thereon, which are the names of the twelve tribes of the children of Israel:

On the east three gates; on the north three gates; on the south three gates; and on the west three gates.

And the wall of the city had twelve foundations, and in them the names of the twelve apostles of the Lamb.

And he that talked with me had a golden reed to measure the city, and the gates thereof, and the wall thereof.

And the city lieth foursquare, and the length is as large as the breadth: and he measured the city with the reed, twelve thousand furlongs. The length and the breadth and the height of it are equal.

And he measured the wall thereof, an hundred and forty and four cubits, according to the measure of a man, that is, of the angel.

And the building of the wall of it was of jasper: and the city was pure gold, like unto clear glass.

And the foundations of the wall of the city were garnished with all manner of precious stones. The first foundation was jasper; the second, sapphire; the third, a chalcedony; the fourth, an emerald;

The fifth, sardonyx; the sixth, sardius; the seventh, chrysolyte; the eighth, beryl; the ninth, a topaz; the tenth, a chrysoprasus; the eleventh, a jacinth; the twelfth, an amethyst.

And the twelve gates were twelve pearls: every several gate was of one pearl: and the street of the city was pure gold, as it were transparent glass.

And I saw no temple therein: for the Lord God Almighty and the Lamb are the temple of it.

And the city had no need of the sun, neither of the moon, to shine in it: for the glory of God did lighten it, and the Lamb is the light thereof.

And the nations of them which are saved shall walk in the light of it: and the kings of the earth do bring their glory and honour into it.

And the gates of it shall not be shut at all by day: for there shall be no night there.

And they shall bring the glory and honour of the nations into it.

And there shall in no wise enter into it anything that defileth, neither whatsoever worketh abomination, or maketh a lie: but they which are written in the Lamb's book of life.

Revelation 22:1–21

And he shewed me a pure river of water of life, clear as crystal, proceeding out of the throne of God and of the Lamb.

In the midst of the street of it, and on either side of the river, was there the tree of life, which bare twelve manner of fruits, and yielded her fruit every month: and the leaves of the tree were for the healing of the nations.

And there shall be no more curse: but the throne of God and of the Lamb shall be in it; and his servants shall serve him:

And they shall see his face; and his name shall be in their foreheads.

And there shall be no night there; and they need no candle, neither light of the sun; for the Lord God giveth them light: and they shall reign for ever and ever.

And he said unto me, These sayings are faithful and true: and the Lord God of the holy prophets sent his angel to shew unto his servants the things which must shortly be done.

Behold, I come quickly: blessed is he that keepeth the sayings of the prophecy of this book.

And I John saw these things, and heard them. And when I had heard and seen, I fell down to worship before the feet of the angel which shewed me these things.

Then saith he unto me, See thou do it not: for I am thy fellow servant, and of thy brethren the prophets, and of them which keep the sayings of this book: worship God.

And he saith unto me, Seal not the sayings of the prophecy of this book: for the time is at hand.

He that is unjust, let him be unjust still: and he which is filthy, let him be filthy still: and he that is righteous, let him be righteous still: and he that is holy, let him be holy still.

And, behold, I come quickly; and my reward is with me, to give every man according as his work shall be.

I am Alpha and Omega, the beginning and the end, the first and the last.

Blessed are they that do his commandments, that they may have right to the tree of life, and may enter in through the gates into the city.

For without are dogs, and sorcerers, and whoremongers, and murderers, and idolaters, and whosoever loveth and maketh a lie.

I Jesus have sent mine angel to testify unto you these things in the churches. I am the root and the offspring of David, and the bright and morning star.

And the Spirit and the bride say, Come. And let him that heareth say, Come. And let him that is athirst come. And whosoever will, let him take the water of life freely.

For I testify unto every man that heareth the words of the prophecy of this book, If any man shall add unto these things, God shall add unto him the plagues that are written in this book:

And if any man shall take away from the words of the book of this prophecy, God shall take away his part out of the book of life, and out of the holy city, and from the things which are written in this book.

He which testifieth these things saith, Surely I come quickly. Amen. Even so, come, Lord Jesus.

The grace of our Lord Jesus Christ be with you all. Amen.

NOW IT IS FINISHED!

18

While We Wait

Now that we know the truth behind Genesis 3:15 and how Satan's plan is at work, what do we do while we wait for the prophecies to unfold? We only need to look at Scripture to find the list of instructions.

1. Bless Israel!

And I will bless them that bless thee, and curse him that curseth thee: and in thee shall all families of the earth be blessed. (Genesis 12:3)

- Find a ministry that operates in Israel advancing the gospel and providing humanitarian aid. I highly recommend Messiah of Israel Ministries (https://www.messiahofisraelministries.org) and the work of Rabbi Zev Porat.
- Visit Israel on a tour. My tours are listed at www.ignitinganation.com/events, or join SkyWatch or Rabbi Zev Porat on their tours.

2. Pray for the peace of Jerusalem.

I was glad when they said unto me, Let us go into the house of the LORD.

Our feet shall stand within thy gates, O Jerusalem.

Jerusalem is builded as a city that is compact together:

Whither the tribes go up, the tribes of the LORD, unto the testimony of Israel, to give thanks unto the name of the LORD.

For there are set thrones of judgment, the thrones of the house of David.

Pray for the peace of Jerusalem: they shall prosper that love thee.

Peace be within thy walls, and prosperity within thy palaces.

For my brethren and companions' sakes, I will now say, Peace be within thee.

Because of the house of the LORD our God I will seek thy good. (Emphasis added)

The peace of Jerusalem is not a something, it is a someone: Yeshua. We long for His return, but we must pray that the scales will fall from the eyes of those who have been deceived by Satan's plan.

3. Repent!

If my people, which are called by my name, shall humble themselves, and pray, and seek my face, and turn from their wicked ways; then will I hear from heaven, and will forgive their sin, and will heal their land. (2 Chronicles 7:14)

If you are a believer in the Jewish Messiah and have harbored anti-Semitic, anti-Jewish, or anti-Israel sentiments, you must repent of this, as it is an unbiblical position.

If you have allowed replacement theology or believe in any way that God has broken His covenant with Israel, then you must ask yourself, "If God can break His eternal covenant with Israel, then why couldn't He break His covenant with me? (John 3:16).

Paul made it perfectly clear in Romans 11:

I say then, Hath God cast away his people? God forbid. For I also am an Israelite, of the seed of Abraham, of the tribe of Benjamin.

God hath not cast away his people which he foreknew. Wot ye not what the scripture saith of Elias? how he maketh intercession to God against Israel saying,

Lord, they have killed thy prophets, and digged down thine altars; and I am left alone, and they seek my life.

But what saith the answer of God unto him? I have reserved to myself seven thousand men, who have not bowed the knee to the image of Baal.

Even so then at this present time also there is a remnant according to the election of grace.

And if by grace, then is it no more of works: otherwise grace is no more grace. But if it be of works, then it is no more grace: otherwise work is no more work.

What then? Israel hath not obtained that which he seeketh for; but the election hath obtained it, and the rest were blinded.

(According as it is written, God hath given them the spirit of slumber, eyes that they should not see, and ears that they should not hear;) unto this day.

And David saith, Let their table be made a snare, and a trap, and a stumbling block, and a recompence unto them:

Let their eyes be darkened, that they may not see, and bow down their back alway.

I say then, Have they stumbled that they should fall? God forbid: but rather through their fall salvation is come unto the Gentiles, for to provoke them to jealousy.

Now if the fall of them be the riches of the world, and the diminishing of them the riches of the Gentiles; how much more their fulness?

For I speak to you Gentiles, inasmuch as I am the apostle of the Gentiles, I magnify mine office:

If by any means I may provoke to emulation them which are my flesh, and might save some of them.

For if the casting away of them be the reconciling of the world, what shall the receiving of them be, but life from the dead?

For if the firstfruit be holy, the lump is also holy: and if the root be holy, so are the branches.

And if some of the branches be broken off, and thou, being a wild olive tree, wert grafted in among them, and with them partakest of the root and fatness of the olive tree;

Boast not against the branches. But if thou boast, thou bearest not the root, but the root thee.

Thou wilt say then, The branches were broken off, that I might be grafted in.

Well; because of unbelief they were broken off, and thou standest by faith. Be not high minded, but fear:

For if God spared not the natural branches, take heed lest he also spare not thee.

Behold therefore the goodness and severity of God: on them which fell, severity; but toward thee, goodness, if thou continue in his goodness: otherwise thou also shalt be cut off.

And they also, if they abide not still in unbelief, shall be grafted in: for God is able to graft them in again.

For if thou wert cut out of the olive tree which is wild by nature, and wert grafted contrary to nature into a good olive tree: how much more shall these, which be the natural branches, be grafted into their own olive tree?

For I would not, brethren, that ye should be ignorant of this mystery, lest ye should be wise in your own conceits; that blindness in part is happened to Israel, until the fulness of the Gentiles be come in.

And so all Israel shall be saved: as it is written, There shall come out of Sion the Deliverer, and shall turn away ungodliness from Jacob:

For this is my covenant unto them, when I shall take away their sins.

As concerning the gospel, they are enemies for your sakes: but as touching the election, they are beloved for the fathers' sakes.

For the gifts and calling of God are without repentance.

For as ye in times past have not believed God, yet have now obtained mercy through their unbelief:

Even so have these also now not believed, that through your mercy they also may obtain mercy.

For God hath concluded them all in unbelief, that he might have mercy upon all.

O the depth of the riches both of the wisdom and knowledge of God! how unsearchable are his judgments, and his ways past finding out!

For who hath known the mind of the Lord? or who hath been his counsellor?

Or who hath first given to him, and it shall be recompensed unto him again?

For of him, and through him, and to him, are all things: to whom be glory for ever. Amen.

4. Embrace the entire Scripture, not just the New Testament.

All scripture is given by inspiration of God, and is profitable for doctrine, for reproof, for correction, for instruction in righteousness. (2 Timothy 3:16)

There has been a major shift within Western churches to advance a New Testament-only narrative. To do so removes the very foundation of understanding, as there was no New Testament at the time of Jesus or any of the apostles. The mere fact that the Gospel of Matthew contains close to one hundred and fifty Old Testament references and the book of Revelation includes almost five hundred Old Testament references is reason enough to continue to embrace the whole Scripture.

Yeshua/Jesus made it abundantly clear in Matthew 5:17 regarding the Law and the prophets (the Old Testament) when He said:

> Think not that I am come to destroy the law, or the prophets: I am not come to destroy, but to fulfil.
>
> For verily I say unto you, Till heaven and earth pass, one jot or one tittle shall in no wise pass from the law, till all be fulfilled.
>
> Whosoever therefore shall break one of these least commandments, and shall teach men so, he shall be called the least in the kingdom of heaven: but whosoever shall do and teach them, the same shall be called great in the kingdom of heaven.
>
> For I say unto you, That except your righteousness shall exceed the righteousness of the scribes and Pharisees, ye shall in no case enter into the kingdom of heaven.

5. Speak out!

And the Lord said, Behold, the people is one, and they have all one language; and this they begin to do: and now nothing will be restrained from them, which they have imagined to do. (Genesis 11:6)

If nothing moved you in this book more than the silence that gripped the Church during the Holocaust, then we must never be silent again. As believers, we are to stand boldly for the truth of God's Word and His promises. As an engrafted Jewish or Gentile believer, you are a part of Israel's spiritual inheritance as being counted among the Children of Israel. We were called to be the head and not the tail, and have been given authority over all the schemes of the enemy. Our silence condemns us, and we must raise our voices above the vitriol.

Genesis 11:6 is God's proclamation that if we act as one body and in one voice, nothing will be impossible for us. I can think of no more empowering words coming straight from the mouth of God.

Final Thoughts

The pages you have read reflect the facts about what was, what is, and what is to come. It is not my intention to condemn, but to provoke every believer to examine where they stand today. Either you are for Yeshua and God's plan for Israel and the Jewish people, or you are a part of Satan's plan to eliminate the seed line that will usher in the Second Coming of Messiah. For many, this may be the first time you have ever read or learned of this diabolical agenda. Regardless of whether you knew or did not know, you cannot straddle the fence. In the words of Yeshua/Jesus Himself, "You are either for me or against me." Now that you know the truth, what will you do with it?

If you are a believer in the promised Jewish Messiah, whether you are a natural branch or an engrafted wild branch, you are now joined together as a part of the Commonwealth of Israel. Therefore, the instructions contained in Numbers 6 verses 22 and 23 apply to you:

And the Lord spake unto Moses, saying,

Speak unto Aaron and unto his sons, saying, On this wise ye shall bless the children of Israel, saying unto them, "The LORD bless thee, and keep thee: The LORD make his face shine upon thee, and be gracious unto thee: The LORD lift up his countenance upon thee, and give thee peace."

And in verse 27, the Lord goes on to say:

And they shall put my name upon the children of Israel, and I will bless them."

Receive this now, in Yeshua's name. AMEN!

From the Heart of the Rabbi

Dear Beloved Reader,

Thank you for taking this journey with me through my history, the history of the Jewish people, and the history of the Church. As difficult as it may be for many to recount the facts of history, my heart is more burdened about today and your standing before the Lord. I wrote this book to illustrate how far we have drifted from God's truth and the rise in what will ultimately eternally separate you from God.

My heart is heavy not because of what has been done, but because so many have fallen into Satan's trap without knowing. It is my prayer that, after reading this book, you will find yourself realizing that you might have been one who heard those dreaded words, "Depart from me, I never knew you." But now you will know the truth—and the truth will set you free.

We have devoted so much of our time to getting people into the Kingdom that we have allowed lies and deception to cloud our understanding of Israel, the Jews, and God's end-time plan for mankind. This book is not written to find fault or condemn any part of Judaism or Christianity. It is not a condemnation of thousands of years of documented history. It is a clarion call to remember the past and learn from it so that we find ourselves on the right side of Heaven.

It is God's desire that none shall perish, and I share that same desire. It is with your eternal future in mind that I have written this book. Many of the chapters might have been hard to read, as they chronicle a demonically inspired agenda to rid the earth of the seed line of Messiah.

My prayer is that those who have accepted Jesus as a part of God's plan of redemption, but who have been ensnared in the teachings of man, will find the strength to grab hold of God's truth and cross over from the goats' side to the sheep's side. It's far better to lose a human friend for rejecting unsound doctrine than to forego your eternal salvation.

I fully expect to receive many comments on the content of this book and the message contained within, but history and the Bible are on my side. I have made every effort to let history speak for itself. But like King David, we too must cry out to God with these words from Psalm 139: 23–24:

Search me, O God, and know my heart: try me, and know my thoughts:
And see if there be any wicked way in me, and lead me in the way everlasting.

I invite you to reach out to me at rabbieric@ignitinganation.com with your comments and questions or to pray for wisdom and understanding. My heart yearns for you not to be on my side, but on the Lord's side so that we can spend eternity together.

May the Lord bless you in all His ways,
With love in Messiah,
Rabbi Eric E. Walker

Glossary of Terms
& Terminology

Abba: Father.

Adam: The first man; derives from the same root as *adom*, meaning "red."

Adom: Red.

Adonai: Used in place of the Tetragram, means the Lord.

Akev: Heel.

Arbabanel: Isaac ben Judah Abarbanel, commonly referred to as Abarbanel, also spelled Abravanel, Avravanel or Abrabanel, was a Portuguese Jewish statesman, philosopher, Bible commentator, and financier.

Armageddon: According to the book of Revelation in the New Testament of the Christian Bible, Armageddon is the prophesied location of a gathering of armies for a battle during the end times.

Ayin: "Eye" in Hebrew.

Bar Kochba: Jewish leader who led a bitter but unsuccessful revolt (132–135 CE) against Roman dominion in Judaea.

Baruch: Blessing.

B'Shem: More often seen as HaShem, "the Name."

Bethlehem: "House of Bread."

Canaan: The name of a large and prosperous ancient country (at times independent, at others, a tributary to Egypt) located in the Levant region of present-day Lebanon, Syria, Jordan, and Israel. The area on the West Bank of the Jordan River—the Promised Land.

Edom (Edomites): Descendants of Esau.

Elohim: When capitalized, God the Father. Lowercased, it refers to other gods.

Esau: Twin born of Jacob and Rebecca described as "hairy" and who sold his birthright to his brother. Jacob.

Essenes: Member of an ancient Jewish ascetic sect of the second century BC–second century AD in Palestine, who lived in highly organized groups and held property in common. The Essenes are widely regarded as the authors of the Dead Sea Scrolls.

Gemara: In Aramaic, "to study and to know." A collection of scholarly discussions on Jewish law dating from around AD 200–500.

Haba: When used in context with a blessing, it means "the person."

Hadrian: Roman emperor (AD 117–138).

Halakah: The religious laws that dictate all aspects of life for observant Jews from the time they wake in the morning to when they go to sleep at night.

Jerusalem: The holiest city in Judaism and the ancestral and spiritual homeland of the Jewish people since the tenth century BCE. During classical antiquity, Jerusalem was considered the center of the world where God resided. The city of Jerusalem is given special status in Jewish religious law.

Josephus: Titus Flavius Josephus, born Yosef ben Matityahu in Jerusalem—then part of Roman Judea—to a father of priestly descent and a mother who claimed royal ancestry. A first-century Romano-Jewish historian best known for writing *The Jewish War.*

Kabbalah: The ancient Jewish tradition of mystical interpretation of the Bible, first transmitted orally and using esoteric methods (including ciphers). It reached the height of its influence in the later Middle Ages and remains significant in some sects of Judaism today.

Keterot: Incense.

Kippa: Also known as *yarmulke,* the round head covering worn by a man.

Kotel: Western Wall, Hebrew Ha-Kotel Ha-Ma'aravi, also called Wailing Wall, in the Old City of Jerusalem, a place of prayer and pilgrimage sacred to the Jewish people. It is the only remains of the retaining wall surrounding the Temple Mount, the site of the First and Second Temples of Jerusalem, held to be uniquely holy by the ancient Jews. The First Temple was destroyed by the Babylonians in 587–586 BCE, and the Second Temple was destroyed by the Romans in 70 CE.

Levite: The tribe of Aaron and his descendants.

Maimonides, aka Rambam: Moses ben Maimon, commonly known as Maimonides and also referred to by the acronym Rambam, was a medieval Jewish philosopher who became one of the most prolific and influential Torah scholars of the Middle Ages.

Marcion of Sinope: An early Christian theologian, evangelist, and important figure in early Christianity.

Masada: "Strong foundation or support" in Hebrew; a natural fortress built on top of a barren, mountainous desert plateau thousands of feet above the Dead Sea. After the destruction of the Second Temple, 960 rebels fled to Masada and ultimately took their own lives to escape enslavement by Rome.

Megillah: Comprised of the Mishnah and the Gemara, it contains the opinions of thousands of rabbis from different periods in Jewish history.

Mishkan: The Tabernacle.

Mishna: "Repetition"; written tersely in the form of short rulings in a language known as Mishnaic Hebrew and is a large collection of sayings, arguments, and counter-arguments that touch on virtually all areas of life.

Nachash: Used in reference to the serpent in Hebrew in Genesis.

Nephilim: The offspring of the fallen angels.

Nisan: First month of the Hebrew calendar.

Orthodox: The branch of Judaism that endeavors to uphold all the Mosaic and Talmudic teachings.

Passover: Feast commemorating Israel's deliverance from Pharaoh as documented in Exodus 12 and commanded in Leviticus 23.

Pharisee: One who believes in the Law of Moses, the Prophets, and resurrection.

Rabbi: Literal translation is "teacher or master"; common usage is similar to "pastor."

Rabbi Sha'ul: Rabbi Saul of Tarsus, referred to in the Scriptures as Paul.

Rabbi Akiva: Akiva developed as a sage during the period after the destruction of the Second Temple (70 CE), a time of transformation for the Jewish community as rabbinic Judaism began to take shape. Since the Temple no longer served as the focal point of Jewish life, the sages (who later became known as rabbis) reconstructed Judaism with Torah study at its center.

Rambam: Moses ben Maimon, commonly known as Maimonides and also referred to by the acronym Rambam, was a medieval Sephardic Jewish philosopher who became one of the most prolific and influential Torah scholars of the Middle Ages.

Rashi: A shorthand way of referring to Rabbi Shlomo Yitzchaki, an eleventh-century French scholar. He wrote one of the first complete explanatory commentaries on the Talmud. Rashi's words are usually rendered in a special font known as Rashi script and always appear on the inside margin of the page.

Ruach Ha'Kodesh: The Holy Spirit.

Sadducees: Those who believe in the Law of Moses and do not believe in the prophets or resurrection.

Sanhedrin: Assemblies of either twenty-three or seventy-one elders appointed to sit as a tribunal in every city in the ancient land of Israel.

Satan (haSatan): The accuser of the brethren.

Scribes: Group of individuals who enjoyed the authority of leadership in Israel. In the New Testament, they are associated with the Pharisees and the high priests as opponents of Jesus.

Sepulcher: A small room or monument cut in rock or built of stone in which a dead person is laid or buried.

Sotah: Tractate Sotah deals with the ordeal of the bitter water—the woman suspected of adultery—as well as other rituals involving speech.

Tallit: Four-cornered shawl with fringe worn as instructed in Deuteronomy 22:12.

Talmud: The Talmud, meaning "teaching," is an ancient text containing Jewish sayings, ideas and stories. It includes the

Mishnah (oral law) and the Gemara ("Completion"). The Talmud is the textual record of generations of rabbinic debate about law, philosophy, and biblical interpretation, compiled between the third and eighth centuries and structured as commentary on the Mishnah with stories interwoven. The Talmud exists in two versions: the more commonly studied Babylonian Talmud was compiled in present-day Iraq, while the Jerusalem Talmud was compiled in Israel.

Tanakh: The name of the Hebrew Bible: TA (Torah), NA (Navaim—Prophets)—CH (Ketuvim [Writings]).

Terah: Abraham's idol-making father.

Torah: The first five books of the Bible.

Tractate: An organizational element of Talmudic literature similar to a chapter.

Yahweh: Anglicized pronunciation of the Tetragram יהוה.

Yeshiva: School.

Yeshua: Hebrew for "Salvation"; the Messiah; Jesus.

Yom Kippur: The Day of Atonement, as described in Leviticus 16 and Leviticus 23.

Zealots: A political movement in first-century, Second-Temple Judaism that sought to incite the people of Judea province to rebel against the Roman Empire and expel it from the Holy Land by force of arms, most notably during the first Jewish-Roman War.

Notes

1. Gaster, T. H.; Dimitrovsky, Haim Zalman; Novak, David; Pines, Shlomo; Vajda, Georges; Greenberg, Moshe; Baron, Salo Wittmayer; Feldman, Louis H.; Silberman, Lou Hackett; Hertzberg, Arthur; and Cohen, Gerson D. (2021, September 30). Judaism. Encyclopedia Britannica. https://www.britannica.com/topic/Judaism.

2. Britannica, T., Editors of Encyclopaedia (2016, April 11). Genesis. Encyclopedia Britannica. https://www.britannica.com/topic/Genesis-Old-Testament.

3. Tanakh (the Hebrew Bible) is Judaism's foundational text. The word *Tanakh* is an acronym of its three parts: Torah (The Five Books of Moses), Nevi'im (Prophets), and Ketuvim (Writings). It contains stories, law, poetry, and teachings about God and humanity. Accessed 11/27/21, https://www.sefaria.org/texts/Tanakh.

4. My Jewish Learning, "About God in Judaism," accessed 11/27/21, https://www.myjewishlearning.com/article/about-god-in-judaism/.

5. Britannica, T., Editors of Encyclopaedia (2020, May 15). Rabbi. Encyclopedia Britannica. https://www.britannica.com/topic/rabbi.

6. Ahlström, G. W. (2020, May 15). Prophecy. Encyclopedia Britannica. https://www.britannica.com/topic/prophecy.

7. The Talmud is the textual record of generations of rabbinic debate about law, philosophy, and biblical interpretation, compiled between the third and eighth centuries and structured as commentary on the Mishnah with stories interwoven. The Talmud exists in two versions. The more commonly studied Babylonian Talmud was compiled in present-day Iraq, while the Jerusalem Talmud was compiled in Israel. Accessed 11/27/21, https://www.sefaria.org/texts/Talmud.

8. Halakhah: The Laws of Jewish Life. Halakhah is the "way" a Jew is directed to behave, encompassing civil, criminal, and religious law. Accessed 11/27/21, https://www.myjewishlearning.com/article/halakhah-the-laws-of-jewish-life/.

9. Britannica, T., Editors of Encyclopaedia (2014, August 21). Mishna. Encyclopedia Britannica. https://www.britannica.com/topic/Mishna.

10. Ibid. (2015, January 1). Gemara. Encyclopedia Britannica. https://www.britannica.com/topic/Gemara.

11. Twersky, I. (2021, July 9). Rashi. Encyclopedia Britannica. https://www.britannica.com/biography/Rashi.

12. Sotah (Hebrew: סוֹטָה or Hebrew: שׂוֹטָה) is a tractate of the Talmud in rabbinic Judaism. The tractate explains the ordeal of the bitter water, a trial by ordeal of a woman suspected of adultery, which is prescribed by the book of Numbers in the Hebrew Bible, accessed 11/27/1. This article incorporates text from a publication now in the public domain: Singer, Isidore; et al., eds. (1901–1906). "Sotah." The Jewish Encyclopedia. New York: Funk & Wagnalls.

13. William Davidson Talmud, Sotah 9b:3. https://www.sefaria.org/Sotah.9b.3?lang=bi.

14. Britannica, T., Editors of Encyclopaedia (2014, April 14). Orthodox Judaism. Encyclopedia Britannica. https://www.britannica.com/topic/Orthodox-Judaism.

15. Bokser, B. Zion (2021, March 26). Moses Maimonides. Encyclopedia Britannica. https://www.britannica.com/biography/Moses-Maimonides.

16. Westman, R. S. (2021, May 20). Nicolaus Copernicus. Encyclopedia Britannica. https://www.britannica.com/biography/Nicolaus-Copernicus.

17. Britannica, T., Editors of Encyclopaedia (2012, October 17). Yeshiva. Encyclopedia Britannica. https://www.britannica.com/topic/yeshiva.

18. Reynolds, F. E.; Kitagawa, Joseph M.; Snellgrove, David Llewelyn; Nakamura, Hajime; Tucci, Giuseppe; and Lopez, Donald S. (2021, April 8). Buddhism. Encyclopedia Britannica. https://www.britannica.com/topic/Buddhism.

19. Strickmann, M.; Ames, Roger T.; and Seidel, Anna K. (2020, April 28). Daoism. Encyclopedia Britannica. https://www.britannica.com/topic/Daoism.

20. Melton, J. Gordon (2016, April 7). New Age Movement. Encyclopedia Britannica. https://www.britannica.com/topic/New-Age-movement.

21. Accessed 11/27/21. https://chopra.com/bio/neale-donald-walsch.

22. Biography.com, "Who Is Deepak Chopra?" Accessed 11/27/21. https://www.biography.com/personality/deepak-chopra.

23. Britannica, T., Editors of Encyclopaedia (2021, August 11). Hebrew Bible. Encyclopedia Britannica. https://www.britannica.com/topic/Hebrew-Bible.

24. Stefon, M.; Chadwick, Henry; Hick, John; Wainwright, Geoffrey; Spencer, Sidney; Crow, Paul A.; Marty, Martin E.; McGinn, Bernard J.; Lindberg, Carter H.; Fredericksen, Linwood; Hogg, William Richey; Benz, Ernst Wilhelm; Pelikan, Jaroslav Jan; and Sullivan, Lawrence E. (2020, November 26). Christianity. Encyclopedia Britannica. https://www.britannica.com/topic/Christianity.

25. Berenbaum, M. (2021, July 1). Holocaust. Encyclopedia Britannica. https://www.britannica.com/event/Holocaust.

26. Sanders, E. and Pelikan, Jaroslav Jan (2021, June 16). Jesus. Encyclopedia Britannica. https://www.britannica.com/biography/Jesus.

27. Hershey, Doug, "Yeshua: The Meaning of the Hebrew Name of Jesus," accessed 11/27/21. https://firmisrael.org/learn/who-is-yeshua-meaning-of-hebrew-name-jesus/.

28. Britannica, T., Editors of Encyclopaedia (2021, June 3). Gentile. Encyclopedia Britannica. https://www.britannica.com/topic/Gentile.

29. A skullcap worn by Orthodox male Jews at all times and by others for prayer,

especially a crocheted one worn by those with a specifically religious Zionist affiliation. Accessed 11/27/21. https://www.dictionary.com/browse/kippa.

30. My Jewish Learning, "Tallit (The Prayer Shawl)," accessed 11/27/21, https://www.myjewishlearning.com/article/tallit-the-prayer-shawl/.

31. Vander Laan, "Mount Moriah," accessed 11/27/21, https://www.thattheworldmayknow.com/mount-moriah.

32. Britannica, T. Editors of Encyclopaedia (2020, December 17). Isaac. Encyclopedia Britannica. https://www.britannica.com/biography/Isaac.

33. Ibid. (2021, July 26). Exodus. Encyclopedia Britannica. https://www.britannica.com/event/Exodus-Old-Testament.

34. Ibid. (2021, March 25). Levite. Encyclopedia Britannica. https://www.britannica.com/topic/Levite.

35. Ibid. (2021, July 16). Yom Kippur. Encyclopedia Britannica. https://www.britannica.com/topic/Yom-Kippur.

36. Lively, Leah, "What Do Messianic Jews Believe and Practice?" Accessed 11/27/21, https://www.christianity.com/church/denominations/what-do-messianic-jews-believe-and-practice.html.

37. Brandon, S. G.F. (2021, March 17). Salvation. Encyclopedia Britannica. https://www.britannica.com/topic/salvation-religion.

38. Britannica, T., Editors of Encyclopaedia (2021, August 31). Satan. Encyclopedia Britannica. https://www.britannica.com/topic/Satan.

39. Ham, Ken, "What Is Biblical Creation?" Accessed 11/27/21. https://answersingenesis.org/creation/.

40. Zaleski, C. (2021, September 29). Heaven. Encyclopedia Britannica. https://www.britannica.com/topic/heaven.

41. Britannica, T., Editors of Encyclopaedia (2020, December 23). Cain. Encyclopedia Britannica. https://www.britannica.com/biography/Cain-biblical-figure.

42. Missler, Chuck, "Meanings of The Names in Genesis 5," Koinonia House, 8/1/2000, https://www.khouse.org/articles/2000/284/.

43. Ibid.

44. Parrot, A. (2021, March 13). Abraham. Encyclopedia Britannica. https://www.britannica.com/biography/Abraham.

45. Zeidan, A. (2021, September 1). Ishmael. Encyclopedia Britannica. https://www.britannica.com/biography/Ishmael-son-of-Abraham.

46. Britannica, T. Editors of Encyclopaedia (2007, June 12). Hagar. Encyclopedia Britannica. https://www.britannica.com/biography/Hagar-biblical-figure.

47. Schorr ,Rebecca Einstein, *"Why Do Jews Circumcise?"* accessed 11/27/21, https://www.kveller.com/article/why-do-jews-circumcise/.

48. Heiser, Michael S., "What the Bible Teaches About a Divine Council," accessed 11/27/21, https://www.miqlat.org/what-the-bible-teaches-about-a-divine-council.htm.

49. Ibid. "What Eden Tells Us about Satan," Gospel Centered Discipleship, 6/12/2020, https://gcdiscipleship.com/article-feed/what-eden-tells-us-about-satan.

50. "Esau," Jewish Virtual Library, accessed 11/21/21, https://www.jewishvirtuallibrary.org/esau.

51. Block, Herbert, "Distinguishing Jacob and Israel," *Jewish Bible Quarterly*, accessed 11/21/21, https://jbqnew.jewishbible.org/assets/Uploads/343/343_jacobis1.pdf.

52. Altein, Yehuda, *Korah, The Rebel of the Bible,* Chabad, circa 2011, https://www.chabad.org/library/article_cdo/aid/246641/jewish/Korah-The-Rebel-of-the-Bible.htm.

53. In the Bible, Baal (also rendered Ba al) was an important Canaanite god, often portrayed as the primary enemy of the Hebrew God Yahweh. The Semitic word "baal" (meaning "Lord") was also used to refer to various deities of the Levant. Accessed 11/27/21, https://www.newworldencyclopedia.org/entry/Baal.

54. Britannica, T., Editors of Encyclopaedia (2013, September 18). Melqart. Encyclopedia Britannica. https://www.britannica.com/topic/Melqart.

55. Ibid. (2018, February 16). Asherah. Encyclopedia Britannica. https://www.britannica.com/topic/Asherah-Semitic-goddess.

56. Mariottini, Dr. Claude, "Jezebel, A Great-Grandmother of Jesus," Dr. Claude Mariottini, professor of Old Testament, April 27, 2015. https://claudemariottini.com/2015/04/27/jezebel-a-great-grandmother-of-jesus/.

57. Genesis 50:20, "But as for you, ye thought evil against me; but God meant it unto good, to bring to pass, as it is this day, to save much people alive."

58. Student, Gil, "Angels and Afterlife," accessed 11/27/21, https://www.torahmusings.com/2012/11/angels-and-afterlife/.

59. Ibid., "You Don't Have to Be a Prophet," Torah Musings, 11/16/2015, https://www.torahmusings.com/2015/11/you-dont-have-to-be-a-prophet/.

60. Wiersbe, Warren, Be Reverent, (Colorado Springs, CO: David C. Cook, 2000) page 25.

61. Heiser, Michael S., "What Does the Vision in Ezekiel 1 Mean?" Logos, 10/1/2021, https://blog.logos.com/vision-ezekiel-1-mean/.

62. Ibid. "Elohim as 'Gods' in the Old Testament." In Faithlife Study Bible. (Bellingham, WA: Lexham Press, 2012, 2016).

63. Telushkin, Joseph, as cited in "Ancient Jewish History: The Great Revolt (60–70 CE), Jewish Virtual Library, accessed 11/21/21, https://www.jewishvirtuallibrary.org/the-great-revolt-66-70-ce.

64. Vander Laan, Ray, "The Jewish Revolts," Focus on the Family, accessed 11/21/21, https://www.thattheworldmayknow.com/the-jewish-revolts.

65. The Temple Institute, Jerusalem, Israel, accessed 11/21/21, https://templeinstitute.org/biblical-commandments/.

66. Pope Paul VI, "Nostra Aetate—Declaration on the Relation of the Church to Non-Christian Religions, The Second Vatican Council," New Advent, accessed 11/21/21, https://www.newadvent.org/library/docs_ec21na.htm.

67. Bieler, Ludwig G. J., St. Ignatius of Antioch, also called Ignatius Theophoros (Greek: "God Bearer"), (died c. 110, Rome; Western feast day October 17); Eastern feast day December 20), bishop of Antioch, Syria (now in Turkey), known mainly from seven highly regarded letters that he wrote during a trip to Rome, as a prisoner condemned to be executed for his beliefs. He was apparently eager to counteract the teachings of two groups—the Judaizers, who did not accept the authority of the New Testament, and the docetists, who held that

Christ's sufferings and death were apparent but not real. The letters have often been cited as a source of knowledge of the Christian church at the beginning of the second century. Britannica, accessed 11/21/21, https://www.britannica.com/biography/Saint-Ignatius-of-Antioch.

68. Roberts, Alexander and Donaldson, James, Editors, "From the 38-volume work: Early Church Fathers—Ante-Nicene Fathers to A.D. 325," Vol. 1, Epistle of Ignatius to the Philippians, Chapter 14, accessed 11/21/21, http://www.pseudepigrapha.com/LostBooks/ignatius2philippians.htm.

69. New Advent, "Fathers of the Church, The Epistles of Barnabas." Chapter 3, accessed 11/21/21, https://www.newadvent.org/fathers/0124.htm.

70. Ibid., chapter 13.

71. Marcion of Sinope (ca. 110–160 C.E.) was a Christian theologian who was excommunicated by the early church at Rome as a heretic; Nevertheless, his teachings were influential during the second century, and a few centuries after, thus forming a counter-point to emerging orthodoxy., New World Encyclopedia contributors, "Marcion," New World Encyclopedia, https://www.newworldencyclopedia.org/p/index.php?title=Marcion&oldid=1013713 (accessed November 24, 2021).

72. Ibid.

73. Rav Shaul, translated from the Hebrew, is "Rabbi Saul" in reference to Rabbi Saul of Tarsus. Most of what we know about the Apostle Paul (also known as Saint Paul or Saul of Tarsus) comes from the writings attributed to him and the Book of Acts.

74. Layman, "Marcion, the Canon, the Law, and the Historical Jesus, Early Church Writings," accessed 11/24/21, http://www.earlychristianwritings.com/info/marcion-layman.html.

75. The Editors of Encyclopedia Britannica, "St. Polycarp, Greek bishop," St. Polycarp, in full Saint Polycarp of Smyrna, (flourished second century; feast day February 23), Greek bishop of Smyrna and Apostolic Father who was the leading second-century Christian figure in Roman Asia by virtue of his work during the initial appearance of the fundamental theological literature of Christianity. Historically, he formed a link between the apostolic and patristic

ages, Britannica, accessed 11/24/21, https://www.britannica.com/biography/
Saint-Polycarp.

76. *Christianity Today*, Christian History, "Polycarp, Aged bishop of Smyrna,"
accessed 11/24/21, https://www.christianitytoday.com/history/people/martyrs/
polycarp.html.

77. Wilken, Robert L., "Tertullian Christian Theologian Alternate Titles:
Quintus Septimius Florens Tertullianus," Born: c.155 or 160 Carthage Tunisia
Died After: 220 Carthage Tunisia, Britannica, accessed 11/24/21, https://www.
britannica.com/biography/Tertullian.

78. Tertullian, "Against Marcio, Book IV." accessed 11/24/21, https://www.
newadvent.org/fathers/03124.htm.

79. Ibid.

80. Anon, "10 Things You Need to Know About Shimon bar Kokhba," accessed
11/24/21, https://resources.finalsite.net/images/v1592287954/wbtlaorg/
j3sygu69stug8nslhodl/BarKokhba-TenThingstoKnow.pdf.

81. Jewish Virtual Library, "Rabbi Akiva ben Joseph (50–135)" accessed
11/24/21, https://www.jewishvirtuallibrary.org/rabbi-akiva.

82. Anon, "10 Things You Need to Know About Shimon bar Kokhba" accessed
11/24/21, https://resources.finalsite.net/images/v1592287954/wbtlaorg/
j3sygu69stug8nslhodl/BarKokhba-TenThingstoKnow.pdf.

83. Bowersock, G. W. "Hadrian "Roman Emperor, Alternate titles: Adrian,
Caesar Traianus Hadrianus Augustus, Publius Aelius Hadrianus," Born: January
24, 76 Rome? Italy? Died: July 10, 138 (aged 62) Baiae Italy, Britannica, accessed
11/24/21, https://www.britannica.com/biography/Hadrian.

84. Wilson, Mark, "James or Jacob in the Bible? Giving Jacob His Due,"
Biblical Archeology Society, 5/7/21, https://www.biblicalarchaeology.org/daily/
biblical-topics/bible-versions-and-translations/james-or-jacob-in-the-bible/.

85. Catholic Encyclopedia, "Eusebius Pamphili, Bishop of Cæsarea in Palestine,
the "Father of Church History"; b. about 260; d. before 341., accessed 11/24/21,
https://www.newadvent.org/cathen/05617b.htm.

86. Summers, Paul, "James Was Not a Disciple of Yeshua (...But Jacob

Was)," Hebrew Streams, accessed 12/9/2021, https://www.hebrew-streams.org/works/misconceptions/havharah-yakobos.html.

87. Schonfield, Dr. Hugh J., "History of Jewish Christianity" Chapter 5, Page 37, Original Date 1936, Re-edited and re-printed by Bruce R. Booker under permission of The Hugh & Helene Schonfield World Service Trust.

88. Catholic Encyclopedia, "St. Hegesippus." A writer of the second century, known to us almost exclusively from Eusebius, who tells us that he wrote in five books in the simplest style the true tradition of the Apostolic preaching. His work was entitled *hypomnemata* (Memoirs), and was written against the new heresies of the Gnostics and of Marcion. Accessed 11/24/21, https://www.newadvent.org/cathen/07194a.htm.

89. Denova, Rebecca. "The Separation of Christianity from Judaism." World History Encyclopedia. Last modified June 21, 2021. https://www.worldhistory.org/article/1785/the-separation-of-christianity-from-judaism/.

90. The Editors of Encyclopaedia Britannica, *"St. Justin Martyr, Christian apologist"* St. Justin Martyr, (born c. 100, Flavia Neapolis, Palestine [now Nāblus]—died c. 165, Rome [Italy]; feast day June 1), one of the most important of the Greek philosopher—Apologists in the early Christian church. His writings represent one of the first positive encounters of Christian revelation with Greek philosophy and laid the basis for a theology of history.Britannica, accessed 11/24/21, https://www.britannica.com/biography/Saint-Justin-Martyr.

91. The identity of Trypho as rabbi Tarfon—the Hebrew name "Tarfon" itself is likely derived from Greek Trifon (Trypho)—has been proposed, but many Jewish scholars do not accept the notion that Justin Martyr's Trypho is Tarfon. They instead consider Trypho a fictional character invented by Justin for his literary goals, accessed 11/24/21, https://everything.explained.today/Dialogue_with_Trypho/.

92. Denova, Rebecca. "The Separation of Christianity from Judaism." World History Encyclopedia. Last modified June 21, 2021. https://www.worldhistory.org/article/1785/the-separation-of-christianity-from-judaism/.

93. Jakób Jocz (1906-1983) was born in Vilnius, Lithuania and studied in

Germany, England and Scotland. He received his Ph.D. and Litt.D. from Edinburgh University, Scotland. He contributed to many professional journals and wrote four other books of Old Testament study and systematic theology. Dr. Jocz was ordained in the Anglican Church, and served for many years as Professor of Systematic Theology at Wycliffe Seminary, Toronto. As a third generation Hebrew Christian he was passionately interest in evangelism amongst Jews. However, he also saw the need for a place of dialogue and sought to get the two communities to understand their past and get past the stereotypes. Jocz most notable works are The Jewish People and Jesus Christ written in 1949 and on the distinctive nature of Israel and Church before God in his 1958 work A Theology of Election: Israel and the Church. He turned his attention in 1968 to the future destinies of both groups in his often reprinted The Covenant: A Theology of Human Destiny., People Pill, accesses 11/24/21, https://peoplepill.com/people/jakob-jocz.

94. Jocz, Jakob, "The Jewish People and Jesus Christ," SPCK (January 1, 1954), page 198.

95. Catholic Encyclopedia, "Ebionites," By this name were designated one or more early Christian sects infected with Judaistic errors. The word Ebionites, or rather, more correctly, Ebionæans (Ebionaioi), is a transliteration of an Aramean word meaning "poor men." It first occurs in Irenaeus, Adv. Haer., I, xxvi, 2, but without designation of meaning. Origen (Against Celsus II.1; De Princ., IV, i, 22) and Eusebius (Church History III.27) refer the name of these sectaries either to the poverty of their understanding, or to the poverty of the Law to which they clung, or to the poor opinions they held concerning Christ. This, however, is obviously not the historic origin of the name. Other writers, such as Tertullian (De Praescr., xxxiii; De Carne Chr., xiv, 18), Hippolytus (cfr. Pseudo-Tert., Adv. Haer., III, as reflecting Hippolytus's lost "Syntagma"), and Epiphanius (Haeres., xxx) derive the name of the sect from a certain Ebion, its supposed founder., accessed 11/24/21, https://www.newadvent.org/cathen/05242c.htm.

96. Ibid, "St. Irenaeus, Bishop of Lyons." Information as to his life is scarce, and in some measure inexact. He was born in Proconsular Asia, or at least in some province bordering thereon, in the first half of the second century; the exact date

is controverted, between the years 115 and 125, according to some, or, according to others, between 130 and 142. It is certain that, while still very young, Irenaeus had seen and heard the holy Bishop Polycarp (d. 155) at Smyrna., accessed 11/24/21, https://www.newadvent.org/cathen/08130b.htm.

97. Bettenson, Henry, "Documents of The Christian Church," page 37, Oxford University Press; 4th edition (November 15, 2011).

98. Catholic Encyclopedia, "Pope St. Victor I," (189–198 or 199), date of birth unknown. The "Liber Pontificalis" makes him a native of Africa and gives his father the name of Felix. This authority, taking the "Liberian Catalogue" as its basis, gives the years 186–197 as the period of Victor's episcopate. The Armenian text of the "Chronicle" of Eusebius (Leipzig, 1911, p. 223) places the beginning of Victor's pontificate in the seventh year of the reign of the Emperor Commodus (180–87) and gives it a duration of twelve years; in his "Church History" (V, xxxii, ed. Schwarts, Leipzig, 1902, p. 486) Eusebius transfers the beginning of the pontificate to the tenth year of the reign of Commodus and makes it last ten years.

99. Smith, Horane, "Letter to Polycrates," *Prevail Magazine*, accessed 11/24/21, https://www.prevailmagazine.org/letter-from-polycrates/.

100. Catholic Encyclopedia, "The First Council of Nicea," First Ecumenical Council of the Catholic Church, held in 325 on the occasion of the heresy of Arius (Arianism). As early as 320 or 321 St. Alexander, Bishop of Alexandria, convoked a council at Alexandria at which more than one hundred bishops from Egypt and Libya anathematized Arius. The latter continued to officiate in his church and to recruit followers., accessed 11/24/21, https://www.newadvent.org/cathen/11044a.htm.

101. Catholic Encyclopedia, "Origen and Origenism," Origen, most modest of writers, hardly ever alludes to himself in his own works; but Eusebius has devoted to him almost the entire sixth book of "Ecclesiastical History." Eusebius was thoroughly acquainted with the life of his hero; he had collected a hundred of his letters; in collaboration with the martyr Pamphilus he had composed the "Apology for Origen"; he dwelt at Caesarea where Origen's library was preserved, and where his memory still lingered; if at times he may be thought somewhat

partial, he is undoubtedly well informed. Accessed 11/24/21, https://www.
newadvent.org/cathen/11306b.htm.

102. Gruber, Dan, "The Church and the Jews (Hanover, NH: Elijah Publishing, 1991, 1997, 2001, 2017).

103. Ibid, Page 14, 2017 edition.

104. Ibid, Page 15, 2017 edition.

105. Ibid.

106. Ibid., Page 16, 2017 edition.

107. Schonfield, Dr. Hugh J., "History of Jewish Christianity" Page 54, Original Date 1936, Re-edited and re-printed by Bruce R. Booker under permission of The Hugh & Helene Schonfield World Service Trust.

108. Catholic Encyclopedia, "Diocletian" Roman Emperor and persecutor of the Church, born of parents who had been slaves, at Dioclea, near Salona, in Dalmatia, A.D. 245; d. at Salona, AD 313.

109. The Great Persecution (303–313), Historai Rex, accessed 11/24/21, https://historiarex.com/e/en/207-great-persecution-303-313.

110. Catholic Encyclopedia, "Constantine the Great." His coins give his name as M., or more frequently as C., Flavius Valerius Constantinus. He was born at Naissus, now Nisch in Servia Nis, Serbia—Ed., the son of a Roman officer, Constantius, who later became Roman Emperor, and St. Helena, a woman of humble extraction but remarkable character and unusual ability. The date of his birth is not certain, being given as early as 274 and as late as 288. After his father's elevation to the dignity of Caesar we find him at the court of Diocletian and later (305) fighting under Galerius on the Danube. When, on the resignation of his father, Constantius was made Augustus, the new Emperor of the West asked Galerius, the Eastern Emperor, to let Constantine, whom he had not seen for a long time, return to his father's court. This was reluctantly granted. Constantine joined his father, under whom he had just time to distinguish himself in Britain before death carried off Constantius (25 July, 306). Constantine was immediately proclaimed Caesar by his troops, and his title was acknowledged by Galerius somewhat hesitatingly. This event was the first break in Diocletian's scheme of a four-headed empire (tetrarchy) and was soon

followed by the proclamation in Rome of Maxentius, the son of Maximian, a tyrant and profligate, as Caesar, October, 306., accessed 11/24/21, https://www.newadvent.org/cathen/04295c.htm.

111. Ibid., "Pope St. Sylvester I (314–335)," accessed 11/25/21, https://www.newadvent.org/cathen/14370a.htm.

112. Ibid., "Eusebius of Cæsarea," Eusebius Pamphili, Bishop of Cæsarea in Palestine, the "Father of Church History"; b. about 260; d. before 341., accessed 11/25/21, https://www.newadvent.org/cathen/05617b.htm.

113. Eusebius of Caesarea, Ecclesiastical History, Alternate titles: "Historia ecclesiastica," AD 312–324, accessed 11/25/21, https://www.britannica.com/biography/Eusebius-of-Caesarea#ref234886.

114. Catholic Encyclopedia, "St. Pamphilus of Cæsarea," Martyred 309. Eusebius's life of Pamphilus is lost, but from his "Martyrs of Palestine" we learn that Pamphilus belonged to a noble family of Beirut (in Phœnicia), where he received a good education, and that he quitted his native land after selling all his property and giving the proceeds to the poor. Accessed 11/25/21, https://www.newadvent.org/cathen/11436b.htm.

115. Gruber, Daniel, *The Church and the Jews* (Hanover, NH: Elijah Publishing, 1991, 1997, 2001, 2017), Page 12, 2017 edition.

116. Catholic Encyclopedia, "St. Papias," Bishop of Hierapolis (close to Laodicea and Colossæ in the valley of the Lycus in Phrygia) and Apostolic Father, called by St. Irenæus "a hearer of John, and companion of Polycarp, a man of old time." He wrote a work in five books, *logion kyriakon exegesis*, of which all but some fragments is lost. Accessed 11/25/21, https://www.newadvent.org/cathen/11457c.htm.

117. Ibid, "St. John the Evangelist," John was the son of Zebedee and Salome, and the brother of James the Greater. In the Gospels the two brothers are often called after their father "the sons of Zebedee" and received from Christ the honourable title of Boanerges, i.e. "sons of thunder" (Mark 3:17). Originally they were fishermen and fished with their father in the Lake of Genesareth. According to the usual and entirely probable explanation they became, however, for a time disciples of John the Baptist, and were called by Christ from the circle of John's

followers, together with Peter and Andrew, to become His disciples (John 1:35–42) accessed 11/25/21, https://www.newadvent.org/cathen/08492a.htm.

118. Gruber, Daniel, *The Church and the Jews*, (Hanover, NH: Elijah Publishing, 1991, 1997, 2001, 2017), Page 12, 2017 edition.

119. Catholic Encyclopedia, "Arianism," A heresy that arose in the fourth century, and denied the divinity of Jesus Christ. Accessed 11/25/21, https://www.newadvent.org/cathen/01707c.htm.

120. Ibid., "The Blessed Trinity." The Trinity is the term employed to signify the central doctrine of the Christian religion—the truth that in the unity of the Godhead there are Three Persons, the Father, the Son, and the Holy Spirit, these Three Persons being truly distinct one from another. Accessed 11/25/21, https://www.newadvent.org/cathen/15047a.htm.

121. Gruber, *The Church and the Jews,* Page 30, 2017 edition.

122. Schaff, Philip, *Eusebius Pamphellius: Church History, Life of Constantine, Oration in Praise of Constantine*, Christian Classics Ethereal Library, accessed 11/25/21, https://www.ccel.org/ccel/schaff/npnf201.iv.vi.iii.xviii.html.

123. Ibid., "Chapter XV—"How Constantine Entertained the Bishops on the Occasion of His Vicennalia," accessed 11/25/21, https://www.ccel.org/ccel/schaff/npnf201.iv.vi.iii.xv.html.

124. Gruber, Daniel, *The Church and the Jews*, Page 34, 2017 edition.

125. Ibid., Pages 35–36, 2017 edition.

126. Durant, Wil, *The Age of Faith: The Story of Civilization, Volume IV*, (New York: MJF Books, June 1, 1993), Chapter IV.

127. The Editors of Encyclopaedia Britannica, "Council of Antioch: Historical Church Council," Council of Antioch, (341 CE), a non-ecumenical Christian church council held at Antioch (modern Antakya in southeastern Turkey) on the occasion of the consecration of the emperor Constantine I's Golden Church there. Accessed 11/25/21, https://www.britannica.com/event/Council-of-Antioch.

128. Catholic Encyclopedia, "Apostolic Canons." A collection of ancient ecclesiastical decrees (eighty-five in the Eastern, fifty in the Western Church) concerning the government and discipline of the Christian Church, incorporated

with the Apostolic Constitutions, accessed 11/25/21, https://www.newadvent.org/cathen/03279a.htm.

129. Schonfield, Dr. Hugh J., "History of Jewish Christianity," Pages 71–72, Original Date 1936, Re-edited and re-printed by Bruce R. Booker under permission of The Hugh & Helene Schonfield World Service Trust.

130. Saltet, L. (1912). Epiphanius of Salamis. In The Catholic Encyclopedia. New York: Robert Appleton Company. Retrieved November 25, 2021 from New Advent: http://www.newadvent.org/cathen/13393b.htm.

131. Saltet, L. (1910). St. Jerome. In The Catholic Encyclopedia. New York: Robert Appleton Company. Retrieved November 25, 2021 from New Advent: http://www.newadvent.org/cathen/08341a.htm.

132. Arendzen, J. (1909). Ebionites. In *The Catholic Encyclopedia*. (New York: Robert Appleton Company). Retrieved November 25, 2021 from New Advent: http://www.newadvent.org/cathen/05242c.htm.

133. Elkasites were members of an ancient Jewish sect, whose name was taken from its founder, Elxai, accessed 11/25/21, http://www.fact-index.com/e/el/elkasite.html.

134. Fortescue, A. (1912). Theodosius I. In *The Catholic Encyclopedia*. (New York: Robert Appleton Company). Retrieved November 25, 2021 from New Advent: http://www.newadvent.org/cathen/14577d.htm.

135. Norman, Jeromy M., "By the Edict of Thessalonica Three Roman Emperors Make Nicene Christianity the Official State Religion of the Roman Empire," 2/27/380, accessed 11/25/21, https://www.historyofinformation.com/detail.php?id=2695.

136. Baur, C. (1910). St. John Chrysostom. In *The Catholic Encyclopedia*. (New York: Robert Appleton Company). Retrieved November 25, 2021 from New Advent: http://www.newadvent.org/cathen/08452b.htm.

137. Translated by J. Walker, J. Sheppard and H. Browne, and revised by George B. Stevens. From *Nicene and Post-Nicene Fathers*, First Series, Vol. 11. Edited by Philip Schaff. (Buffalo, NY: Christian Literature Publishing Co., 1889.) Revised and edited for New Advent by Kevin Knight. http://www.newadvent.org/fathers/210208.htm.

138. Ibid.

139. Portalié, E. (1907). Life of St. Augustine of Hippo. In *The Catholic Encyclopedia*. (New York: Robert Appleton Company). Retrieved November 25, 2021 from New Advent: http://www.newadvent.org/cathen/02084a.htm.

140. Hillerbrand, H. J. (2021, November 6). Martin Luther. Encyclopedia Britannica. https://www.britannica.com/biography/Martin-Luther.

141. Bouwsma, W. J. (2021, July 6). John Calvin. Encyclopedia Britannica. https://www.britannica.com/biography/John-Calvin.

142. Translated by Marcus Dods. From *Nicene and Post-Nicene Fathers*, First Series, Vol. 2. Edited by Philip Schaff. (Buffalo, NY: Christian Literature Publishing Co., 1887.) Revised and edited for New Advent by Kevin Knight. http://www.newadvent.org/fathers/1201.htm.

143. Specht, Die Lehre von der Kirche nach dem hl. Augustinus, Paderborn, 1892.

144. *Imprimatur.* +John M. Farley, Archbishop of New York, *The Catholic Encyclopedia*, Volume II, "Saint Augustine of Hippo," accessed 11/25/21, http://traditionalcatholic.net/Tradition/Calendar/08-28.html.

145. Portalié, E. (1907). Life of St. Augustine of Hippo. In *The Catholic Encyclopedia*. (New York: Robert Appleton Company). Retrieved November 25, 2021 from New Advent: http://www.newadvent.org/cathen/02084a.htm.

146. Translated by Marcus Dods. From *Nicene and Post-Nicene Fathers*, First Series, Vol. 2. Edited by Philip Schaff. (Buffalo, NY: Christian Literature Publishing Co., 1887.) Revised and edited for New Advent by Kevin Knight. http://www.newadvent.org/fathers/1201.htm.

147. Gruber, Daniel, The Church and the Jews, (Hanover, NH: Elijah Publishing, Copyright 1991, 1997, 2001, 2017), Pages 204–205, 2017 edition.

148. Huddleston, G. (1909). Pope St. Gregory I ("the Great"). In *The Catholic Encyclopedia*. (New York: Robert Appleton Company). Retrieved November 25, 2021 from New Advent: http://www.newadvent.org/cathen/06780a.htm.

149. Cohn-Sherbok, Dan, *Messianic Judaism: A Critical Anthology* (New York, NY: Bloomsbury Publishing, 2/11/13) Chapter 1, "Early Jewish Christianity."

150. Butler, R. U. (1912). Pope Bl. Urban II. In *The Catholic Encyclopedia*. (New

York: Robert Appleton Company). Retrieved November 25, 2021 from New Advent: http://www.newadvent.org/cathen/15210a.htm.

151. Weber, N. (1912). Waldenses. In *The Catholic Encyclopedia*. (New York: Robert Appleton Company). Retrieved November 25, 2021 from New Advent: http://www.newadvent.org/cathen/15527b.htm.

152. Butler, George, "The Change of the Sabbath, Was It by Divine or Human Authority?" Southern Pub. Association, 1904, Page 148.

153. Great Schism of 1054—Cardinal Humbert of Silva Candida's excommunication of Patriarch Michael Cerularius. From Byzantium: Church, Society, and Civilization Seen through Contemporary Eyes (Geanakoplos) pgs. 208-209, ¼.2018, accessed 11/25/21, http://deepinwonderland.blogspot.com/2018/01/1054-schism-cardinal-humbert-of-silva.html.

154. Ott, M. (1910). Pope Innocent III. In *The Catholic Encyclopedia*. (New York: Robert Appleton Company). Retrieved November 25, 2021 from New Advent: http://www.newadvent.org/cathen/08013a.htm.

155. Pennington, K. J. (2021, July 12). Innocent III. Encyclopedia Britannica., accessed 11/25/21, https://www.britannica.com/biography/Innocent-III-pope.

156. Britannica, T. Editors of Encyclopaedia (2021, October 18). William Edward Hartpole Lecky. Encyclopedia Britannica, accessed 11/25/21. https://www.britannica.com/biography/William-Edward-Hartpole-Lecky.

157. Lecky, William Edward Hartpole, "History of the Rise and Influence of the Spirit of Rationalism in Europe, Volume 2" University Press of the Pacific (July 1, 2001) Honolulu, Hawaii, pages 40–41.

158. For seventeen years, Fr. Juan Antonio Llorente worked as a "mole" in the Madrid office of the Spanish Inquisition, ultimately rising to the position of Secretary-General. With unquestioned access to centuries of Inquisition files, Fr. Llorente wrote the first-ever history of the Inquisition. After the conquest of Spain by Napoleon's forces in 1808, Lllorente seized the opportunity and published his work., PBS, accessed 11/25/21, https://www.pbs.org/inquisition/llorente.html.

159. Baker, Dr. Todd D., "Exodus from Rome Volume 1: A Biblical and Historical Critique of Roman Catholicism, Volume 1," iUniverse, May 1, 2014, Page 67.

160. Leclercq, H. (1910). Fourth Lateran Council (1215). In *The Catholic Encyclopedia*. (New York: Robert Appleton Company). Retrieved November 25, 2021 from New Advent: http://www.newadvent.org/cathen/09018a.htm.

161. Ott, M. (1909). Pope Gregory IX. In *The Catholic Encyclopedia*. (New York: Robert Appleton Company). Retrieved November 25, 2021 from New Advent: http://www.newadvent.org/cathen/06796a.htm.

162. Hunt, Dave, *A Woman Rides the Beast*, (Eugene, Oregon: Harvest House, 1994) p. 231, www.harvesthousepublishers.com, Page 231.

163. Spanish Inquisition. (2020, February 16). New World Encyclopedia, Retrieved 18:32, November 25, 2021 from https://www.newworldencyclopedia.org/p/index.php?title=Spanish_Inquisition&oldid=1032451.

164. Britannica, T. Editors of Encyclopaedia (2021, October 30). James II. Encyclopedia Britannica. https://www.britannica.com/biography/James-II-king-of-Aragon-and-Sicily

165. Schonfield, Dr. Hugh J., *"History of Jewish Christianity"* Page 80, Original Date 1936, Re-edited and re-printed by Bruce R. Booker under permission of The Hugh & Helene Schonfield World Service Trust.

166. Kirsch, J.P. (1912). Council of Vienne (1311–12). In *The Catholic Encyclopedia*. (New York: Robert Appleton Company). Retrieved November 25, 2021 from New Advent: http://www.newadvent.org/cathen/15423a.htm.

167. Jewish Virtual Library, "Zamora," Encyclopaedia Judaica. © 2008 The Gale Group, accessed 11/25/21, https://www.jewishvirtuallibrary.org/zamora.

168. MacCaffrey, J. (1907). Council of Basle. In *The Catholic Encyclopedia*. (New York: Robert Appleton Company). Retrieved November 25, 2021 from New Advent: http://www.newadvent.org/cathen/02334b.htm.

169. Britannica, T. Editors of Encyclopaedia (2013, September 23). Marrano. Encyclopedia Britannica. https://www.britannica.com/topic/Marrano.

170. Britannica, T. Editors of Encyclopaedia (2016, February 16). converso. Encyclopedia Britannica. https://www.britannica.com/topic/converso.

171. Millard, Dr. Catherine, "Book of Prophecies of Christopher Columbus", Messianic Jew – Original Manuscript with English/Hebrew Translation. Introduction © 2015; 2019.

172. Lehmann-Haupt, H. E. (2020, December 17). Johannes Gutenberg. Encyclopedia Britannica. https://www.britannica.com/biography/Johannes-Gutenberg.

173. Britannica, T. Editors of Encyclopaedia (2020, May 15). Reformation. Encyclopedia Britannica. https://www.britannica.com/event/Reformation.

174. Britannica, T. Editors of Encyclopaedia (2020, May 18). Dominican. Encyclopedia Britannica. https://www.britannica.com/topic/Dominican-order.

175. Azcona, T. de (2021, March 6). Ferdinand II. Encyclopedia Britannica. https://www.britannica.com/biography/Ferdinand-II-king-of-Spain.

176. Highfield, J. (2021, November 22). Isabella I. Encyclopedia Britannica. https://www.britannica.com/biography/Isabella-I-queen-of-Spain.

177. Britannica, T. Editors of Encyclopaedia (2021, September 12). Tomás de Torquemada. Encyclopedia Britannica. https://www.britannica.com/biography/Tomas-de-Torquemada.

178. Schonfield, Dr. Hugh J., *"History of Jewish Christianity"* Page 93, Original Date 1936, Re-edited and re-printed by Bruce R. Booker under permission of The Hugh & Helene Schonfield World Service Trust.

179. Translated from the Castilian by Edward Peters, "Edict of the Expulsion of the Jews (1492)" accessed 11/25/21, http://www.sephardicstudies.org/decree.html.

180. Britannica, T. Editors of Encyclopaedia (2014, April 17). Chaldean Catholic Church. Encyclopedia Britannica. https://www.britannica.com/topic/Chaldean-Catholic-Church.

181. Jewish Virtual Library, *"Jewish Holidays: Tisha B'Av"*, accessed 11/25/21, https://www.jewishvirtuallibrary.org/tisha-b-av.

182. Britannica, T. Editors of Encyclopaedia (2021, February 21). Babylonia. Encyclopedia Britannica. https://www.britannica.com/place/Babylonia.

183. Stacey, J. (2021, March 13). John Wycliffe. Encyclopedia Britannica. https://www.britannica.com/biography/John-Wycliffe.

184. Britannica, T. Editors of Encyclopaedia (2021, January 16). Miles Coverdale. Encyclopedia Britannica. https://www.britannica.com/biography/Miles-Coverdale.

185. Hillerbrand, H. J. (2021, November 6). Martin Luther. Encyclopedia Britannica. https://www.britannica.com/biography/Martin-Luther.

186. Britannica, T. Editors of Encyclopaedia (2019, July 3). Augustinian. Encyclopedia Britannica. https://www.britannica.com/topic/Augustinians.

187. Spalding, J. C.; Nelson, E. Clifford; Marty, Martin E.; Bainton, Roland H.; and Chadwick, . Owen (2021, August 17). Protestantism. Encyclopedia Britannica. https://www.britannica.com/topic/Protestantism.

188. Gallaher, J. G. (2020, December 7). Leo X. Encyclopedia Britannica. https://www.britannica.com/biography/Leo-X.

189. Britannica, T. Editors of Encyclopaedia (2021, August 7). Johann Tetzel. Encyclopedia Britannica. https://www.britannica.com/biography/Johann-Tetzel.

190. Britannica, T. Editors of Encyclopaedia (2021, October 24). Ninety-five Theses. Encyclopedia Britannica. https://www.britannica.com/event/Ninety-five-Theses.

191. Chenu, M. (2021, March 3). St. Thomas Aquinas. Encyclopedia Britannica. https://www.britannica.com/biography/Saint-Thomas-Aquinas.

192. Britannica, T. Editors of Encyclopaedia (2021, February 10). Summa theologiae. Encyclopedia Britannica. https://www.britannica.com/topic/Summa-theologiae.

193. Gruber, Daniel, "The Church and the Jews," Elijah Publishing, Hanover, NH, Copyright 1991, 1997, 2001, 2017, Pages 211-212 – Chapter 39. excerpted Thomas Aquinas' Summa Theolgica, 2017 Edition.

194. Heinemeyer, W. (2021, November 9). Philip. Encyclopedia Britannica. https://www.britannica.com/biography/Philip-landgrave-of-Hesse.

195. Gruber, Daniel, The Church and the Jews, (Hanover, NH: Copyright 1991, 1997, 2001, 2017), Pages 264–265, 2017 edition.

196. Luther, Martin, *That Jesus Christ Was Born a Jew, 1523,"* accessed on 11/25/21, https://www.uni-due.de/collcart/es/sem/s6/txt09_1.htm.

197. Ibid.

198. Martin Luther and the Jews, "From Luther's 'On the Jews and Their Lies'," accessed 11/25/21, https://www.laits.utexas.edu/bodian/re-MartinLutherAndJews.html.

199. Britannica, T. Editors of Encyclopaedia (2021, August 23). Anabaptist. Encyclopedia Britannica. https://www.britannica.com/topic/Anabaptists.

200. Bromiley, G. W. (2021, October 7). Huldrych Zwingli. Encyclopedia Britannica. https://www.britannica.com/biography/Huldrych-Zwingli.

201. Britannica, T. Editors of Encyclopaedia (2015, June 25). Moravia. Encyclopedia Britannica. https://www.britannica.com/place/Moravia.

202. It is in the northern part of the state and is considered to be the cultural center of the Westphalia region. It is also a state district capital. Münster was the location of the Anabaptist rebellion during the Protestant Reformation and the site of the signing of the Treaty of Westphalia ending the Thirty Years War in 1648. Today it is known as the bicycle capital of Germany.

203. Dyck, C. J. (2021, January 27). Menno Simons. Encyclopedia Britannica. https://www.britannica.com/biography/Menno-Simons.

204. Britannica, T. Editors of Encyclopaedia (2021, August 23). Mennonite. Encyclopedia Britannica. https://www.britannica.com/topic/Mennonite.

205. Bouwsma, W. J. (2021, July 6). John Calvin. Encyclopedia Britannica. https://www.britannica.com/biography/John-Calvin.

206. Calvin, John, *Institutes of the Christian Religion* (Carol Stream, IL: Tyndale House Publishers; Revised edition, January 1, 2008).

207. Gruber, Daniel, The Church and the Jews, (Hanover, NH: Copyright 1991, 1997, 2001, 2017, Pages 233–251, 2017 edition.

208. Paras, Emily, "The Darker Side of Martin Luther," Constructing the Past, accessed 11/25/21, https://www.iwu.edu/history/constructingthepastvol9/Paras.pdf

209. Britannica, T. Editors of Encyclopaedia (2021, August 19). Council of Trent. Encyclopedia Britannica. https://www.britannica.com/event/Council-of-Trent.

210. Murphy, F. Xavier (2021, November 6). Paul III. Encyclopedia Britannica. https://www.britannica.com/biography/Paul-III.

211. Ferdinandy, M. de (2021, September 17). Charles V. Encyclopedia Britannica. https://www.britannica.com/biography/Charles-V-Holy-Roman-emperor.

212. Durant, Wil, *The Age of Faith: The Story of Civilization*, Volume IV, (New York: 1993, MJF Books), Chapter IV, "The Triumph of Protestantism," 1542–55.

213. Britannica, T. Editors of Encyclopaedia (1998, July 20). Erastianism. Encyclopedia Britannica. https://www.britannica.com/topic/Erastianism

214. Ibid. (2021, August 14). Paul IV. Encyclopedia Britannica. https://www.britannica.com/biography/Paul-IV.

215. Green, David B, *"This Day in Jewish History | 1555: Pope Paul IV Orders Jews to Live in a Ghetto,"* Haaretz, accessed 11/25/21, https://www.haaretz.com/jewish/1555-roman-jews-banished-to-ghetto-1.5295240.

216. https://www.haaretz.com/jewish/1555-roman-jews-banished-to-ghetto-1.5295240.

217. Britannica, T. Editors of Encyclopaedia (2021, July 19). Shabbetai Tzevi. Encyclopedia Britannica. https://www.britannica.com/biography/Shabbetai-Tzevi.

218. Britannica, T. Editors of Encyclopaedia (2021, March 7). John Toland. Encyclopedia Britannica. https://www.britannica.com/biography/John-Toland.

219. Lucci, Diego, "The Law of Nature, Mosaic Judaism, and Primitive Christianity in John Locke and the English Deists," accessed 11/25/21, https://er.ceres.rub.de/index.php/ER/article/view/8354/7704.

220. Zurlo, Dr. Gina A., *"A Little Bit of History: The World Christian Encyclopedia,"* Gordon Conwell Theological Seminary, January 15, 2020, accessed, 11/25/21, https://www.gordonconwell.edu/blog/a-little-bit-of-history-the-world-christian-encyclopedia/.

221. Britannica, T. Editors of Encyclopaedia (2020, January 3). Coptic Orthodox Church of Alexandria. Encyclopedia Britannica. https://www.britannica.com/topic/Coptic-Orthodox-Church-of-Alexandria.

222. Meyendorff, J. (2020, August 20). Eastern Orthodoxy. Encyclopedia Britannica. https://www.britannica.com/topic/Eastern-Orthodoxy.

223. McKenzie, J. L.; Marty, Martin E.; Oakley, Francis Christopher; Frassetto, Michael; Cunningham, Lawrence; Pelikan, Jaroslav Jan; and Knowles, Michael

David. (2020, November 11). Roman Catholicism. Encyclopedia Britannica. https://www.britannica.com/topic/Roman-Catholicism.

224. https://www.salvationarmy.org/ihq/ecclesiology.

225. Assemblies of God official website, accessed 12/25/21, https://ag.org.

226. History of Calvary Chapel, accessed 11/25/21, https://calvarycca.org/history/.

227. Fairchild, Mary. (2021, September 8). Development of Christian Denominations. Retrieved from https://www.learnreligions.com/christian-denominations-700530.

228. Lapham, Steven Sellers, "Ten U.S. Churches Now Sanction Israel—To Some Degree, and with Caveats," Washington Report on Middle East Affairs, March/April 2019, pp. 51–53, accessed 11/26/21, https://www.wrmea.org/2019-march-april/ten-us-churches-now-sanction-israel-to-some-degree-and-with-caveats.html.

229. Facts about Israel: Truths About Our Future, "No Two-State Solution in the Bible." accessed 11/26/21, https://www.factsaboutisrael.uk/no-two-state-solution-in-the-bible/.

230. Amari, Dr. Rafat, "Is Mohammed a Descendant of Ishmael?" "Islam in Light of History," Religion Research Institute, 11/30/04, excerpt from article accessed 11/26/21, http://rrimedia.org/Resources/Articles/is-mohammed-a-descendant-of-ishmael.

231. Firestone, Reuven, "Muslim-Jewish Relations," 1/4/16, Oxford University Press, Powered by PubFactory, accessed 11/26/21, https://oxfordre.com/religion/view/10.1093/acrefore/9780199340378.001.0001/acrefore-9780199340378-e-17.

232. Executive Services Directorate, Washington Headquarters Services, Joint Chiefs, Course Materials, Perspectives on Islam and Islamic Radicalism, accessed 11/26/21, https://www.esd.whs.mil/Portals/54/Documents/FOID/Reading%20Room/Joint_Staff/13-F-0117_DOC_09-course-materials-perspectives-on-Islam_and_Islamic_radicalism.pdf.

233. Britannica, T. Editors of Encyclopaedia (2021, September 21). Nazi Party. Encyclopedia Britannica. https://www.britannica.com/topic/Nazi-Party.

234. Bullock, A.; Bullock, Baron; Lukacs, John; and Knapp, Wilfrid F. (2021, April 26). Adolf Hitler. Encyclopedia Britannica. https://www.britannica.com/biography/Adolf-Hitler.

235. Britannica, T. Editors of Encyclopaedia (2020, January 27). baby boom. Encyclopedia Britannica. https://www.britannica.com/topic/baby-boom-US-history.

236. Berenbaum, M. (2021, July 1). Holocaust. Encyclopedia Britannica. https://www.britannica.com/event/Holocaust.

237. Yad Vashem, The World Holocaust Remembrance Organization, accessed 11/26/21, https://www.yadvashem.org.

238. United States Holocaust Memorial Museum, *"Displaced Persons"* accessed 11/26/21, https://encyclopedia.ushmm.org/content/en/article/displaced-persons.

239. Britannica, T. Editors of Encyclopaedia (2021, October 6). Kraków. Encyclopedia Britannica. https://www.britannica.com/place/Krakow.

240. Memorial And Museum Auschwitz-Birkenau Former German Nazi Concentration And Extermination Camp, accessed 11/26/21, http://auschwitz.org/en/.

241. Ibid.

242. United States Holocaust Memorial Museum, "Poles," accessed 11/26/21, https://www.ushmm.org/collections/bibliography/poles.

243. Britannica, T. Editors of Encyclopaedia (2021, October 5). Roma. Encyclopedia Britannica. https://www.britannica.com/topic/Rom.

244. McCauley, M.; Dewdney, John C.; Conquest, Robert; and Pipes, Richard E. (2020, November 10). Soviet Union. Encyclopedia Britannica. https://www.britannica.com/place/Soviet-Union.

245. The Voice/Vision Holocaust Survivor Oral History Archive, The University of Michigan-Dearborn, Mardigian Library, accessed 11/26/21, http://holocaust.umd.umich.edu/lul/Readings/Lecture-The%20sound%20of%20silence.pdf.

246. NPR, "Records from Once-Secret Archive Offer New Clues into Vatican Response To Holocaust," accessed 11/26/21, https://www.npr.org/2020/08/29/907076135/records-from-once-secret-archive-offer-new-clues-into-vatican-response-to-holoca.

247. Coppa, F. J. (2021, October 5). Pius XII. Encyclopedia Britannica. https://www.britannica.com/biography/Pius-XII.

248. Stefon, M. (2021, September 24). Francis. Encyclopedia Britannica. https://www.britannica.com/biography/Francis-I-pope.

249. Philip Pullella—Philip Pullella is senior correspondent for Reuters in Rome. He has been a journalist for more than thirty-five years. An American of Italian origin, he has been based in Italy for Reuters for the past 30 years.... He was born in southern Italy and he and his family emigrated to New York City in 1958 at the age of four. Accessed 11/26/21, Google search, biography.

250. Reverend Father Norbert Hofmann, SDB, Secretary for the Commission for Religious Relations with the Jews, accessed 11/26/21, http://www.christianunity.va/content/unitacristiani/en/dicastero/organico/personale.html.

251. Pullella, Philip, "No 'Smoking Gun' in Wartime Archives of Pius XII on Holocaust, Vatican says," accessed 11/26/21, https://www.reuters.com/article/us-pope-archives-holocaust/no-smoking-gun-in-wartime-archives-of-pius-xii-on-holocaust-vatican-says-idUSKBN20E294.

252. Times of Israel, "In 'Confession of Guilt,' German Catholic Church Admits 'Complicity' with Nazis," 11/2/20, accessed 11/26/21, https://www.timesofisrael.com/german-bishops-said-to-admit-complicity-in-nazi-actions-in-new-report/.

253. Reich, Walter, former director of the United States Holocaust Memorial Museum, in a speech given on October 22, 2014.

254. Fathers of the Church, "The Epistle of Barnabas," accessed 11/26/21, https://www.newadvent.org/fathers/0124.htm.

255. Brown, P. R. L. (2021, January 1). St. Ambrose. Encyclopedia Britannica. https://www.britannica.com/biography/Saint-Ambrose.

256. Attwater, D. (2021, September 10). St. John Chrysostom. Encyclopedia Britannica. https://www.britannica.com/biography/Saint-John-Chrysostom.

257. Boycott, Divest, Sanction. "The Boycott, Divestment, Sanctions (BDS) movement works to end international support for Israel's oppression of Palestinians and pressure Israel to comply with international law." Accessed 11/26/21, https://bdsmovement.net.

258. Swindell, Daniel. "The Hundred Years' War of Arab Propaganda,"

Times of Israel, 7/25/21, accessed 11/26/21, https://blogs.timesofisrael.com/
the-hundred-years-war-of-arab-propaganda/.

259. Shukeiry, Ahmed. Head of the PLO, to United Nations Security Council,
May 31, 1956, accessed 11/26/21, https://emetnews.org/palestinian-myths/.

260. NGO Monitor, "NGOs and Antisemitism," accessed 11/26/21, https://
www.ngo-monitor.org/reports/ngos_and_antisemitism/.

261. Antidefamation League, "To Stop the Defamation of the Jewish People,
and to Secure Justice and Fair Treatment to All...," accessed 11/26/21, https://
www.adl.org/who-we-are/our-mission.

262. Ibid., "Antisemitic Incidents Hit All-Time High in 2019,"
accessed 11/26/21, https://www.adl.org/news/press-releases/
antisemitic-incidents-hit-all-time-high-in-2019.

263. Rashida Tliab, Rashida Harbi Tlaib is an American politician and lawyer
serving as the U.S. Representative for Michigan's 13th congressional district since
2019. The district includes the western half of Detroit, along with several of its
western suburbs and much of the Downriver area. Accessed 11/26/21, https://
tlaib.house.gov.

264. Ilah Omar, Ilhan Abdullahi Omar is an American politician serving as the
U.S. Representative for Minnesota's 5th congressional district since 2019. She
is a member of the Democratic–Farmer–Labor Party. Accessed 11/26/2021.
https://omar.house.gov.

265. Alexandia Ocasio-Cortez, Alexandria Ocasio-Cortez, also known by
her initials AOC, is an American politician and activist. She has served as the
U.S. Representative for New York's 14th congressional district since 2019, as a
member of the Democratic Party. Accessed 11/26/21, https://www.ocasiocortez.
com/splash.

266. Zurcher, Anthony. "Israel-Gaza: The Democrats' 'Tectonic' Shift on the
Conflict" BBC News, 5/21/21, accessed 11/26/21, https://www.bbc.com/
news/world-us-canada-57161929?xtor=AL-72-%5Bpartner%5D-%5Bbbc.
news.twitter%5D-%5Bheadline%5D-%5Bnews%5D-%5Bbizdev%5D-
%5Bisapi%5D&at_medium=custom7&at_custom2=twitter&at_

custom1=%5Bpost+type%5D&at_custom4=7078605C-B9C7-11EB-8BA3-
BDF74744363C&at_custom3=%40BBCNews&at_campaign=64.

267. Ward, Benjamin, "Europe's Worrying Surge of Antisemitism," Human
Rights Watch. Accessed 11/26/21, https://www.hrw.org/news/2021/05/17/
europes-worrying-surge-antisemitism#.

268. Truth About Israel, "The Comprehensive Guide to the Truth About the
United Nations," accessed 11/26/21, http://www.thetruthaboutisrael.org.il/
qanda/comprehensive-guide-truth-united-nations/.

269. Magid, Jacob, "Progressive Dems Introduce Bill They
Say Aims at Keeping 2-State Solution Alive," *Times of Israel*,
9/24/21, accessed 11/26/21, https://www.timesofisrael.com/
progressive-dems-introduce-bill-aimed-at-keeping-two-state-solution-alive/.

270. Aman, John, "Soros' Cash Helps 'Flip' Evangelicals away from Israel,"
WND, 9/29/21, accessed 11/26/21, https://www.wnd.com/2021/09/
soros-cash-helps-flip-evangelicals-away-israel/.

271. Cramer, Philissa, "Antisemitism Fears Made 40% of US
Jews Change Their Behavior Last Year—Survey," Times of Israel,
10/26/21, accessed 11/26/21, https://www.timesofisrael.com/
antisemitism-fears-made-40-of-us-jews-change-their-behavior-last-year-survey/.

272. Koenig, William, American author and White House correspondent,
author of *Eye to Eye: The Consequences of Dividing Israel*, which has been placed
in the hands of every President since George H. W. Bush I.

273. Koenig, William, *Eye to Eye: The Consequences of Dividing Israel*, Christian
Publications; Revised edition (August 27, 2017).

274. Joel Richardson is the author of several books, including *New York Times*
bestselling *Islamic Antichrist: The Shocking Truth About the Real Nature of the
Beast*. He is an internationally recognized expert on biblical prophecy, the Middle
East, and Islam, and is a human rights activist and a commentator for WND.
Accessed 11/26/21, https://store.joelstrumpet.com.

275. Bill Salus, author, radio host, speaker. Accessed 11/26/21, http://www.
prophecydepotministries.net.

276. Tibi, Ahmad, "Deputy Speak of the Israeli Knesset," accessed 11/26/21, https://main.knesset.gov.il/en/MK/APPS/mk/mk-personal-details/208.

277. Britannica, T. Editors of Encyclopaedia (2021, November 10). Bashar al-Assad. Encyclopedia Britannica. https://www.britannica.com/biography/Bashar-al-Assad.

278. Pentecost, Dwight, *Things to Come: A Study in Biblical Eschatology* (Grand Rapids, MI: Zondervan Academic, MI, Later Printing edition (August 1, 1965), Page 480.